About 'Among the Mountain Laurels'

"[This] story is both tragic and uplifting...and beautifully told in these pages. It is a real document of faith and perseverance, inspiring to all of us. [Pauline is] truly the essence of a 'good mountain woman'; tough and true and tender all at once. I'm sure many others would love to read [this] story as well."

> *Lee Smith - award winning author of 15 books of fiction, including the recently released novel 'On Agate Hill'. Among her most accomplished novels about the Appalachian region are 'Oral History' and 'Fair and Tender Ladies'.*

"An instant classic about strong women who survive in a mountain land scarcely, if ever, written about."

> *Frank Ritter - author and journalist for half a century with The Tennessean in Nashville.*

Dedications

For Edwina Harber-Burkhart, Kimberly Lynn Harber, Jacqueline Duvall Harber-Hensley, my loving daughters who sparked my human spirit to persevere spiritually, educationally, and economically, and to battle renal failure and transplants, not once but twice. To live for them intensified my fight for life.

For William Roy Jeffries III, Brian Codey Hensley, Lindsey Ruth Hensley, and Hannah Grace Burkhart, my grandchildren, the sunshine of my golden years.

For Milford Lee Scroggins, Ashley Morgan Scroggins, and Corey Danielle Scroggins, who by pure providence entered my life at the ages of three, four, and six as a result of tragedy. Never could a bond of love be greater.

For Ralph Harber, my husband, who graciously respected my free spirit.

Thanks

A special thanks to Judith Victoria Hensley, my mentor, who knew there was a story in my heart and gracefully inspired me to find the writer that existed within. To her I will be forever grateful.

Thanks to the family who gave to me their 17 year old son's kidney as he was suddenly taken from life in June of 1983. Perhaps some day we shall meet.

Thanks to Elizabeth Ann Gross Smith, who handed me a writer's market book over 15 years ago and said, "You have a story to tell."

Thanks to Rhonda Long Robinson for her unending encouragement and support.

Memoriam

In memory of Daddy and Momma, Henry Hensley and Ruthie Smith Hensley, who nurtured my mountain roots, which enabled me, like the mountain laurel, to weather the storms of life. Also in memory of their daughter-in-law, Jackie Blanton Hensley, their great-granddaughter, Ruby Mae Beard, and their niece, Mary Jane Verhey. My first cousin, George Hamlin, who was a second dad to me.

Among the Mountain Laurels
A Testament to the Human Spirit of a Harlan County Woman

Pauline Hensley Harber

Among the Mountain Laurels

This book is a memoir. Some names may have been changed to protect identities. The incidents described are written from the memories of the author. Comments or statements within these pages are solely the responsibility of the author; Ascended Ideas accepts no legal responsibility for their authenticity. Wherever possible, permission has been obtained to use images or names.

Copyright © 2007 by Pauline Hensley Harber

All rights reserved, including the right to reproduce this book or portions thereof in any form.

An Ascended Ideas original

Ascended Ideas ePublishing
PO Box 120
Coldiron, KY 40819
http://www.ascendedideas.com

ISBN: 0-9795103-1-7

Cover by Judy A Mason

Some cover photos by Judith Victoria Hensley

Printed in the United States of America

CHAPTER 1

Deep in the Appalachian mountains of southeastern Kentucky in Harlan County lies a little valley called Martin's Fork. To the eyes of an outsider it might seem to be the end of the world; to me it is, and always has been, my earthly refuge.

In the serenity of my home, settled snuggly beneath the beautiful mountains adjacent to the clear rippling waters flowing from the Wild River, I awakened to a lovely July morning. The cool, fresh air breezed through the window and the lingering scent of dew-wet honeysuckle growing along the fence row perfumed the air. Sprinkles of sunshine danced through the sheer curtains of the open window. I was seldom greeted by that sunrise kiss, but I had stayed in bed until nearly eight this particular morning.

Slipping into a white eyelet lace dress, I buttoned down the entire front. It had princess style short sleeves and fit moderately at the waist before flaring out slightly as it lengthened to my ankles. I felt pretty. I knew the white enhanced the color that had returned to my complexion, as well as my shiny dark hair. While adorning myself, my thoughts were positive knowing that I was once again physically able to walk down the stairs on my own. I was home. I was safe.

A sense of peace flowed through me as I made my way down the stairs and entered the dining room. Bright light from the morning sun beamed through the glass doors and made the creamy Victorian lace curtains look ever so soft as they blended with the sandy sage walls and the shiny, light colored wood floor.

As I walked into the kitchen, the peach and cream linoleum sparkled in the glowing sun, the semi-sheer peach curtains edged with cream lace flowed with the mountain breeze. Through the kitchen door near the outer edge of the yard, I could see God's creation. The multicolored wildflowers were covered with droplets of moisture, swaying in the wind that softly moved from the west. Huge oak trees stood majestically adjacent to them, yet did not block the black barn with its tin roof and the grassy fields stretching across the grounds until they rolled out of sight.

I soon had the percolator rhythmically spitting out the aroma of freshly brewed Folgers. In the past, that scent would draw my husband, Ralph, to the kitchen table to talk while I cooked breakfast and packed his lunch for the day. More and more of late, he lingered in other parts of the house, avoiding breakfast at the table and coming out only when his food was packed in layers into the Igloo cooler that held his lunch and snacks for the working day. The bottom layer was made of fresh fruit, usually apples, and then lunch sandwiches. Carefully resting on top of that were treats to last him until he returned home, exhausted from his coal hauls between Black Star and the tipple at Pathfork late in the day.

On that particular morning not even the hiss of eggs and sausage frying in the cast iron skillet or the tempting smell of homemade biscuits in the oven could lure him to the table to sit. Ralph made his way to the kitchen and picked up the coffee thermos, egg sandwiches wrapped neatly in tin foil, and the cooler. His eyes betrayed the weariness within him and his face was etched in sadness. His dark, curly, thick hair was beginning to show traces of gray. At six feet, Ralph had always stood tall and handsome, noticeable in any crowd; but today his shoulders were drooping slightly and he seemed bent in some unfamiliar way. He left by way of the kitchen door without uttering a word.

This man was my love, my companion, my rock. He had stood by me through every hospital stay, paid my medical bills without complaint, and showed me in a thousand ways that he was mine and I was his. Ralph made me feel secure. He worked hard to make the extra money that covered the expenses that go with a chronic illness. I appreciated his unselfish way of making sure the money was there for my needs and for our girls. His love, his reliability, and his determination made me feel very special in spite of the physical and emotional trauma I had walked through over the past three years.

The stillness and the beauty of morning had always been a cherished time for me. On that morning, with everything so quiet, I almost had to hold my breath and listen hard to hear anything stirring outside or in. Out the back window, the mountains towered above our home. Table Rock and Chimney Rock stared down from the mountain summit like ancient sentinels guarding our little world; their stony strength stood out among the dancing trees.

My heart seemed to fill up with inexplicable joy as I looked at those familiar natural works of art there on the mountain. I could look and look at their stark beauty and never get enough. They had weathered the storms, the centuries of time, yet they stood solid in their places, unchanging to our eyes while seasons rolled in and out around them. As I stood there gazing out the window, Psalm 121, "*I will lift up mine eyes unto the hills from whence cometh my help,*" gently flowed through my mind. After drinking in the natural beauties that surrounded me, I was ready to start my day with gladness.

I could not bring myself to go back to bed after Ralph left for work, knowing I could not allow another minute of another day to escape me. While experiencing mere existence while living on dialysis, not being able to see the beauty around me, I was separated far too often from my real world. I lay in bed each day after dialysis gaining only enough strength to return the following day. I was simply surviving. This poor quality of life separated me from my life of joy, my teaching career, my mountain surroundings, my church, my ability to help people in need, my need to do things for and with my children and their friends. Once again living a normal life made me feel as though the trauma I had walked through was only a dream.

Warmth and joy stirred inside me as I looked through the big window on the north side of the house. In the field outside, the grass glistened as though sprayed by a heavenly mist while the horses quietly grazed in a world of their own.

Suddenly, I realized that I hadn't heard the coal truck's engine start. As I walked down the stairs into the family room, I could see through the door that the truck was still parked near the garage. I walked to the patio and to the carport to see what was going on. Only a problem with the truck would have kept Ralph home this long. Then I saw him.

This man that had been a part of my life since we were twenty-one; this man had been so strong; who had worked hard for many years to educate both our children and me; who had built our home with his own hands; this man who had never bought new vehicles, boats, or taken trips or spent money on himself; this man who had always been there for me during dialysis, nephrectomies, and transplants; this man sat slumped in an old gray rocking chair under the carport. Like rain pouring over Table Rock, silent tears ran rivulets down the creases of his weathered and beloved face.

"We'll make it, Ralph," I said in a faltering voice, "We've been through hard times before and we're still here to tell the tale. We'll make it through this." Although he looked like that same man, there was a sad hopelessness in my spirit that he would be changed forever.

I wanted to say, "Get up and go! Don't give in to this pain gripping your life." Anger and sadness flowed through me like a winding river.

This strong man was crumbling in silence before me. My presence and my struggle for the right words were only intensifying his pain. I wanted to pray this darkness away, but I sensed that, in this moment, he was in a place where I could not go.

I retreated as quietly as possible to the house fighting back tears with every step until I collapsed on the couch and gave in to the torrent of emotions that overtook me. I wept bitterly for Ralph and for myself. I wept for our girls who had always known only their father's strength, and I cried for all the broken dreams of a lifetime. I cried for the lost sense of security I had embraced when the last of my two kidney transplants appeared successful. I cried for an uncertain future.

There had been many days of emotional pain and adjustment behind us, and now there would be many days of pain and adjustment ahead. I feared that I had a mountain to climb this time that might be beyond my strength. Just as I had never made the climb to Table Rock and Chimney Rock, I wasn't sure I could climb up from this dark valley.

I didn't want Ralph to see me falling apart. I didn't want to add my pain to his or add any burden of guilt for the sorrow this was bringing me or to the weight he was already carrying. I thought the best thing I could do for Ralph was to leave him to be alone.

I drove the two miles to my mother's house; one of the longest drives of my life. That familiar refuge beckoned me. As I rounded the curve and saw the little white house with its tin roof sitting as it had since before the day a midwife delivered me into this world in a back bedroom, a glimmer of hope returned that everything would be alright.

I had pulled myself together as much as possible before I got out of the car and made my way up the stone steps, through the screened in porch to the back door and into the living room. There I found my mother sitting in a rocking chair in the corner, with the morning light filtering through the window onto her silver hair, casting noonday shadows straight down across her face.

"I'm sittin' here, not worth the salt that goes in my bread," she said as she looked out the window. "Cain't even keep my own house clean. Cain't get up and go. Cain't do none of the things that once brought me pleasure. I wish the Good Lord would just take me out of here if He's done with me. Ain't good for nothin' like this."

"If the good Lord was done with you, He would've already called," I told her. "You just don't know what a help you are to people with your prayers and your kind words. We need you, and I guess the Lord knows it better than you do."

My mother had always been a pillar of the community and everybody knew that, except maybe her. From the time she drew her first breath in a cabin in the shadow of Black Brush Mountain, she had been a survivor among her eight brothers and sisters, with all the rest already buried in Britton Graveyard. She had reared five children of her own and five of her sister's. There hadn't been a weak bone or a lazy streak in her whole body that I could remember until Parkinson's disease finally overtook her.

I wanted to go to her and put my head in her lap as I had done when growing up. I wanted to pour my heart out to her, tell her all my fears, and let her soothing voice and words of wisdom work their magic in me. I wanted to feel the touch of her work-worn hands on my hair, patting my face like she did when I was a child. I needed her so much, but I couldn't let her know.

She had unwillingly been thrust into her second childhood. Unable to care for her house or herself as she wanted, she needed me. Somewhere in time, I had slipped into her shoes and she into mine. My mother had a strong will and unique ways that were never to be forgotten by anyone that had known her.

I said, "Momma, I will clean your house and you will feel better."

I did and a spark of joy returned to her face. I hugged her around the shoulders before I gathered my keys to leave and laid my cheek against hers. "I'll see you later."

Glancing across the river as I drove back to my house, I reflected on how the mountain laurels were blooming with their delicate clusters of small, light pink flowers and green shiny leaves by the clear mountain streams. After surviving the cold harsh winters, the storms, the raging winds, the dark nights, and the deep snows, they looked as though they had never been touched by anything other than the sunshine and fresh air that flowed their way.

The peak season for blooming was ordinarily the last of May, but these blooms still flaunted themselves in July. Suddenly I realized that I, too, could survive regardless of how hard life's storms raged. Being raised a mountain girl with a strong faith in God had made me a strong willed woman.

CHAPTER 2

It became more and more necessary for me to find a refuge, a cleft in the rock, to hide myself until this storm passed over. Over time, early morning strolls down the Martin's Fork Road by the river became a safe place for me to reflect over the years of my life and draw strength from the knowledge that I had already survived so many hardships.

Walking through this deep valley, hidden between the ridges of Brush Mountain and Stone Mountain, the breezes from their craggy summits found me and breathed strength into my being. Like the old eagles, I rode the winds to soar again. The musical ripple of shallow water over rocks and the fragrance of blue Sweet Williams, honeysuckle, and wild roses growing near the bank carried me back through the years to the days of my childhood. Memories of a happier time came to comfort me.

~~~~~

In the nineteen forties and fifties, the valley, so beautifully surrounded by mountains, provided peace, protection, and a sense of belonging for those of us who called it home. Progress had not made its way into Martin's Fork. A single dirt road weaved its way through the trees and rocks along the course of the river, even crossing in and out of the water at times.

The mountains stood so very tall, hovering over the valley on every side as it stretched east to west for about twelve miles. The Wild River originated out of Stone Mountain at the head of Martin's Fork, snaking its way through the valley until eventually it converged with the Poor Fork and the Clover Fork about twenty odd miles downstream to form the headwaters of the Cumberland River. The river was as clear as the crystal that graced Florence Hamlin's china cabinet. Every rock and gravel of the riverbed was visible beneath the shallow water. Our Wild River was pure enough for man and beast alike to drink from.

When night fell upon the valley, quietness settled over Martin's Fork, with the exception of the sound of moisture dropping from the trees or the sad sound of the owls calling to each other through the stillness. At times there were no sounds at all. It was as if the whole world was asleep. The only light came from the moon and stars. In the full phase of the moon, one could walk anywhere without a lantern or flashlight. This was my world; I knew no other.

As I worked in the cornfields with my sisters and brothers, I often passed the slow days by thinking about the spot in the Martin's Fork River that we called the Spring Hole. As my hoe dug into the soft soil, row after row, I envisioned the swinging bridge that hung high over the water at the lower end of the swimming hole where the water began to shallow. The mountain laurels with their shining leaves and pink blossoms shimmered teasingly on the banks as the clear water glistened in the sun. The river seemed so still, as if it especially awaited the nine hot and tired children who had hoed corn all day long.

Mary Ruth was the oldest; she was thirteen when she came to live with us. I still remember thinking how fair and beautiful she was with her long blonde hair and delicate figure as she walked beside me and held my hand.

Rodney was the oldest boy, tall, thin, and sandy headed. He had a frail look about him due to health problems, but that didn't stop him from feeling that his age gave him a certain amount of control and responsibility over the rest of us.

Frank, one of the five who came to us after Aunt Liddie died, seemed to be the one who felt her loss deepest. Surrounded by the rest of us, he still seemed lonely and insecure. He often retreated to the hill above our house to cry in private.

Next to Frank was Sam, mischievous and full of life; anything you could think of, Sam was into it. He was our wild child, riding horses bareback across the open field and through the mountains, whooping and hollering as he went.

I was a little younger than Sam and Frank. The ten of us from two families brought together were shuffled like a deck of cards, with not many months in between the ages of several of us.

Willard was tall, thin, dark haired. He had a pleasing personality and dreams of being somebody when he grew up, like a ball player or something really important. He had a passion for life and big ideas for his future.

Harold was a high-tempered, frail, little, blonde-headed boy. The other kids often picked on him, knowing they could get a rise out of his temper. Harold was always responsible; no one ever had to tell him twice to do anything. You could tell him once and count on it getting done right the first time.

Esco and Morine were so close to the same age, teachers often thought they were twins. Esco had a crown of dark curly hair and struggled with a stuttering problem. He told me once that after he came to live with us he had seen his mother after she died standing at the foot of his bed in a white chiffon gown. Esco was only five when his mother died. When he was older he learned to milk the cow and Momma noticed that he brought home less and less milk each day, so she decided to find out what was going on. She learned that Esco's dog, Junior, was getting his belly full of milk by standing nearby with his mouth open while Esco squirted it full.

Morine was the baby for nine years until Wilhelmina was born. All of the older children kind of spoiled her. She was a tiny little blonde headed girl with fine features who loved to play, but didn't like to work. The rest of us let her get away with that because she was the baby, but when she got a little older, she got stuck washing out the inside of the clear Mason jars we used for canning because her hands were smallest and could easily slip inside the jars with a cloth to make sure they were clean and ready to receive the fruits of the new annual harvests.

When Wilhelmina came, we were all older. We all spoiled her so that she didn't have to do much of anything that would have been considered work. I took care of her and played with her as if she was my baby.

"When I finish this row, the swimmin' hole is callin' my name," Rodney would say.

"Last one in's a rotten egg!" Mary Ruth would call over her shoulder as she dropped her hoe and took off like a scalded dog toward the swimming hole, blonde waves of hair streaming behind her as she ran.

When our day's work was done and our blood cooled, we swam and bathed our tired bodies in the clean, clear water. Momma never allowed us to jump into the cold water if she was with us until we had rested long enough to cool down. She had it in her mind that it wasn't good for us to change our body temperatures too suddenly.

"Make sure you wash good," she'd say. "Cleanliness is next to Godliness!"

We took soap and washcloths with us and when our swimming was done, we bathed our tired bodies in the river before returning home. Momma made soap for us to use for other things, but she always bought white bars of Ivory soap for us to use for bathing. Because Ivory soap floated, there was never a danger of losing the bars in the rocky river bottom where the water hole was deeper. Somehow, this daily swimming and bathing in the river seemed to wash away anything that was wrong in my life. Troubles seemed to float away as the water washed over and past us towards a destination unknown to us.

When free from working the fields, I walked through the big grassy field to the swinging bridge that hung high over the shallow water at the lower end of the Spring Hole. I knew in my heart I was a blessed young girl to live in a place of such peace and indescribable beauty.

I was a thin, fair skinned girl with long black hair, nearly always wearing a pretty little flowery cotton dress my mother made for me from feed sacks on the old treadle Singer sewing machine. I loved my mother's homemade clothes. She designed them from looking at a store bought garment or the pictures in the Sears-Roebuck and Alden's catalogues. I fit right in with the girls who only wore store bought dresses.

I often walked through the field alone or sat on the swinging bridge and stared into the mountains seeking answers, wondering what awaited me beyond them. I wondered if I would ever see the world that existed beyond Martin's Fork, and if I did what would it be like, and how would I get there?

Sometimes I could hear the train as it passed through the tunnel only a few miles away. The lonesome sound of the whistle blowing then answering itself as it bounced off the rocky cliffs stirred a longing in me for places and things I didn't know. I could hear it, but I had never seen that long metal serpent that called so forlornly to us who lived along the valley. The loneliest cry of the train's whistle came in the darkness. We were usually in bed by dark because we had to get up early the next morning to help with gardening and preserving food in summer or to do chores before we left for school in other seasons.

On rare occasions, we left the coal oil lamp burning and stayed up past dark. That was a special treat for us. For some reason I dreamed about my future more when the lamplight was glowing. The last voice we heard before the light was put out was Momma's. We all knew to join in with her in the Lord's prayer:

"Our Father, which art in Heaven.

Hallowed be Thy name.

Thy kingdom come.

Thy will be done,

On Earth as it is in Heaven.

Give us this day our daily bread

And forgive us our debts

As we forgive our debtors.

Lead us not into temptation,

But deliver us from evil.

For Thine is the kingdom

And the power,

And the glory,

Forever.

Amen."

Regardless of how hard our week's work had been, we were up bright and early come Sunday morning, getting ourselves ready for church. We really didn't have clothes that could be called Sunday best, but they were always clean.

We must have looked like we were playing follow the leader with ten of us children following along behind our tall, dark haired mother as we all walked through the little valley of Martin's Fork on Sunday mornings on our way to Bethel Baptist Church. We paired up and talked as we walked up the dusty road.

Every Sunday, regardless of the weather, our procession made its way from our little house on the side of the hill, down the valley for about two miles to Bethel Baptist church. The church bell ringing in the hand made steeple, warned us to hurry as it echoed through Martin's Fork. When we neared the top of the hill, we got our first glimpses of the white, tin-roofed church sitting in a huge grassy field adjacent to the cool clear river that ran so free.

"Come on in, children," Wick Hamlin would say as he stood in the doorway ringing the bell. "It's time to take up meetin'." His words were as welcome and familiar as the sound of the bell. Sunday mornings were always spent in the little Baptist church learning values that would carry us through our lives.

Momma said, "No matter what happens to you in life, you will always come back to what you have learned in our little church. The Bible says, you might depart, but you will come back!"

Preacher Neal came from Tennessee on the weekends to act as our pastor, staying with first one and then another in the community, returning to Tennessee during the week to work. He was soft spoken and never got loud, but his words were full of meaning. It was a great treat when Preacher Neal took a turn staying at our house. Even my daddy, who never went to church, would try to make sure there was a special treat to eat when Preacher Neal came, like mutton from our little flock of sheep.

Preacher Neal had a way of making us children feel as if we were special and that our lives were important. Because we were good children, he felt that God would bless us with good lives as adults. He sat and talked about the Bible with Daddy. My daddy read the Bible and knew it. He wasn't a Christian, but he could talk to Preacher Neal about the Lord and about the Bible and it was never something he resented.

Wick Hamlin was the overseer of the church; he led it when we didn't have a pastor and made sure that everything was taken care of and done in order. We knew it was time for service to start when he would go to the platform.

"I thank God that He has spore us and we are gathered together here for another Sabbath Day," he'd say. Then he'd say, "Turn to page so and so…" and turn the service over to whoever was leading the singing if he wasn't the one leading it himself. His son, Clarence, played the guitar and he'd start the singing with the rest of us joining in.

Little coal oil lamps were spaced equally around the walls of the church. A tiny metal plate stood between the lamp and the wall to protect the wood and caused the flames to dance, casting off a soft light that made everything look peaceful and calm.

Sometimes, Wick's daughter, Gladys, would play guitar and sing a special song for us. I thought she was as beautiful as any movie star I'd seen in a magazine. Her long brown hair hung in a fashionable cut just below her shoulders and her peachy complexion seemed to glow in the soft church light. Gladys had actually sung over the radio and was probably the closest thing to a movie star that I had ever seen. When I looked at her, I knew that when I got old enough, I would find my own fashionable, movie star look.

In church, we just had the music of guitars and voices and many times we sang without any kind of instruments. The congregation sang beautiful harmonies out of paper-backed hymnals in their old time voices to the words of *Amazing Grace*; *I'll Fly Away*; or maybe *Are You Washed in the Blood of the Lamb*. Every once in a while someone in the congregation would cry out praising the Lord. They had old fashioned "hand shakes" at times, just to let each other know that we were among family and friends, that we were loved, and we could feel the Holy Spirit moving sweetly among us.

Henry Hensley (Daddy)

Ruthie Smith Hensley (Momma)

CHAPTER 3

The little four-room house we ten children shared with Momma and Daddy had no plumbing – which meant that there were no indoor bathroom facilities, and no running water in the house. We carried water in five gallon lard buckets or metal water buckets from the stream that ran down the mountain near the house. In the summertime when that stream of water went dry, we had to go to the Stone Mountain side to get it, which was a lot more trouble.

We used a wheelbarrow to bring the covered buckets of water in, because we could fit more in the wheelbarrow than we could carry at one time. This job was assigned to two children at a time.

When the buckets were near dry, Momma would call, "Children, it's time to get water."

There was no dragging around or arguing, someone gathered the buckets and headed for the spring.

There was no electricity in Martin's Fork. We used coal-oil or kerosene lamps. Yet, if we traveled a mere twenty miles east of the head of Martin's Fork, we could have found modern conveniences in Harlan. Twenty miles seemed far off, since we had very little transportation in the nineteen forties. Momma and Daddy didn't own an automobile. Only a few people in our valley had cars and daddy had to hire someone to take us to town if we went.

Mary Ruth, Morine, and I got to go with him in the car to Cawood where he would be dropped off and catch another ride on to Leatherwood. Uncle Sid had a little Henry J Ford and we all packed in it to get to ride to Cawood with Dad. Cawood was a little place, but the colored lights over Fowler's grocery store fascinated me. I imagined the lights to be like those I'd heard about in the big city.

People in Cawood had wells.

In spite of the difficulty in transporting water, at our home we practiced the "cleanliness is next to godliness" rule. We did our laundry once a week by carrying our clothes to the river where we built a fire to heat water and used a washboard to scrub our clothes clean. We could use all the water that we wanted to use because it 'ran free'.

I loved washday; it was never a chore, but a fun day. It was a day to hear and feel the calmness as the shallow, clear water ran peacefully and calmly over the rocks. I was able to look upon the banks of the river, arrayed with greenery accented by a touch of blue Sweet Williams growing wild. Beyond this, the grassy fields stretched out before the backdrop of mountains that looked as though they touched the blue sky. Little escaped my young eyes. I loved the beauty of nature with all my heart and soul and made time to appreciate my surroundings in spite of a work day.

Once the water was boiling, we put the white clothes in the big galvanized washtub along with homemade lye soap. We would take a battle stick and chug the clothes up and down every once in a while to make sure they were getting thoroughly clean.

Quilts didn't have to be boiled, but were placed in tubs of warm water. Momma would call, "Paulie, you can jump up and down barefoot in the tub of quilts; that will be a fun way to get them clean." I jumped and jumped and loved every moment of the time it took to get them clean.

We talked as we worked and made happy plans for the future which made the day's work pass quickly.

"Come Fourth of July," Momma might say, "we'll take us some chicken over to Cloud Branch and have us a picnic. We'll invite our friends, Daisy and Golden Daniels, to go with us."

I could picture it clearly.

Cloud Branch lay between two ridges. The land was grassy and level with a clear stream that ran through heading for Martin's Fork River. A huge oak tree stood in the middle, making the area perfect for a picnic. All of us children would help stack rocks in two rows lying parallel to each other. Between the two rows we would build a fire for cooking. On top of that, we would lay a metal rack big enough to set the frying pans on for frying chicken and cooking green beans and potatoes fresh out of the garden.

As we dreamed of the day we would go to Cloud Branch, we kept the questions coming to keep Momma talking.

"Can we stack the rocks to make a fireplace?"

"Can we play in the branch?"

"Can we carry the watermelon?"

"Can we play in the woods?"

"Can Frank take Pup?"

On and on the questions poured out and Momma answered kindly to each one we thought of as we painted fine pictures in our minds of what that day would be like on Cloud Branch. When we ran out of questions, she sang for us.

"*I know there is a land of beautiful flowers,*" she would sing. It was her favorite and we loved to hear her voice carrying the words away up into the sky. She could sing as sweet as a bird's song, with no other music but the sound of her voice.

The work passed pleasantly.

Colored clothes were washed in another tub. First Momma got a good firm grip of the wash board in one hand, then took the lye soap and scrubbed over the board two or three times, leaving the soap on the board. Next, she took one item of clothing and scrubbed it up and down over the soapy board, turning the item in different directions to make sure it was thoroughly cleaned.

Both colored and white clothes were rinsed in the clear water of the river and wrung by hand. These were taken home to hang out to dry on the clothesline that stretched between two trees or posts on the hill above the house. The next day we would sprinkle them down with water, and then roll them so they would stay damp as we ironed them. They turned out very slick and smooth.

~~~~~

I was a happy child, living in my own little world. I played in the streams that ran off the mountains and passed through the edge of our yard and finally emptied into Martin's Fork River.

Playtime consisted of a lot of pretending. I unraveled twine from a cow feed sack, wrapped it around the end of a cane pole and pretended I had a real fishing pole. Walking up and down the rocky stream, I looked for calm pools of water where I caught minnows with my bare hands. These would be my catch of the day.

I strung them on a big latch pin and called, "Kitty, kitty!" The little kittens came running for their tasty meal.

Because there weren't enough coal mining jobs near home, my dad was gone during the week. He worked as many shifts as he could get Monday through Friday and then came back for the weekend. I missed him terribly while he was gone.

One of the things he loved to do when he was home was whittle. The last piece of wood he whittled on before he left I would put in a secret place so that I could return and touch it during the week while he was away. Every time I had to watch him leave us, I would be heartbroken. I still remember his tall, lanky form, his blond head, and his long strides as he'd walk around the bend in the road that took him out of sight for another week. I always watched until he was gone. Afterwards I felt such loneliness as I sat behind our little white house and choked back the tears.

While Dad was away, Mom was in charge. For a time there were only four children, but after mom's sister, Aunt Liddie, died suddenly from undiagnosed causes, our family inherited five new members. The children's father had preceded Aunt Liddie in death, so they were orphaned; there were four boys and one girl – ages five, seven, nine, ten, and thirteen. We were five, seven, nine, and thirteen at the time. My baby sister, Wilhelmina, arrived later.

The day of Aunt Liddie's funeral in December of 1949 is one that I will never forget. Before the funeral, the aunts and uncles sat in the small dimly lit kitchen of Liddie's house around a homemade table. They were trying to make decisions about who would take which child.

One family member said, "I think we should divide the three older children and send the two younger children to an orphanage."

My daddy, a big man standing well over six feet tall, never had much to say, but when Daddy spoke, people listened.

"I'll not let these five children be separated! I will take them all," Daddy said, even though the children belonged to my mother's sister and it would mean a lot more load for him to carry all the way around.

"It'll be a different story when you start trying to put food on the table," one uncle said.

When Daddy stood up from the table, we all knew the conversation was ended and Daddy had settled the matter in his own way. There would be no objections from any of the other relatives.

Daddy said, "I am not worried about putting food on the table; I know what I can do." He paused for a moment, "I already know what it's like to feel alone and *be* alone in the world. My own father died a few days before I was born. I know the sadness of a childhood always feeling unloved and lonely."

Everyone always said about my daddy, "Henry was cheated of his childhood. That's why he has such a big heart - especially for unfortunate children."

~~~~~

The stories of Daddy's childhood always made me cry - one story in particular was about his first dress up outfit.

I envisioned my daddy as a little boy, frail and sad as he walked through the fields, across the streams, and through the apple orchard to Aunt Jenny and Uncle Floyd's house. Aunt Jenny gave him a coat, shoes, and an entire outfit, including a dress up hat. He had had so little during his youth that to be able to receive an entire store-bought outfit was more than he ever dreamed. I could imagine after Aunt Jenny washed his old clothes and put them in a bag, he would have thrown it across his shoulder, a smile of gratitude still lingering as he left to show his grandmother, Ada, the new clothes.

Jenny would say, "Henry, me and your uncle Floyd love you. Now you come back and see us; we will always be here for you."

~~~~~

Aunt Liddie had lived up a hollow near the foot of the mountain with her five children in a three room boxed house. A boxed house was made of rough lumber inside and out. That was the cheapest, fastest way the coal company could throw up a house for the workers to live in while they were working in the mines during the week. There had not been any mining in that hollow for a good while when Aunt Liddie got permission to move into the deserted house. With her being laid to rest, it would be empty once again.

Aunt Liddie's funeral took place on a blue December day. She was laid out in the back room of that little boxed house in a navy blue dress with a little white flower in the pattern. Her coffin stood in the place where the beds had been. When time came for the funeral, they took her to the church for the preaching and singing, then on to the Britton Graveyard for the burial. I know they all cried, but the only sound I could remember was the sorrowful cries of my mother as they laid her sister to rest.

After the funeral, my cousin, Mary, and I walked down the winding road that lay between the mountain and the river to my house and, as of that day, Mary's new home. As we walked an old borrowed truck passed us, carrying the children's belongings and four sad little boys in the back, shivering from the cold wind and the even colder memory of seeing their mom for the last time that day as she was laid to rest on a nearby hillside beneath the lonesome pines.

I found it hard to believe that suddenly I had five more siblings, but it was exciting. I had always gone to their home to play and now I had them all the time.

I thought as we walked, *I have me a big sister.*

I was sad over Aunt Liddie, but also excited about having a new sister and four brothers.

Aside from the belongings in the borrowed truck, the only other possessions the children owned had been a milk cow and a small dog named Pup. Pup was white with a couple of large black spots. All the boys loved Pup, but Frank loved him most. When an uncle took the milk cow and Pup, claiming them as rightfully his, it nearly broke the boys' hearts. They didn't mind the cow so much, but Frank grieved over the dog as if he had lost his best friend.

Our little four-room house had a front and back porch and inside we had wall-to-wall beds. Mary Ruth and I put five year old Esco in the bed between us. Frank and Rodney, who were the oldest boys, slept together, while Harold, Willard, and Sam shared a bed. Morine shared the bed with Mom while Dad was away working at the mines. We were stacked in like cordwood.

One cold January night, our little world was lit up by the full moon when we were awakened by a sad howl at the bottom of the yard. Running out to the front porch in their long johns, the boys discovered it was Pup.

They were yelling, and laughing saying, "It's Pup, it's Pup!"

Traveling about twenty miles across one mountain, over ridges, through the woods, across the creeks, Pup had found his way to us. He must have gone first to the little boxed house in the School House Hollow and then come to the only other place he had known where the children might be found.

What a joyous time it was when Pup came home! Frank wore a smile no one had seen for such a long time. The others were jumping up and down, but Frank had Pup right around the neck, hugging him and loving him and whining a happy whine right along with Pup.

"Won't nobody take this dog, I reckon," one of the boys said. "And if they do, he *knows* where home is."

After the celebration of Pup's return, we resumed our lives as usual, with Pup always on Frank's heels.

Bottom, left to right: Aunt Jenny, baby Edith, Uncle Floyd and Frances
Top, left to right: Aunt Ada and Henry Hensley (Daddy)

Front, left to right: Rodney, Harold, Morine, Pauline
Top: Momma

Pauline, Frank, Rodney, Morine

CHAPTER 4

With Daddy boarding away at Leatherwood to work in the mines during the week, Momma took care of everything. She must have been an angel, or close to it, never complaining and quarreling very little, with a quiet way of letting us know who was in charge and disciplining when necessary.

Everybody had a job to do. Some of us carried water. Some slopped the hogs. Some gathered kindling. Some carried in coal. Some cooked. Some washed dishes. Some gathered eggs. Some cut weeds. Just about any job you could think of, there was somebody at our house who knew how to do it.

Living on a limited income, Momma knew she had to shop wisely. Once a month she hired someone that owned a car to take her to Harlan. Her purchases were always the same: one hundred pounds of pinto beans, one hundred pounds each of flour and meal, and fifty pounds of lard. As she traveled back home from the town, she would say, "I'm so thankful to know I can feed my nine children for another month."

Every day we cooked a huge kettle of pinto beans on a coal-burning cook stove for about four hours. No matter how hot the weather, the beans still had to be cooked. We couldn't have survived without soup beans and corn bread, which supplied our bodies with protein. The beans and soup tasted delightful, and we only complained if we didn't have them. Momma, at the age of thirty-one, learned very quickly how to prepare three meals per day for nine children.

On holidays when we had special food such as chicken and dumplings, green beans, and banana pudding, we would ask, "Where are the pinto beans?"

Our bedtime snack consisted of a few leftover pinto beans, onions, and water, or maybe canned peaches; there were always plenty of canned peaches. We finished the potatoes, cornbread, fried sauerkraut, and chowchow at our regular meal. I loved sitting at the table covered with a shiny oilcloth, talking, laughing, and eating beans left over from supper.

After a belly full of pinto beans and the gas that followed, the results at bedtime with so many children crowded in one room brought giggles that could be heard throughout the house.

~~~~~

I loved fried chicken so much that I often waited until the chickens went to roost in the holly tree above our house at night to catch a fresh fryer for breakfast. After the chickens were settled in, I very quietly began climbing the tree in hopes that I could grab one by the legs. I eased my hand through the holly branches and disturbed them something fierce. One flew out of the tree and I made my way back down the tree and chased it until I caught it.

Now, the hardest part for me was wringing the chicken's neck. There are times a chicken will play dead, jump up, and run away. I had experienced that, too. The chicken staggered like it had drunk from a moonshine still; I had failed to break its neck. I usually did a good job, but this chicken didn't fall limp right away.

The fire had already gone out in the cook stove since it was the end of the day and there was no way to heat water for scalding the chicken in order to pluck its feathers. I endeavored to skin the chicken without the regular scalding. I took feather, skin and all off at the same time! This was very hard, but I managed. I was determined to put that chicken on the table for breakfast!

Carving the chicken also involved a struggle, but I succeeded. After washing it, I placed the chicken in cold salt water and the next morning Mom fried it for breakfast. As I ate my piece of chicken at breakfast, I enjoyed every crumb and knew I had been rewarded well for my effort of making it possible to have fried chicken with our gravy and biscuits.

We always had enough to eat, but not so much that we ever got past being thin. We never had anyone in our family counting calories or worrying about being overweight, which was really good for all of us.

~~~~~

I was told that I had a pleasing nature, so I was chosen to do special errands. Sometimes I walked barefoot in my little flowered dress, trailing down the dusty road to Roosevelt Daniels' small country store to get ten bottles of RC Cola. Even though I was already quite tired from a day of picking berries, hoeing corn, and helping prepare food for the winter, I was proud to be the one chosen to go on this errand.

I walked back with my arms wrapped around the brown paper bag of RCs, holding onto them as though I was scared to death of losing one. What a treat it was when we all sat around drinking those tall bottles of cold soda, checking the bottle after every sip to see how much was left. I could feel myself coming alive as I drank my RC.

Occasionally, Momma baked jam cakes from the berries we had picked in the summer and preserved as jam. She took flour, eggs, milk, vanilla extract, baking soda, sugar, shortening, and our summer blackberries made into jam. She would make three or four layers and create a very tall cake. I was often allowed to stir the batter. I was the only child who seemed to be interested in hanging around to watch her bake and knew where there was a cake being made there would be a bowl and a spoon to lick.

The icing was made from brown sugar and fresh butter that was boiled to caramelize. It had such a wonderful sweet, old-fashioned taste; nothing else in the world tasted like it. The recipe was her own, based on what ingredients she had to make do with.

When the smell of a cake baking reached the other noses in the household, there were plenty of children gathered who wanted to lick the bowl and spoon if it wasn't already licked clean.

"How long 'till it's done?" we'd all ask.

"How long 'till its cool?"

"Is company coming?"

"Are you making it just for us?"

And we loved it when Momma's answer was, "We don't have to have company just for a special treat. We are special enough."

When box suppers were held at the school, Momma's jam cakes always brought in some of the highest bids.

"That's not one of your Momma's famous jam cakes hidin' in that box, now is it?" the men would tease as we carried our box in proudly. Everybody loved her jam cakes, especially Cliff Williams, the auction man.

One day, Momma made a blackberry cake and set it on the front porch to cool. When we returned for it, our old hound dog, Luke, had managed to get on the porch and help himself to this tasty treat. I couldn't comprehend why.

"Mom," I said. "How can that ugly hound be so greedy?"

"I guess he likes my jam cake, too!" she laughed.

The bits he had left behind were covered with his slobber and not fit for anyone to eat.

I was so mad at that dog for eating up our cake that the next time I had to make cornbread for him to eat I did it without putting any seasoning in the bread at all. He just sniffed at it and walked away.

My dad said, "That's pretty bad when a dog won't even eat your cornbread. You'll have to do better than that if you ever expect to catch a husband!"

I told him what I'd done and why. Instead of quarreling at me for wasting the ingredients of the cornbread, he just laughed.

~~~~~

We butchered pork at hog killing time once a year. Even so, we had meat on our table only for a short period of time. We raised our meat, butchered, cured, and ate it before it had time to spoil because there was neither refrigerator nor freezer to keep fresh meat in. The pork was salted down and put in the smokehouse. Mom always saved the best until last, which were the hams.

I loved it when Daddy came home for the weekend and Momma went to town, because he knew how much I loved fried ham. The two of us took the hacksaw and went to the smokehouse to cross cut the ham in pieces so large that one would cover the bottom of a big iron skillet. We fried it until it was brown and tender and enjoyed every bite, then joked about what Momma would say.

One winter Dad was away at work, as usual, and Momma was home with the children. It was a cold, snowy night and all of us sat around the small fireplace that cast a dim light through the room.

Momma said, "Let's cut the ham in the morning and have biscuits, gravy, and ham!"

I fell asleep thinking of waking up to the smell of ham frying and walking into the kitchen, feeling the warmth of the heat from the coal burning cook stove and seeing the perfectly shaped biscuits sitting on the end of the stove keeping hot until the gravy was made from the ham drippings.

When morning came, Momma took her knife from the drawer, her key hanging from a nail on the wall, and dashed out through the snow to the smokehouse to find the lock broken. When she opened the door, she discovered that the hams were gone.

We were so sad on that cold, snowy winter morning when we discovered that the special food that we had worked all year for and looked so forward to eating was gone.

As we all gathered around the fireplace to talk about it, Momma said, "Children, I'm afraid to leave our meat in the smokehouse, but we have no place else to keep our pork."

I never saw Momma more disappointed than she was that morning.

Later, a nearby neighbor, Jake Clouse, related to Momma, "I saw two men go into the mountains just as darkness began to hover over the trees, heading around the ridge toward your home."

He revealed their names to Momma. The thieves probably sold the hams for a small price.

~~~~~

When spring returned to the mountains, preparations for the next winter's storehouse of food began all over again.

I enjoyed the seasons in which we grew, harvested, and prepared our food for the winter. I especially enjoyed late June when blackberries were ripening on the vine. We went far into the mountains and found flat pieces of land where wild blackberries were growing. The one thing that bothered me most was that everyone's pails filled up before mine.

Frank always aggravated me about being too delicate to compete as well as I wished. "Pauline, you're slower than smoke rising off of poop. You'll never get your bucket full, as slow as you are!"

I couldn't seem to hoe my row of beans, corn, or potatoes as fast as the others, but Mary always hoed back to meet me on the same row while some of the boys made fun of me. I knew they loved me, but had to entertain each other in some way.

As we weren't fortunate enough to own our own gardening land, we went to the head of hollows at the foot of the mountains and found small plots of flat land to garden. We raised large crops of corn on other people's land in exchange for part of the crop. My six brothers felt as though they had grubbed everyone's land on Martin's Fork. While other boys were fishing, swimming, and playing, my brothers were learning responsibility.

We canned as many as thirteen bushels of peaches at one time, made a hundred quarts of blackberry jelly and jam, and strung or canned numerous bushels of green beans. We used an empty Spam can to chop many heads of cabbage into sauerkraut and we canned everything we could get our hands on.

The boys dug a big hole in the ground under the house where we put our potatoes for the winter. I really dreaded having to go to the tater hole.

Momma would call out, "Who wants to go to the tater hole?"

I wanted to please Momma so badly that I grabbed the potato pan and off to the tater hole I went. Not everything was so easily "put up" for winter as potatoes.

Two large washtubs sat on the ground below the porch, and many fruit jars were piled near the tubs of water. I was elected the 'jar washer' until Morine was old enough. I would rather have been up on the porch that faced the beautiful mountains than down below washing jars. I was missing some of the excitement and laughs that went on around the tower of green beans that were being strung. I could hear everything, but it wasn't as exciting as being in the middle of it all. After the jars were clean, I joined the bean-stringing group.

Momma very seldom got irritated with us. The worst time was when we were all sitting around a mountain of green beans, stringing and breaking, and after a while, out of boredom, the boys began an occasional throwing of some part of the bean at each other. When the boys continued for too long, Mom began to get a little aggravated.

She would always say, "I wish I was in Yurp (Europe)."

I thought, *Oh, my! Where's Yurp?* It sounded so far away that I always felt uneasy when she made that statement.

Our family, being as large as it was, had to store lots of food to get us through the year. In spite of all the food we preserved, there was a period of time during growing season that we ran out and could not have survived without pinto beans and corn bread.

~~~~~

In September, after harvest season was over, school started back.

The school that we attended didn't have a lunchroom, so mom bought our lunch items at a little grocery store. Each of these items cost a nickel. We usually got an apple, cake, and a bag of chips, which were packed into a large grocery bag.

I was only nine years old, but toted that big bag onto the school bus, because the others were too embarrassed. My feelings were always hurt because the other children counted all nine of us everyday when we got on the bus. Carrying that big bag didn't bother me nearly as much as being counted.

Everyone sat with a grin on their face, not meaning to hurt anyone by repeating in unison, "One, two, three…" until they reached nine.

At lunch, all my sisters and brothers gathered around a long wooden table on the stage of the Baptist church, which also served as our school. During lunchtime, I stood at the table and passed out each brother and sister's lunch items. It always seemed that someone had sneaked into our lunches at recess and taken out one or two things. After handing out everyone else's, I took what was left. Sometimes that would be only one item, but I was happy to have what was left.

Before we had gotten our new brothers and sister, I often took cornbread and milk in a shiny Karo syrup bucket. When lunch time came, I was always embarrassed to get the bucket out of the closet because one girl, using a demeaning tone of voice, had asked me if I brought cornbread and milk to school. After that remark, I sort of stayed to myself during lunch, sometimes not eating lunch at all. My brothers didn't mind eating at school because they could drift out into the woods next to the river near the school with the other boys and have lunch. As a rule, the girls stayed in or nearby the schoolhouse during lunch.

At that time, I was probably six or seven years old. Each day, I would walk home from school by myself – about a two-mile walk. One afternoon when walking down the dusty road that lay by the river, I was extremely hungry. Carrying my lunch bucket with me, I remembered the milk and bread. Immediately, I opened my bucket and began to eat, the bread had broken down into small crumbs in the milk. After three or four bites, I thought I heard a car approaching, hurriedly I tried to close the bucket and, in the process, I spilled my lunch that tasted so heavenly. As I looked at the milk and cornbread gently flowing down the dirt road, I realized that I only thought I had heard a car coming. I had two miles to walk and it would be hours before supper.

Ethel Hamlin and Sam Twinam On porch: Esco Hensley and Pup - 1953

CHAPTER 5

In the early nineteen fifties we were all stricken with measles. What an adventure that turned out to be!

People in our community told Momma, "You'd better keep them children in almost total darkness or the measles will go back into their skin and you will have a bunch of blind youngins."

Momma probably knew better but couldn't take any chances. I will never be able to understand how she kept nine children in two small semi-dark bedrooms, with some running a fever, some vomiting, and others needing something.

One thing that was hilarious was when Sam vomited in five year old Esco's ear. Now, Esco couldn't talk plain so imagine how funny it was when he began jumping about, screaming "Ruf (Ruthie)! Sam puked in my yur!"

We all laughed so hard. Our bout with the measles came in the spring of the early fifties and we were quarantined in our bedrooms about fourteen days. I will never forget the day I walked onto the front porch.

Everything seemed so bright because I hadn't been outside in so long. The mountains looked like they were made of green velvet. The air was so pure and clean; even though we lived in semi-poverty, we were blessed with God's gift of purity. One thing for sure, you never missed what you never had of material things.

Our house sat on a little plateau, sort of on a hillside, which was a part of the Martin's Fork Valley and near the river. We were surrounded by mountains on four sides with big fields just below us as our little valley spread out on both sides of the river. It was heavenly to look into the mountains after being isolated for so long. Having measles taught me to appreciate nature more than ever because it was as though for the first time my eyes and my inner soul absorbed the entirety of the beauty that surrounded me.

After everyone was well, we resumed the hard work of survival.

~~~~~

Four years passed and Momma became pregnant for the fifth time. When I was a youngster, pregnancy was very personal and secretive. Being only thirteen, I knew very little about pregnancy. I noticed that Momma was acting differently, so I became suspicious when she bought a couple of maternity dresses.

One Sunday evening when I went to visit my grandmother, who was ailing from rheumatoid arthritis, she called me to her bedside, "Pauline I have something that I must tell you. Your mother is with child."

Grandma said, "Honey, you will have to take care of your momma. Having a child at thirty-five will be dangerous and she might die."

Secretly, I had worried from my earliest remembrance that Momma might die and leave us as Aunt Liddie had left her children.

Grandma said, "Do everything you can do to help her."

Later Grandma told Aunt Fannie, "Pauline turned as white as a sheet when I told her that her momma was with child."

I took Grandma seriously and began immediately to take on a greater responsibility. At this time, I was in the seventh grade.

I began to miss school one day a week to do laundry and ironing, which wasn't easy, although we no longer used a washboard. We were fortunate enough to have a wringer type washer that ran by gasoline, but water had to be carried from the spring or river, depending on the weather.

Grandma had a hard life of her own. She had given birth to one of her children when she lived at the top of a mountain—or almost at the top. The only ways to and from her house were two separate footpaths. One led to a coal camp on one side of the mountain and the other down the mountain to Martin's Fork Valley.

One day she said, "Let me tell you a true story about myself. I was home alone when I began to have labor pains, knowing that my baby was about to be born, I put together everything I needed: a couple of white sheets, water, scissors, etc, then, laid down on the scrubbed puncheon floor, and delivered my child. Your grandpa wasn't worth a hill of beans. He made a little moonshine now and then, but sat by the fire sleeping most of the time while I carried in the firewood. We had to move across the mountain to Virginia one time because the revenuers got so hot on your grandpa."

Grandma Emily said. "He did work at a government distillery one time up by the old red house, they called it. At least he got purty good pay, but that didn't last too long." The hardships that Grandma endured probably caused her to be over-protective of Momma.

I certainly took what she said to heart. I got up in the morning before I went to school, cooked breakfast for nine children, washed dishes, made beds, and swept the floors. Also, I was responsible for seeing that everyone looked decent before leaving for school. In the little four room cabin I would call repeatedly each morning, "Get up boys, breakfast is ready; your clothes are by your bed."

The boys dressed, made a dash for the big table with benches that were made from rough wood bought from the sawmill. They loved my homemade biscuits and gravy. Sometimes when there was no milk because the cow had gone dry, I used water instead to cook breakfast, they didn't complain as long as their bellies were full.

One night, in an effort to save a little time the next morning, I patted the sausage out, put them in the skillet, and set it in the bottom of the cabinet to stay overnight so I could just pop skillet and sausage on the stove in the morning before school. It was so cold in the kitchen there was no worry of the meat spoiling. The only trouble was, the sausage sure smelled good to the old tomcat. He managed to twist the latch on the cabinet door and had his fill. There was no meat for the boys that morning, only gravy and biscuits, but they didn't care - not them. They weren't hard to please.

In my daddy's own way, he let me know that I was his special little girl. He came home one weekend and noticed that I didn't look well. I was growing thinner all the time and had become pale and weak eyed. I was unstable on my feet, and had to force myself to put one foot in front of the other to keep going. I knew something was wrong because I was having dizzy spells and would hurry to the bed to lie down before I fell down.

Daddy said, "Ruthie, you need to take Paulie for a checkup, she doesn't look well."

So she hired someone to drive me to the doctor. I had no idea what was wrong. I hadn't told anyone that I was passing out. Still, I wasn't afraid of what the doctor would say, I thought that whatever was wrong with me was a part of life and I'd get over it. Dr. Buttermore did a complete workup.

"Ruthie," he said "Blood tests reveal that Pauline has rheumatic fever and will have to be hospitalized."

What he called a hospital turned out to be more like a big fine house. It was called the Annex and was only two stories tall. There was a beautiful grassy yard fenced in by a stone wall and had a large concrete porch with brick columns where patients could sit outside in the fresh air. There were no critically ill patients in the Annex.

Having never stayed more than one night away from home, I was miserably homesick. The two weeks I had to stay seemed like an eternity. We lived about twenty miles from the hospital and the trip had to be made on winding, curvy roads.

In spite of the condition of the roads and all of the work that Momma had to do, she said, "Paulie, I will come every day during the week, I will hire someone to bring me."

Every day when she started to leave, I wanted desperately for her to stay. But Momma had given her word and I knew she would be back the next day. She would manage, somehow, to get there.

Daddy stopped on the weekends as he traveled home from work. He brought me pork chop sandwiches and Orange Crush soda pop from a restaurant in town. This made me feel so special and appreciated. It was almost worth being sick to get such special attention.

After recovering from my illness, I continued to do for Momma as her pregnancy progressed. No one knew how I worried. I was afraid I couldn't do all that needed to be done. I was so afraid she might die and leave me.

At this point, I really missed my cousin, Mary, who had since gotten married and who had always helped to do the work. Because of a sense of mountain pride that was part of our heritage and culture, the boys weren't asked to do the girls' chores and Morine was too young. Boys did outside work and girls did the inside chores, except for working the fields and gardens. We all knew our place.

The year that Momma was pregnant was a hard year, but Christmas that year was an unforgettable one. It was tradition at our Baptist Church to draw names if one could afford it, and exchange gifts. I sat anxiously waiting to hear my name, eagerly watching each child go up to receive their gift. As I sat, not knowing if there would be a gift for me, but having great anticipation that there might be.

Finally, someone called, "Pauline Hensley."

I walked down the isle to receive my gift. The box was small and beautifully wrapped in shiny red and gold paper. Upon returning to my seat, I nervously and excitedly opened the tiny box. It was the most beautiful watch I had ever seen and I certainly never dreamed I would own one. The gold band and crystal face of the wristwatch glistened as it reflected the light. My hands trembled as I removed it from the box.

I looked all around, "Who did this?"

I looked from one face to the other. Everyone was silent. When my eyes fell on Lewis Hamlin, his sneaky little grin said it all. I knew he was the one who had done this act of kindness. Lewis was Momma's nephew, one of Aunt Fannie's sons. He had bought the watch for me and put it under the Christmas tree, but his name wasn't on it. He gave this little mountain girl the happiest Christmas ever.

As a little boy, life had not been easy for Lewis; his dad had died when he and his four brothers were very young. Ed, George, Clinton, and Elmer along with Lewis had great love and compassion for Momma's children. They knew what it was like to be economically deprived as a child.

The months slowly passed until my baby sister, Wilhelmina, was born, and I adored her. She was a beautiful baby and I cared for her as if she was my own. I took care of her so well that one day when she was learning to put sentences together, she said, "You are my 'Little Momma' and the other one is my 'Big Momma'."

Daddy usually took me to the coal camp where he worked for a couple of weeks each year. The visits started when I was about twelve years old. He boarded with the Caldwell's, Shorty and Dolly, who had a daughter, Marcella, about my same age. They lived in a coal camp company house at Leatherwood, owned by Blue Diamond Coal Company. My dad was charged two dollars a day; they fed him meals, packed his lunch, gave him a room of his own to sleep in, and were like a real family to him. After we got to know them well, they'd drive him home almost every weekend and stay with us until they went back on Sundays. We had a ball. Dolly helped Momma cook and we all shared the chores. We looked forward to their coming and never got tired of them. They took care of Daddy while he was away from us and we took care of them when they brought him home.

On my visits with Daddy to the Caldwell's house, I was pampered as though I was an only child. Life was so different there. They had sandwiches and ice cream and all kinds of things that we considered delicacies at home. It seemed like they could just go to the commissary and get anything in this world they wanted. They drew out scrip and shopped like there was no end to how much they could buy, but all of this did not stop my becoming homesick for my loving family and the comfort of my own home.

Every year when I visited, Dad gave me money to buy something for myself. However, the trip that I took three months after Wilhelmina was born was different. I couldn't buy for myself, regardless of how badly I wanted a new outfit. I spent my money on my baby sister. I just couldn't resist buying a beautiful, mint green, frilly dress and black patent leather shoes for her and could hardly wait for my visit to end so that I could take the dress and shoes home and see my sister in them.

Needless to say, there was a special bond between Wilhelmina and myself. I never dreamed that one day she would grow up and risk her life to save mine.

CHAPTER 6

I began high school when Wilhelmina was very young. She was my pride and joy. There were thirteen years and ten months between us and I felt as if she belonged to me because I took care of her so much. I bathed her, fed her, worried over her when she was sick, and did everything for her that I could.

Momma managed to get us fairly decent clothes for school and gave us twenty-five cents a day for lunch. At age fourteen, I wasn't very pretty; at least I didn't think so. I was tall and thin, and it seemed that being short was the way to be in 1955. I lived in misery. When I walked down the hallway between classes, I felt that people were always staring at me. At five feet nine inches tall, I towered over almost all of the girls and most of the boys. I was convinced that boys preferred shorter girls.

As my high school years passed, I began to feel a little better about myself. During my junior year, Dad gave me money to order pastel cotton material. Momma made gathered skirts with wide waistbands and cute blouses to match and she also bought lace can-can slips for fullness. I wore a wide leather belt to accentuate the blouse and skirt outfits. These homemade clothes were not thought too much of, but with the right kind of body shape, long and thin, the full skirts in pastel colors were an asset, not a liability.

I wore my hair loose and natural and in an occasional ponytail. Nature was really kinder to me than I realized as a teenager, because I did have a long, thin body, pretty black hair, and perfectly straight teeth.

I really wanted to wear lipstick. All of the other girls wore it, but Momma had a church going friend that didn't believe that Christians should wear lipstick. I figured if I wore lipstick I would have to backslide. Momma would have felt really embarrassed around her best friend had I shown up with red lips.

Finally, one day at school I said to my friend, "Christine, may I use your makeup?"

"Sure," she said.

I put on powder, mascara, and lipstick.

Wearing makeup made me feel really pretty but guilty. I didn't profess to be a Christian anymore. I really dreaded to walk through the door at home. I finally got up the nerve not to rub my lipstick off before I got home and walked in the back door into the kitchen where Momma was cooking supper.

One look and Momma was shocked. She said, "Had I known you were going to put that lipstick on I wouldn't have let you go to high school!"

From that day on I wore pink lipstick, red lipstick, or light orange lipstick depending which color blended with the color of my clothes. Hot Coral Red by

Revlon was my favorite color. I liked it as soon as I saw it on my lips because it was a soft red.

Later on Momma said, "I had a dream that stirred my heart. If you never do no more than wear lipstick you will be a good one, Paulie."

Momma no longer cared what her friend said or thought. Momma was a wise woman.

Every night I dragged in the number two washtub. I still had to carry and heat water for this nightly routine. I had two big pans that I filled with spring water and heated on the coal stove, washing my hair in one and rinsing it in the other. I treated my hair as if it were very special. Then I bathed in the washtub.

I was blessed with a healthy complexion and took very special care of my face even though it meant carrying and heating even more water. I washed my face in hot water – as hot as I could tolerate – then rinsed in cold water. After that ritual, I used Woodbury face cream to keep my skin tone even and soft. No matter how tight things were financially, Momma tried to make sure that I had that special cream for my face.

I had turned seventeen in June of 1957. Believe it or not, my first date came a few weeks after my birthday.

Daddy had always said, "Paulie, no dating until you are seventeen."

I graciously obeyed. However, I had been writing to Ken, who lived in our community, for a short while when we were younger. He was a couple of years older and had joined the Coast Guard as soon as he was old enough, trying to escape the problems he experienced at home while growing up. He wrote to me from San Juan, Puerto Rico when I was fifteen.

"You can write letters," Momma would say.

And I did.

However, when I found out he was getting leave, I stopped writing. After he returned to base, I continued to write back. Young girls loved writing soldiers; it gave us something to look forward to. The month I turned seventeen he was sure I would stop writing, and knew the time had come that I could date, so on that leave he surprised me.

On my first date I wore a beautiful pink, princess style dress with my long dark hair in a ponytail with little pink roses wrapped around the band that held it. Ken was tall, blond, muscular, and handsome in his Coast Guard uniform. Our date went well, but I still laugh about my first kiss. Obviously, he was experienced in kissing and I wasn't. I failed to breathe through my nose and pulled away half scared to death. I was about as naive as they came.

He was on leave for a couple of weeks so we dated and had fun. I remained innocent in every other way, but I sure got a lot better at kissing! Every girl has a first love – this was mine. Eventually our lives went in different directions and our relationship ended.

At the end of my third year of high school, Dad became disabled after having worked twenty-five long years in the coal mines. At the age of forty-three, he began collapsing in the mines, and still had nine children in school. He kept going back to the mines until he could no longer perform his duties as a coal miner. After being hauled out several times, he had to give up. Dad wasn't able to get any type of income for several years. The only income we had was a little over a hundred dollars that Momma received from Social Security for her sister's children.

Times really began to get hard. We had no lunch money. In the 1950s our school didn't have a cafeteria and free lunches were unheard of in our area. Across the tracks from the school was a little coal camp store owned by a couple called Buck and Mary Allen. Lunches could be bought for twenty-five cents, but I couldn't afford to buy lunch anymore. I entered my senior year knowing that there couldn't possibly be any money available for any of the things that I would need.

I remember Momma saying, "Paulie, I don't eat lunch either. I cannot bear to eat anything when I know my children are hungry."

I found that during my lunch period, being hungry wasn't bad, but explaining why I wasn't going across the tracks to the store with my friends was hard. I hid out in the restroom during lunch, hoping that no one would ask why I didn't go to the store.

The hour seemed endless.

We filled our stomachs with Momma's wonderful cooking when we arrived home. When she called, "Its supper time," we wasted no time getting to the table.

I realized that a high school diploma would be the foundation of whatever endeavors might be in my future. I vowed, "Unless tragedy stops me, I will complete my senior year, regardless of what I have to do without."

A classmate, Adeline Middleton, must have realized that my disappearance at lunch was saying that something was wrong. "Come on, lets hit the snack shack," she would say.

She never asked me where I was during lunch, but she always bought me a snack in mid-afternoon, and as we sat in class often gave me paper without my asking. I will never forget the little things she did; I truly loved her as a sister. She had gotten married as a sophomore, but was determined to finish high school. Her husband had a good job working construction and she had money for the things she needed plus extra. She was certainly an unusually considerate person at her age and used such tactfulness in doing good deeds for me.

~~~~~

Every May in our region, the Mountain Laurel Festival was held in Pineville, Kentucky. One princess candidate was chosen from each high school and competed for the honor of Princess at the annual Mountain Laurel Festival held at Pine Mountain State Park in Bell County, Kentucky. Two attendants were chosen annually from each high school to make up the Queen's Court. The Queen was selected from among candidates representing each state college throughout Kentucky. The Queen was then crowned at the Mountain Laurel Festival. I was chosen to be an attendant in the Queen's Court, which was a great honor for me.

Marietta Rogers, a very nice teacher who knew how hard I worked at home and what an undertaking it had been for me to go to school, at a special called meeting of teachers to vote for participants from the senior class said, "I nominate Pauline Hensley. She is a deserving young lady who has striven to finish school."

The teachers agreed and voted for me. This was so exciting, as I had never taken part in extra-curricular activities of any kind. To say the least, I was elated to be among those chosen for this special honor. After the excitement subsided somewhat, I began to worry about getting to the festival and how I would purchase the proper attire for the event. I knew we had little extra cash, if any.

My cousin, Clinton, lived in Corbin. This was a short drive from the festival site at Pine Mountain State Park. He and his wife came to visit his mother, my Momma's sister, Aunt Fannie. I shared my Mountain Laurel Festival excitement with Clinton and his wife, Mary.

"Will you spend the week of the festival with us?" they asked.

Staying with them also meant I would have transportation to the event. This was more than I had hoped for.

Momma managed to get up enough money to buy the material for my dress. Our neighbor, Molly McArthur, heard about the Mountain Laurel Festival and that I was going to be an attendant and wanted to help. She was an excellent seamstress.

She said, "Paulie, do you have someone to make your dress for the festival?"

"No, I sure don't," I replied.

"Then I will do it for you."

Molly had the dress completed within a week. She was so proud of her handiwork. The gown was as elegant as a designer gown.

Excitement engulfed me as I thought about the festival and the long, pink dotted Swiss gown that I would be wearing. The gown was gathered full at the waist, sleeveless, with a semi-low cut neckline. A one-inch wide belt made of green velvet tied into a bow in the front with ribbon hanging almost to the hem of the floor length gown, and there was a matching green velvet headband. The colors of my gown and accessories matched the blossoms and leaves of the mountain laurel that grew wild at the site where the festival would be held.

I had always loved the wild blooming flowers in the mountains. As a little girl walking the two miles home from school, if I spotted a wild flower growing somewhere along the path, I made my way to it even if I had to wade the river or climb the hills. I just had to touch or pick it. Mountain laurels were my favorite.

With their soft pink blossoms, mountain laurels stood out among the other trees in the spring. They were probably among the smallest trees in the mountains. Their green leaves shined, their clusters of small, pink flowers were so soft to touch and their sweet fragrance was heavenly. The laurels were fragile, yet strong. The big timber didn't smother them out because they grew near the edge of streams where sunlight made its way to them. Mountain laurels reminded me of the beautiful, strong women in my family, who weathered the storms of life in the same way the laurels weathered the storms of nature.

When the day finally came for the Mountain Laurel Festival, I arrived at the amphitheatre and made my way to the dressing rooms where the other girls were getting dressed. I felt misplaced and insecure for a moment. I dressed in my pink and green gown and combed my long, dark hair, placing the green velvet band in just the right spot. I wore light make-up. My lips were glistening with shiny pink lipstick and my cheeks were rosy without adding blush. When we were ready to walk around to the amphitheatre that was built on a slightly rolling hill surrounded with mountain laurels, I suddenly felt relaxed and gracefully walked the pathway to the Queen's Court.

While participating in the festival, I knew the other attendants came from a world so different to mine they could not imagine what this event meant to me. Regardless of their cultural advantages or their financial status, they could not have possibly felt any better inside than I did that day. I felt as pure, innocent, strong-willed, and as beautiful as the bouquet of mountain laurels I carried. I knew at that moment that I had a source of energy within that would always be there to encourage me to fight my battle for survival and a better life.

I wasn't crowned queen, but I certainly felt like a princess.

~~~~~

After my graduation, Dad's health continued to deteriorate and he applied for disability social security. In spite of reports submitted on Dad's behalf, they didn't enable him to qualify for disability. As time passed, the doctors decided to send Daddy to Virginia to an institution for the mentally disturbed.

When I was crying over Dad, Momma said, "Paulie, your Daddy gets so nervous and angry when the company doctors claim that he don't have no medical problem."

When they took him away, he said nothing, but his eyes told it all. The emptiness in them echoed in the emptiness of my heart.

Meanwhile, Dad's sister, Ada, and her husband, Mack, came to visit us from Akron, Ohio, and provided the needed transportation for Momma and me to visit

Daddy. I dressed in a simple straight, white cotton dress and wore my hair long, loose and natural to make this journey. I wanted to look pretty for my dad.

Radford, Virginia would be the furthest I had ever been from Martin's Fork. I was pretty excited about riding in Uncle Mack and Aunt Ada's big car. Uncle Mack seemed to glide through the Virginia country talking rather loud. He was making every attempt to be a good sport and even stopped occasionally to do snapshots beside the road. This being my first trip to another state, it seemed far longer than it really was. Hazard and Harlan were the only towns I had ever been to.

After passing through the moderately sized city, which looked really big to me, Uncle Mack said, "I see the hospital on the right."

"My, how beautiful!" I said.

I was so excited when I looked on the loveliness of the perfectly groomed rolling hills. A long blacktop drive meandered up the incline with pretty bushes and flowers in just the right places. The big red brick building with white shutters and trim stood beautiful in the splendor of the fair country. It almost made me forget its purpose.

I said, "Uncle Mack that is a beautiful place, are you sure this is it?"

"Yes, this is it," he said, but sounded a little sad.

When we entered the institution, a young man in white began to unlock doors. We went through an eternity of doors, making the hospital feel more like a prison than a healing place. I had definitely been in the dark as to what kind of hospital my dad was in. I hadn't begun to realize the confinement of this place I thought was so beautiful.

Dad was brought through a door that had to be unlocked before he entered the small visiting room where we waited. He had nothing to say and seemed oblivious to our presence. He hardly resembled the man who was once so tall and strong and had worked so hard for us. We were allowed to visit for only a short time. We all seem to be at a loss for words. I just sat there in that little room feeling helpless and dad just stood there so forlorn. His blue eyes were the saddest eyes I had ever seen. They almost looked gray that day.

As I walked away I didn't look back. Only as we were driving down the hill did I glance back at the red brick facility that now looked cold and desolate. Suddenly a feeling of hopelessness swept over my spirit.

Momma seemed very sad as we drove back to Martin's Fork.

I said, "Momma, why did this happen to my daddy?"

She didn't respond because she didn't have the answer.

I was trying desperately to figure things out. My dad had been a man who loaded tons of coal by shovel every day of the week and often worked sixteen hours in a double shift. He had worked so hard for us and had been so strong. I couldn't imagine what had brought him so low. No one explained to me that daddy had been given shock treatment prior to our arrival, which accounted for the distant look on his face.

In 1959 much stigma was placed on mental problems. As we drove, I felt a gnawing deep in the pit of my stomach, a feeling of sadness beyond words. I knew that my dad didn't have a mental problem. From the time he was seventeen years old, he had crawled into a three-foot high coal mine under the mountains and loaded coal until every nerve in his body had been shattered and his strength was gone at the early age of forty-three. The strong, muscular man that had been such a profound part of our lives was now bowed from the hardships of days gone by.

As we drove I remembered so vividly the time that Dolly Caldwell said, "Pauline, would you like to see the entrance to the mines where your daddy works."

I said, "Yes."

We drove into the mountains to the Blue Diamond Coal mine, Dolly stopped, "This is it."

My heart wept as I looked at the dark hole that went under the mountain. At age fifteen I asked, "My dad is so tall, how does he pick and shovel coal in there?" Then I realized he didn't walk - he crawled.

After that experience I never stopped worrying over my daddy.

He had spent his childhood without a father and was left with a mother who had no way of providing for him. There wasn't a welfare system, so survival was hard. On the rare occasions when Dad spoke of his childhood, it was easy to comprehend that he had no childhood. He had always picked up the load in front of him and carried on. He was not a quitter even though his life had not been easy.

I grieved for my dad when remembering the sadness in his eyes. Even in a crowd, he had always looked so sad and alone. For many years I have relived that day, in a small room behind locked doors; how I felt a hurt that squeezed my heart with ultimate sorrow and how my tall blonde haired, blue-eyed hero was in a place I could not go.

I will never forget the sadness of looking through his eyes into his soul and for a moment feeling what he was feeling. I hugged him and said, "Good bye, Daddy. I love you."

He just stood there in silence.

Pauline Hensley (Harber) - senior year of high school

CHAPTER 7

In our lives, some people seem to pass through quickly, but there are those rare individuals who are there for a lifetime. My cousin, George Hamlin, who was like a second dad to me during the periods when Daddy was away working at the mines, was one of those individuals. It seemed like he had always looked after me from the time I was a little girl. Momma and Aunt Fannie always lived relatively close to each other; therefore her children were really close to Momma's children.

George's confidence in me from my childhood until this day has been a source of strength and encouragement. Shortly after I graduated high school and had my visit with Dad in Radford, Virginia, George and Gene came for a visit.

"Pauline," they said, "Do you want to go to Nashville with us and look for work?"

I pondered a little and said, "I love and appreciate you for asking. The answer is yes!"

A day or so after we arrived in Nashville, Gene made cute little short sleeved jackets tapering in a curved design at the waist. Momma had sewn simple straight, sleeveless sheath style dresses for me of black, blue, red, pink, yellow, black and white checked - all of cotton. With white linen jackets white gloves and dress up pumps I looked somewhat sophisticated.

I walked the streets of Nashville for five weeks looking for general office work, nearly wearing my shoe leather off. The heat of the July sidewalks was wilting as I walked from place to place trying to find work. Every day as George or Gene drove me into the city to drop me off for another day of job hunting.

I would say, "Gene, the fear of big city life in Nashville tries to grip me. It makes the security of the mountain's embrace seem like another world. But I won't give into my insecurities!"

"Polly, you can do it!" Gene would say.

"If you believe in me, I must believe in myself."

With only one year of typing and shorthand, I believed that I had the type of personality for a receptionist's position if someone would give me a chance. Scraping the bottom of the barrel, I finally gave up and went to an employment agency that required ten percent of your pay for a number of weeks in return for assisting in finding a job for their contacts.

Finally in July of 1959, I went to Dr. Pepper Bottling Company in north Nashville and applied for a receptionist and general office worker position. The owner, Mr. Ozier interviewed me.

He said to the office manager, "She looks good to me. Hire her."

Mr. Ozier was one of the most professional and respectful men I had ever met. The job paid forty dollars a week. I brought home thirty-three dollars and twenty cents, which was a lot of money to me. It was the most money I had ever had in my life except for one time that Dad gave me fifty dollars to buy school clothes for my junior year in high school.

I could hardly imagine that the big city had opened its door and accepted me as part of the office work force. It was a mark of great accomplishment for a mountain girl who still felt greener than the trees of home.

Again Gene came to my rescue, "Polly," she said, "We are going shopping."

She took me to a huge department store in the mall near her home. I left the store with a new fall wardrobe, beautiful colors of skirts and sweaters, shoes to match, even a winter coat.

I said, "How can I find the words to express my gratitude?"

"You don't have to, Polly. I know you are grateful."

Eventually, I moved from my cousin's house to the city of Nashville, and lived in the YWCA where the rent was four dollars per week. George and Gene had been so gracious to me and I knew that I was welcome to stay with them, but at the same time told them, "I want you to have your own space and to be proud of me for making my own way."

They replied, "You will never know how proud we are of you! We love you."

I was able to pay my rent, buy bus fare to work, and send four dollars home to buy my brothers and sisters lunch for school. I couldn't bear the thought of the younger ones that were left going hungry.

The YWCA housed young women who were away from home and provided the safety of chaperones, locked doors, and the security of knowing we were not alone. There were probably a hundred girls living in the building, with a housemother on each of the four floors. Everyone started with a roommate. Mine was Evelyn Berryman who was a country girl from Tennessee. She was an exotic beauty like I had never seen before and I admired her greatly. She reminded me of Sophia Loren and seemed so sophisticated to me. She exuded confidence in every move she made, every step.

Almost immediately she said, "I will be glad to show you around the big city."

On warm, breezy evenings after work, Evelyn and I walked into the city and soaked in every bit that we could hold of architectural structures, scenery, trains passing below the bridge, and storefront windows. One of our favorite haunts was Church Street where all the department stores tempted our dreams and our wallets. I opened my first account and was able to buy beautiful dresses off the rack, like I had never seen before coming to Nashville.

My first purchase was a green silk dress with a walking jacket. The walking jacket was just a few inches shorter than the dress that edged the bottom of the knee. I bought it especially to wear to the big Baptist church we had located in west Nashville. For the first time, with a beautiful French hair style, twin pearl earrings, necklace, and matching ring, black patent leather heels, matching purse, white gloves - in those days you just weren't dressed up without wrist length gloves - and my new dress, I felt just as stylish as any of the uptown Nashville girls. My YWCA roommates, Evelyn, Flo, and I walked gracefully through the city, confident of our elegance. We made our way to church. Having gone to church all of my life, I felt that I absolutely had to find a church to go to on Sunday mornings.

After our first visit I said, "Girls, I long for the familiarity and closeness of my friends and loved ones in our little white chapel at Martin's Fork."

It seemed that every Nashville church was huge beyond my imagination with cavernous sanctuaries and balconies. The congregations were so large, it wasn't easy to make friends or easily get acquainted with anyone.

I said to Flo and Evelyn, "West Baptist serves the purpose of paying respect to our Lord Jesus."

Flo said, "You are so right."

At that time I really didn't profess salvation, however my upbringing still lingered with me; I held on to my values. So, Evelyn Berryman, Florence Cottrell, and I made our weekly pilgrimage to the uptown Nashville Baptist Church and back again, content with our own company.

~~~~~

The YWCA was very near the capitol building in downtown Nashville. It was common for small groups of us to walk to Capitol Hill where the breeze blew gently and the beautiful capitol building sprawled before us. Late in the evening, just at dark, we sat on Capitol Hill, talking of our homes, our families, and our dreams.

There were so many young girls in Nashville at that time who worked office jobs that it looked like a female evacuation at 4:00 p.m. on weekdays. Everyone walked or rode buses to get back to their apartments or to the YWCA after work.

I remember hearing someone say, "If you happen to be in downtown Nashville at 4:00 on a week day, it looks like God has set all his little angels loose on the city."

The YWCA was also near Sewart Air Force Base and Fort Campbell Army Base. The USO Club transported young girls by bus to the bases where there were always dances that the YWCA girls were invited to, as well as USO dances at the ballroom in the YWCA. All of the young men were lonely for a pretty face to talk to and to remind them of home. Events were well chaperoned and decent. There was absolutely no drinking or misconduct. The young military men were the finest kind of gentlemen, always polite, always respectful.

~~~~~

The first date I had in Nashville came when George, his daughter, Teresa, and I went to the Tennessee State Fair. I chose to wear black Capri pants with a white, three quarter length sleeved blouse and style my hair in a pageboy, as I'd had it trimmed a little. We indulged ourselves in several activities then decided to do something more relaxing. As we watched a show of performing horses, my attention was primarily focused on the event, although I felt that I was being observed.

A tall, muscular fellow standing near us watching the show introduced himself, "Hi, I'm Bill McCormick."

He extended his hand to shake mine. I tried to respond gracefully.

We watched for a bit, trying not to look too interested in each other. Casually, we began to share comments about the amazing performances. We were very relaxed as we talked. Sometimes in life there are people you meet that you just feel you have always known. This tall dark stranger didn't make me feel that he was a stranger.

Bill asked, "May I call you sometime?"

Teresa was about ten years old at the time and blurted my telephone number right out to this dark eyed, dark haired stranger. I felt the blush start at my neck and spread to the top of my head. He grinned but didn't write the number down. I thought he was probably doing a little innocent flirting and would never remember that phone number.

I was wrong.

I wasn't use to getting many telephone calls. George and Gene rarely called. I never got calls from home because, at that time, telephone service had not been extended beyond Cawood, nine miles east of Martin's Fork; it would be a long time before the telephone lines would reach home.

So when one of the girls yelled down the hallway, "Pauline! You have a phone call!" I had a notion that it might be Bill McCormick.

"How would you like to go to a square dance on Saturday night?"

"I'd be delighted," I said, trying not to sound overly excited.

"I'll be playing in the band with my brothers. Do you mind?"

"That will be fine. Do you have a band?"

"Well, you might say so. We play country and bluegrass. Maybe you've heard of us…The McCormick Brothers."

I hadn't been exposed to that much bluegrass music, so I didn't have a clue who they were. But when he told me he played bass fiddle for Johnny Cash, I couldn't believe it. Johnny Cash was BIG; he was everybody's favorite "man in black".

Suddenly it hit me that this fellow wasn't just a tall, good looking stranger, but a genuine Nashville celebrity.

I could hardly wait to tell Cousin George the next time I saw him. George certainly wasn't as naive as I had been about country music. He knew immediately who the McCormick Brothers were and was very excited. By the time he finished telling me about their music, their songs, that they'd been on the Grand Ole Opry, and that they had several recordings, I wondered how in the world this had happened to me – to be asked out by someone so well known.

When he came to pick me up, I was ready and waiting. I had pulled my hair up on my head loose and casual. I chose a stylish forest green, polished cotton dress with a full skirt for swirling on the square dance floor. I tried to find a color that would be complimentary to my hazel eyes, reflecting the green in them.

One of the girls called for me. "You have a caller," she grinned and raised her eyebrows.

Bill was waiting for me downstairs in the lobby to walk me to his car. He looked like a square dancer straight from the Grand Ole Opry and country music scene. Being a gentleman, he opened the door of his big car and I tried to slip in gracefully. With the top laid back, it seemed that everyone we passed on the way to the square dance was staring at us. At first I felt conspicuous, like something was wrong with us to make everybody look. Finally, I realized that they were looking at Bill McCormick, Nashville musician, Johnny Cash's bass fiddle player, country music celebrity. I was proud to be riding in his big car, be his date, and on the way to a real Nashville event.

We dated for some time and our relationship turned serious. But I wasn't ready to fall in love with anybody.

"I really don't understand the way you guard your feelings. Is there a reason as to why you can't fall in love with me?" he would ask on more than one occasion.

There was more to life for me than falling in love young, marrying young, and never seeing any other parts of the world. As much as I loved the mountains, I had to experience what was beyond. I often felt pulled in two directions. Part of me wanted adventure… to see and do things in the wide world, and part of me wanted to pack up and head back to the mountains that held all things dear and familiar, but I never voiced these words to Bill McCormick.

CHAPTER 8

Early on a Saturday morning, I heard an unexpected page over the intercom.

"Pauline Hensley, you have a visitor," the girl called to my room. "Would you please come down?"

I wasn't expecting anyone and I couldn't imagine who had come calling. Entering the lobby I was very surprised to see my guest.

"Would you like to go to Martin's Fork?" Ralph asked.

It was an invitation I couldn't refuse. I only got to go home about every six weeks on the bus, and I was glad to get a ride with Ralph in his little green convertible.

After spending the weekend, I chose to ride the Grey Hound bus back to Nashville.

My longings had not changed to see other places and experience adventure. I pretty well dismissed Ralph from my mind. Nashville's social opportunities were calling me. I enjoyed my job and felt that I was doing well, although I didn't feel very secure about it being a long term employment.

I decided to join the Marines. So, I went down and took the exam and talked to the recruiting officers. As determined as I was to join, the only explanation I can offer for why I didn't is that my mother prayed it away. She was so distressed when she heard my decision that she went into a constant state of prayer that I would change my mind. Every desire for military life left me.

The recruiting officers I had met remembered me. I received an unexpected call from them one day.

"Our committee is responsible for organizing a welcome for Hugh O'Brien and Alice Laun; the Champaign Lady from the Lawrence Welk Show. Would you like to go with us and be the one who officially welcomes Hugh O'Brien to Nashville when he gets off the plane?"

"I would be honored!"

It didn't take long for me to know a golden opportunity when it was thrown in my lap. It was hard to imagine that this had come my way when there were so many girls in Nashville that it could have gone to.

The appointed day finally arrived and the weather was wonderful. It was summer and the breeze was stirring. I wanted to look perfect. My dark, shiny hair was arranged in a lovely French hairstyle. I wore a beautifully feminine pastel pink and white dress that I purchased from Fox Apparel, matching pink gloves, and soft colors of make-up that complimented my outfit.

Flo smiled and said, "Pauline, you look so glamorous! You look just perfect for this special day!"

~~~~

When we arrived at the airport, there were officials and dignitaries everywhere. Hugh O'Brien was an ex-marine, and even though he starred in the television series, Wyatt Earp, and had done several movies, he never forgot his military background.

Winston Churchill's distant nephew was among the dignitaries. He wore a top hat, a black tuxedo, carried a cane, and held a shot glass of whiskey in his hand. He was loud and flamboyant, constantly cracking jokes to the crowd.

I wasn't saying anything, but just watching the actions of all the people. I had never been involved in anything like that gathering before and hadn't been around that type of crowd.

When the airplane's door opened, my eyes were set in one direction. Women came first, other passengers, and then Hugh O'Brien. I guessed him to be in his early thirties. He was extremely handsome and actually much better looking in person than he was in the cowboy costume he wore for the Wyatt Earp television series.

The female marine walked beside me to introduce us to each other. He extended his hand and took mine. When we posed for pictures, he put his arm around me. He was gracious and soft spoken.

The atmosphere, the sunshine, and the gentle breeze were perfect as the marine sergeants and I followed in a separate car to the Coliseum. Upon arrival I was allowed to go back stage in the hustle and bustle that goes on before a performance. Although I never really had time alone with him to carry on a conversation, it was an exciting event in my life.

When I got back to the YWCA, everybody was waiting and flocking in to see me, asking all kinds of questions.

"What was he like?"

"Did he kiss you?"

"Are you going to see him again?"

The next day someone handed me a photograph of Hugh O'Brien and myself together. The committee had left the picture downstairs for me at the front desk. Of course the girls occupying the fifth floor heard and crowded in to see the pictures. Chapel, a red head that occupied the room near mine came in to see what was so exciting. One look at the picture and she dropped the coke that she held in her hand.

"I am so sorry," she said. "But I can't believe this happened to someone I know! You look just like a real movie star standing beside of him!"

~~~~

Nashville was an exciting place, and I had certainly had some interesting moments, but had begun to grow restless and was thinking about leaving. My social life consisted of chaperoned USO dances at the YWCA, the Air Force Base, and Army Base. I was constantly meeting new people. Everyone I dated began to feel very temporary.

During one of the USO dances I met Jim Ed Brown, a paratrooper from California. His ways were comfortable and his smile was big and pleasant. He was tall and had dark brown hair. He almost always looked as if he was smiling. Talking to him was very natural.

"What are your plans when you leave the service? Will you be going back to California?" I asked.

"I'm going back to California eventually, but at the moment I'm writing songs. My dream is to be a singer," he replied.

Although it never turned in to a big romance, we became friends and continued to see one another and enjoyed each other's company.

My restlessness was mounting. I had begun to feel like I just wanted to get away from Nashville. There was more of the world to see than one city.

The expectations of my job were unrealistic compared to my training and pay. More and more responsibilities were shoveled on to me as well as more demanding expectations. My supervisor had begun to find fault with me and complained to the manager of the company. No matter how hard I tried, she still found fault in everything I did.

"Now, Polly," Gene said, "women on the job sometimes become jealous and they will stab you in the back. Be on the lookout!"

One day the manager of the company came over to my office from advertising. He told me how great I was in public relations and able to stay out of conflicts that went on between employees. He continued to brag about me, then handed me my severance pay.

As much as I had wanted to leave Nashville, I hadn't wanted to leave under those circumstances. The news came to me as a great shock. I was not financially prepared to make a move anywhere at that point.

Pauline Hensley and actor Hugh O'Brien

CHAPTER 9

After I had cleared out my belongings, I walked out of the office with as much dignity as I could muster. My heart was broken, and I thought I would choke before I could be left alone to cry. As I walked down Fourth Avenue North, warm tears silently streamed down my face and I realized thirty-three dollars and twenty cents from my last paycheck was all the money in the world I had to depend on, and office jobs were scarce. As I made my way down the street I vowed to myself that I would not run back home or to my cousin's house. At that moment I had no idea what I was going to do.

When I returned to the YWCA, Flo and Evelyn were there. Being from similar backgrounds, they could certainly identify with my predicament and kept reassuring me that everything was going to be all right.

"Let's go out and have dinner!" Flo said.

"Good idea. That will cheer you right up!" chimed in Evelyn.

They worked on my hair and make up, but I still had to wear sunglasses to hide my tear-reddened eyes. I went through the motions of the evening trying to be polite and as cheerful as possible with my two friends, but I couldn't wait to be alone.

In that small YWCA room on the west side of the building, I crouched on a window seat staring through the darkness to the city lights that spread as far as I could see, wondering what was out there for me. My hurt was so deep. I felt that I had failed. Although with my background and very little training I had come a long way, I still felt rejected.

Suddenly, I decided that I didn't want to live in Nashville anymore. As the night progressed, I still sat on the window bench looking out over the city of Nashville, nursing my wounds. I managed to think of the exciting things I had encountered during my time in the big city. I had enjoyed the USO dances, and had been much honored that a committee with the marines had chosen me to welcome Hugh O'Brien and Alice Laun to Nashville. Most importantly, I had acquired work experience.

I was tired of dealing with the negatives I was experiencing in Nashville. As a little girl I dreamed of growing up and being a model or a movie star. In my heart, I knew that California would eventually be my destination. That night sitting in the window, I began to make plans.

The following day, Jim Ed Brown and I walked to the theater on Church Street. I said, "I am leaving for California in a few days."

He replied, "I will be returning to California in eight months or so and definitely will look you up."

"I'll be looking forward to that!" I said.

"I'll show you around California," he promised.

When my cousin Elmer, George's younger brother, found out what happened with my job, he gladly volunteered to loan me enough money to purchase a plane ticket to California and buy a beautiful outfit. The dress was black knit with a silk lining, long sleeves, turtleneck, straight, and knee length, accented with a soft black leather belt that tied in the front, with extra length that made the dress look more elegant, black shoes, and a matching purse. I pulled my hair up in a popular style. I wanted to look sophisticated as I traveled across the country and when I got off the plane in California.

I was tall and relatively thin at the time, although I had put on a few pounds in Nashville. I was happy with the extra weight since I was tired of being too thin. I suppose that I was born with a certain amount of grace. This, I was told, I had inherited from my Dad's half sister, Mary Scott. I certainly had never had the opportunity to attend a finishing school. While on the flight to California, I received numerous compliments. I almost forgot that I was a mountain girl underneath the polished exterior.

The passenger sitting with me introduced himself as Sherrill Donavon. He worked in the aircraft industry and performed in the western television shows as a walk-on actor for a sideline. His presence made it seem that California was full of new and exciting possibilities.

One of the blessings of being from the mountains is that our huge families had been dispersed from coast to coast, but still cherished family ties. When I arrived at the airport in San Diego, my cousin Mary and her husband, Verlin, met me. He was in the Navy and stationed in San Diego. We drove back to their home where Mary had a little room ready and waiting for me. My clothes had been shipped ahead and she had already put them away, trying to make me feel welcome in their little duplex.

I loved sunny California and I wanted my family problems to be far behind me. My family had very little income and I grieved over their well-being. Even though I tried to outrun the hardships of my youth, Momma always wrote about every problem. I always knew what was going on - the poverty, the struggles, and my father's illness.

Jobs were not easy to find in California. I searched for a few days, and finally went to the state employment office. This office sent me to Sun Swim Pools to apply for a job as receptionist. I was hired and loved the job. I did my job well and was complimented.

Being young and attractive put me in a position to get a lot of attention. I was constantly teased about my mountain dialect, but always in a flattering way. I finally realized that when I was kept on the phone during a business call that the caller was enjoying my accent.

If I heard it once, I heard it a hundred times, "I love the way you talk!" or "What part of Texas are you from?" I suppose I sounded like a Texan to some.

Sherrill Donavon and I continued as friends and enjoyed passing time together going out to dinner, horseback riding, or just visiting with Mary and Verlin in their home. We were never more than friends, but I enjoyed his company.

Verlin was an officer in the Navy, and we sometimes went to events on the base. One evening I met a young officer with incredible good looks and winning ways, quiet but charming. From the beginning, I was impressed with Officer Jack Challender. He talked to both Mary and me casually for quite a while, and eventually asked for my phone number. We began to see each other on a weekly basis and talked on the telephone often.

In the evenings after work, I began to search for a finishing school and chose the Patricia Stevens Modeling School. I found it to be a very prominent modeling and finishing school. Since I had always wanted to become a model, this seemed like the next logical step.

I learned all of the important things a model needed to know - how to walk, sit, and stand; how to dress; the right styles for your body shape and size; the right colors of clothes and cosmetics to match your coloring; how to walk and pivot on the runway; how to wear your hair and make it shine. This knowledge of worldly ways empowered me to believe in appearance as an asset.

The swimming pool company that I worked for also owned an advertising company. This worked out nicely because the advertising company took care of all the publicity for the pool company. When an ad campaign was being launched, they called in Jack Vissers, who was a local celebrity. He was commentator for the Rose Bowl game in Pasadena in 1961.

When Sun Swim Pools opened a new campaign, Jack Vissers recommended they use me for their campaign model, and I gladly accepted. Being used in television and newspaper advertisements led to my being asked to be in the Miss San Diego Pageant, which was a part of the Miss California and Miss America Pageants.

As exciting as this was, I had to face the reality that I had no particular talent. I had looks and personality, but no talent. I accepted the fact that without some sort of talent I didn't have a chance. Maybe the potential was there, but there was no time for development so I withdrew from the beauty pageant idea.

I was still dating Jack Challander and was content to star in the newspaper and magazine ad campaigns and the commercials for television. The commercials were also part of a promotional presentation for Magnabond Coating. A company from back East came to sunny California to promote their product.

Some ads showed me in pretense coating the pools and the idea was, "Magnabond Coating is so easy to apply, even a lady can do it…"

I worked for the swimming pool company until the economy got bad, then was laid off. So again, I began searching for work.

I landed a job with a firm that proofread and typed government documents. This job did not last very long since I had only one year of typing in high school. The boss tried to let me down easy. He came to my desk, told me how beautiful my eyes were, and suggested I get into modeling. The compliment was nice, but at that time I needed a job. Before leaving the building, I went to the ladies room and cried until I was ill.

Again, I covered my swollen eyes with sunglasses and walked away feeling empty. As I walked to the bus stop, I wondered if I was a total failure, but I knew inside that I wasn't. I hadn't had proper training to be a typist in an area of work where precision was so important. In spite of my rationalizations, nothing seemed to remove the inadequacy I was experiencing at that moment.

I felt so alone in the big city, with very little money and not enough training to hold down a well paying job. I was very thankful to have Jack in my life. He was only twenty-four, had a promising career, and was very polite and handsome. We played golf, bowled, and visited with Mary. He was always telling me that I was the type of girl that he always dreamed of having for a wife, and how he would be anxious to see his captain's face when he came for dinner and saw his wife for the first time, and that he loved taking me golfing and bowling to show me off to his friends.

Our relationship was not intimate but innocent and lots of fun, until he didn't show up for a date one night. I knew that something was terribly wrong. He supposedly lived on ship and didn't have access to a phone for incoming calls.

That evening, a still voice compelled me to pick up the directory and look for his name. There it was in black and white. I dialed the number and a lady answered. I asked the usual questions, and learned from the conversation that I had reached the correct number for the Jack I was dating. I found myself having a conversation with Jack's wife from whom he had been separated for a time even before I met him. I also learned that they had two little boys.

I was devastated, regardless of the separation. The disappointment was almost unbearable. *Why did I fall for this one?* I asked myself.

I was very confused, but not too confused to realize that if there was any chance at all that this family could be together that I must get out of the picture. My heart hurt as deep as if I had been physically wounded.

I found myself almost running to get to the ocean, the closest thing to nature. As the waves white capped onto the sandy beach, I stood in the cool dusk of evening feeling the mist from the ocean, and the tears streaming down my face as I prayed, *Please, God help me to let go.*

I had no job and had been involved in a deceitful relationship that had to end at that moment. I wouldn't allow myself to continue seeing Jack even though I cared deeply for him.

During the next few days, I received very ugly telephone calls from the wife. No matter how much I tried to explain to her that I had not known Jack was married and that they were separated, she was rude and did not comprehend my innocence. I suppose it has been and always will be hard for some women to believe that innocence does exist in relationships.

During my hours of hurt, confusion, and desperation, I began to think of all the problems at home. Momma could always use a helping hand, so I decided to head for Martin's Fork, knowing that in the valley beneath the mountains I would be walking back into poverty and hardship, but also into a loving family who would not fault me for having had to try my wings.

In my heart I knew that I had to leave California and leave my dreams of being a model behind. I was afraid that my feelings for Jack might overrule my convictions. I knew that I must follow my heart and return to my mountains. I also knew that Jack was living in a world of what could have been, had he not made a commitment so very young.

I decided to return by bus because I wanted to see the countryside. The trip home was enjoyable and, as I crossed Arizona, New Mexico, Texas, Arkansas, and Tennessee, even somewhat adventurous. I met people from various states as we crossed the deserts, cities, and farmlands.

The weather was cool and windy when I arrived in Knoxville, Tennessee, nothing like the California sun. During the three hour ride home from there, I began to experience a sickness in the pit of my stomach. I thought I had been sure about leaving California, but at that moment I wasn't. I knew because of the distance, I'd never go back. The closer I got to home, the worse I felt, but deep inside my soul, I was sure that I had made the right choice. Doing what is right doesn't always make us happy at the time.

I was twenty-one years old when I returned home. After having been gone two years, I knew that life at home would not be the same as before. Sitting on the porch in the quietness, I stared at the mountains, streams, and rivers, realizing those past times that I thought of as hard times really made up the better part of my life. For the moment, I felt that I had never left Martin's Fork. The time I had spent away in Nashville and San Diego seemed like a dream.

I was like the caterpillar, turned butterfly, which had been forced back into the cocoon.

I walked from the porch, crossed the stream of water that I spent many days playing in as a child, past the honey bee gums that sat on the hillside above the house and into the mountains that were full of redbud and dogwood trees in full bloom and looking so delicate in their given places. After walking high into the mountain I sat on the cool ground to rest.

As I breathed the fresh air and looked toward the valley I began to think of California, of the good times that Jack and I had shared and how sad I was when I made the decision to end our relationship and leave California. I found myself carving our initials on the trunk of a large oak tree knowing they would remain forever, but also knowing I would never contact him again, nor would he contact me as he would never know where I was.

Doing the right thing in life is not always easy, but I knew that my self-respect, values, and morals would not let me down. As I walked back home I felt deep in my heart that I must let go of the past and live for the future. My destiny was in God's hands and would be good as long as I followed my heart. Those values I had learned from my mother, and in the little white Baptist church that still sat by the river with acres of green pasture behind it, lingered within me through the years.

CHAPTER 10

Many times over the years I wondered how my life might have turned out differently if I had not come home to the mountains and to my family. My personal convictions are that each person has a God given destiny. If we go by that inner voice, we pretty well know the path that we should take, and if we choose to take the wrong path, we are usually given the opportunity to get back on the right track and head in the direction we were supposed to go.

It was that inner knowledge that my destiny lay in the embrace of the mountains of Martin's Fork that gave me peace about the decisions I had made and my choice to return to my homeland.

I had only been home for a few weeks when Ralph came for a visit. He had lost his boyish look in our time apart, and now carried himself like a man. Even though we had dated before I went to Nashville, I looked at him through new eyes. It wasn't long until we began dating again.

We were just so much a part of each other's lives that he assumed that we would get married. So did everyone else. I wasn't sure.

One day Ralph and I were riding together on his cousin's Tennessee Walker. I was wearing a skirt, so I had to sit side-saddle behind him. I began to slip off, but I wouldn't let go of Ralph's shirt. I was holding on for dear life, but couldn't stop the fall. Ralph slid off with me.

There we sat in the middle of the field, laughing our heads off. The curl in the center of Ralph's forehead had fallen down from his neatly combed locks. As I brushed the curl back from his face, he stopped smiling and turned serious.

"Pauline, we belong together. I've known it since the first day I saw you on the school bus our junior year when my family had first moved back from Ohio." He reached out and took my hand in his. "Will you marry me?"

I paused for a moment and looked deep into his blue eyes, made up my mind and answered his question. "Yes."

"I always knew that we'd get married some day," he said.

~~~~~

We were married within a few months in a quiet service held in a minister's home.

Ralph's grandparents, Katie and Pee Pace, said they wanted us to live with them for a while. They said they needed our company.

"It just doesn't make good sense for you two to go off and live somewhere alone when there is plenty of room in this big house for the both of us to live and not scrounge each other one little bit," Granny Pace argued.

The economy was terrible and Ralph ended up losing his job. I became very depressed after we moved in with his grandparents. They were very good to me, but I was miserable. I felt degraded, ashamed, and looked down upon. I knew that a few people were making comments that Ralph and I would never have or amount to anything. Their biggest argument was that he was already out of work and we'd never move out of his grandparents' house. There is one thing about mountain people in a tight knit community and that is no matter how much people love you, there are those who watch your life and give their opinions to each other too freely. Eventually you hear about it and feel the sting, but when tragedy comes they are truly there for you.

Our lives seemed so fruitless. Every day consisted of rising early, cooking breakfast, cleaning house, doing laundry, sitting on the porch and talking, preparing the evening meal, and going to bed early. One day bled in to the next, a continual monotony.

"Early to bed and early to rise, makes one healthy, wealthy, and wise," Papaw Pace quoted.

It was the repetition in the routine of what seemed endless days that frustrated me. We had gone to high school, but neither of us had any special training. I could never express the misery that invaded my life during those early months of marriage. I had never anticipated that Ralph would be facing unemployment and we would not be able to be independent so early in our marriage.

When nothing opened up for us in Harlan County, Ralph left going north to try to find work. The economy was bad and people were jobless everywhere. He came back without a job. I continued to do chores on the small farm, but was restless. I sometimes had thoughts of what might have been had I never returned.

The months slowly passed. Ralph picked up odd jobs such as working for Dr. Buttermore, a well-known doctor in the mountains of Harlan County. At this time, I was pregnant with our first child. The time was close for her birth and we had very little money and no health insurance. I had no prenatal care, but it had been decided that Dr. Buttermore would deliver the baby at the old Harlan hospital. I knew I could not afford the new facility that had been built.

Being as naïve as I was, I didn't know what to expect when going into labor. Around 12:00 a.m. on April 17, I began having contractions. My tossing and turning in the bed awakened Ralph.

"Maybe if you would stop tossing and turning so much, you could go back to sleep!"

I tried to lie still and did pretty well until about seven in the morning. Ralph finally concluded that maybe I wasn't doing so well. He went into the living room to get his grandmother. She recommended that we get my mom and go to the hospital.

The hospital was at least a forty minute drive. As we traveled the curvy roads, I began to wonder if we were going to make it.

"I'm not going to make it," I related to Ralph and Momma.

"Do you want to go to Dr. Buttermore's office first?" he asked.

"NO! Please," I said, "GET ME TO THE HOSPITAL!"

Upon entering the hospital lobby, Ralph talked to admissions and they began talking finances. By this time I was sitting on a chair quietly weeping, feeling like a misfit because of our financial situation and at the same time undergoing unbearable pain. The more they talked, the worse I got.

The receptionist became aware of my turmoil and decided to forget the financial arrangements until later. They didn't send for a wheelchair, but opted to send me up on the elevator.

I was immediately taken to the labor room; the nurse began prepping me and realized the baby was coming. Apparently she saw Dr. Cawood pass by, so she stepped out of the room for a minute.

My mother was beside herself. "You'd better come back! She's ready to have this baby!"

I entered the hospital lobby at 7:55 a.m. and Edwina was born at 8:12 a.m. Dr. Buttermore hadn't made it to the hospital so Dr. Cawood delivered my baby. I had never laid eyes on him before. He just happened to be close by.

One look at my gorgeous baby girl, Edwina, seemed to make all bad feelings go away. She was so beautiful with her thick, dark hair and big blue eyes. At this time, there was only one other baby in the nursery - the grandchild of a department store owner in Harlan. Not unexpectedly, the attention of the hospital staff was very focused in their direction.

I wasn't in good health and was anemic due to no prenatal care, and needed close medical attention for several days. Being so weak and dizzy, I had to hold onto things to walk. Nevertheless I was dismissed from the hospital the following morning after Edwina's birth. Before my dismissal, I overheard a nurse talking with the administrative office. From her end of the conversation I gathered that they were checking to make sure that my husband hadn't made a get away with us. I felt like a culprit of some type even though Ralph had gone to the bank and borrowed money to pay the hospital bill. After the office called to inform the nurse that the bill had been paid, everything changed. The nurse came in and offered her assistance in helping us get ready to leave. I thanked her and told her that I could manage fine on my own.

I was stubborn and hurt - so stubborn that I refused to be taken to my car by wheelchair. Mountain pride walked me to the car instead. It is said that one must face the reality that respect and monetary resources go together.

Nevertheless, the joy of having Edwina made other problems dim and I knew that God had given us a very special gift. When she was two months old, Ralph found work in Columbus, Indiana. His job involved the construction of an interstate highway. We moved to Indiana, found a nice clean apartment to live in and were very happy with our new baby and our new existence. After living there several months, winter came and Ralph was laid off. We returned once more to the mountains of our birth.

After staying in Martin's Fork for a few months, Ralph went to Kansas City, Missouri to look for work. He found a job building tunnels and Edwina and I joined him a couple of weeks later, moving across the river to Kansas City, Kansas.

During this year, I became pregnant with our second child. Because of a decline in building tunnels, Ralph was laid off again. We then moved to Frankfort, Indiana, where he began work in a factory. On December 12, at 12:12 Kimberly Lynn was born. The medical circumstances surrounding Kimberly's birth were much better than the treatment received in Kentucky. Due to our changing jobs so much, we had no insurance, but the hospital administration trusted us to pay the bills, which we did, so I left the hospital feeling great. My health was much better, and I was very happy with our new daughter.

Having two children and no help was very exhausting. With the passing of time, my fatigue worsened but I was determined to do the very best that I could with my little girls. In what seemed to be becoming our way of life or a pattern for us, Ralph walked in around 11:30 p.m., at the end of second shift.

"Pauline, I have been laid off from the factory due to lack of seniority. Several men are without jobs."

I relived the same disappointment I had encountered so many times.

I said to Ralph, "I just don't know how I can handle this. I hate being forced back to share someone else's home."

"I will find work somewhere," Ralph said.

We returned to Martin's Fork for a short time until Ralph found work in Rocky Mountain, North Carolina, building tunnels. He rented a very large old house for us because this was the only place that he could find.

At one time, this house had probably been fabulous, but it had been rented for a number of years and was very run down. The ceilings were about twelve feet high and the rooms were painted dark green. We cleaned the house and tried to make it as pleasant as we could. The house reminded me of a morgue.

Nevertheless, I tried hard to make the environment as stable as I could for the children. I worked very hard at trying to maintain my sanity, but felt it slipping. I didn't drive, and I was totally dependent on Ralph to take me wherever I needed to go. He was always sick with a headache after breathing rock dust from working in the small tunnels. If I made it to the grocery store once a week, I was fortunate.

Going out to dinner occasionally was not pleasant anymore since Ralph was never in a good mood. With the passing of time my depression deepened. I came to the conclusion that the only solution was to get out of this type of existence.

Being born into semi-poverty and semi-illiteracy, I had managed to graduate from high school, had done office work, and modeled when I was in California. It seemed I was regressing instead of progressing.

As I occupied this dark monstrosity of a rundown house day after day, I began to think about how we could escape. We needed change. Ralph wasn't happy. The girls weren't happy. I wasn't happy. In my heart, I knew there had to be more to life than this for our little family.

At Pauline's College Graduation

Lewis Hamlin, Harold Hensley, Esco Hensley, Ralph Harber

Front: Kimberly and Edwina Harber

Back: Mary Ruth, Janet Delbeck, Cherylann Bargo, Janet Pace, Wilhelmina, Paula, Gerri Harber, Pauline Harber

CHAPTER 11

During my hours of despair in North Carolina when Edwina was four years old and Kimberly thirteen months, I began to entertain the possibility of going to college. I wondered what Ralph would say about this idea.

It would probably mean that we would have to live apart. I pondered and dreamed about it for a while, realizing that I was twenty-five years old and that I didn't need to wait much longer in making a decision. Ralph and I had often talked about how we would stop moving around and return to the mountains to rear our children. We knew that without a job in the mountains to support us, we would not be able to fulfill this dream.

Finally, I became bold enough to present my idea to Ralph. One evening as we were sitting in the dining room of that big old house I said, "Ralph, I just can't live like this anymore. We never get to see you. You are not happy when we do see you. You always have a headache from the stress of building tunnels. This is not good for any of us. I've been wondering for a long time how you would feel about me going to college?"

I pointed out to him that I could get my degree in education and that getting a teaching job in Harlan County would be a sure thing. When I finished college and began a teaching career he could come back and find work.

Ralph reacted in a calm manner. "If you are sure this is what you want, I will see that you make it financially."

Filled with excitement, I had to decide which college I would attend. My first priority was to find a college in Kentucky not far from Martin's Fork, so I chose a very outstanding mountain college. The University of the Cumberlands in Williamsburg, Kentucky was only two hours away from home.

With the decision made, I contacted the college, received all admission applications and completed enrollment. After receiving a letter of acceptance, I made the necessary arrangements to enter college in January of 1966.

The children and I returned to Martin's Fork. I learned to drive a car only a few weeks before entering college. I knew I would have to be able to drive myself wherever I needed to go if I was going to live on my own. My sister-in-law, Gerri Harber and her friend Roy Lee Long, who had worked and lived in Williamsburg, drove us to the city to find a place to live. I found a brand new apartment - one that had never been lived in. It was completely furnished, and I thought that I had died and gone to heaven; for the moment at least.

Gerri agreed to move down with me and care for the children during the hours I attended school. Shortly after school started, I got my driver's license, and Ralph bought me a white Cadillac convertible. The car was in excellent condition with power windows, power seats, and red leather interior. One would have never guessed that it was ten years old.

After loading our belongings, Edwina, Kimberly, and I drove out of Martin's Fork in that big convertible with the top laid back, the wind blowing our hair, laughing and talking as we headed toward our new way of life. Gerri and I tried to add the special touch to our apartment. Everything was so clean and comfortable. I began orientation on Monday and classes Tuesday. It was such an accomplishment just being there!

As my college days progressed, I often felt guilty about spending so much time away from the girls, but in my heart I knew that I was doing the right thing. My girls would also have a better chance for success if I received an education. I tried very hard when I was with them to make up for the six hours a day that I spent away. Still, my mental condition was much better for dealing with life and with my children than it had been the past four years.

During my youth, I wasn't exposed to very many books or any other type of media, but I possessed an inward motivation and a deep felt loneliness that told me I had to do something with my life. During my primary years, it was unheard of that someone from our community would be a college graduate. In my spirit, I knew that my education should not come to a halt after high school.

I was told during my senior year of high school that I should go to college. Mrs. Ingram, a beautiful, dark haired, fair skinned, petite, young lady who taught in the business department called me to her desk.

She said, "Pauline, you have the ability to do well in college, and should try to go to Eastern Kentucky University."

I was very flattered and considered this to be one of the nicest compliments that I had ever had.

I graciously said, "Thank you, Mrs. Ingram; you will never know what this means to me."

However, since Dad had collapsed in the mines and we had no income, I knew that this was impossible. Nevertheless, the words that Mrs. Ingram spoke to me lived in my mind for years to come. Seven years had passed before this opportunity came my way. I couldn't believe that I was in college.

At times, I sat in the classroom and looked around at other students and told myself, *You're in college. You actually are!*

The joy was unspeakable. Most of the college students of that day were three to six years younger than me, and from different states, communities, and towns. Their age difference seemed of little significance, but it was obvious their cultural background was somewhat different than mine even though many of them were from Kentucky. I felt that I had grown up among the forgotten.

As a college student, I worked hard. Of course, with two children to care for, there were times when my responsibilities were too great. Also, money had to be managed carefully. But I decided that as long as Ralph kept money coming, and God gave me the necessary strength, that there was no reason for my not making it. This is where I placed confidence.

Ralph sent all the money he could, and I stretched it as far as I could. Paying rent, tuition, books and a baby sitter really added up. There were times when I didn't have enough to eat, but I managed to see that the girls did. I had made it through hard times before and I knew that I could do it again. This time, I knew that I would be greatly rewarded when my goals were reached. My life would be different.

The time was difficult, but the years passed quickly. Ralph came as often as he could. Gerri Lynn and I took the children home to Martin's Fork every weekend possible. It was good for the girls to be in a different environment, surrounded by family members who loved them. It was good for me to have the freedom to study while the girls were lavished with attention.

Only six months would pass before my cousin, Jack Hensley, who inspired me to choose the University of the Cumberlands, developed aplastic anemia. At the time he was dating Gerri. Because of his illness, he had to drop out of college and return to Martin's Fork. He died six months later. Gerri never returned with us to Williamsburg. The memories of Jack were too painful in that place. She went north trying to escape the heartache. She found a job and an apartment and began to make a life of her own. We missed Gerri terribly, but I was blessed to find a wonderful sitter for the girls, Freda Ashton. Freda kept the girls for the remainder of my time in college.

The closer I got to graduation, the clearer I saw Utopia in my mind. I would be twenty-eight years old when I received my degree. I could only see visions of a perfect life with Ralph and our girls when Ralph and I landed good jobs in Harlan County.

During my senior year in college, I became pregnant with our third child. The symptoms of pregnancy overwhelmed me. While in class one morning, I began feeling very uncomfortable and began hemorrhaging. I asked to be excused and drove to the hospital as it was only a couple of blocks away.

My doctor, Dr. Pitman, said, "Pauline, I feel that the outcome of this pregnancy is inevitable. You will most likely lose the baby."

After being dismissed from the hospital, I returned to Martin's Fork for a week. When I returned to Williamsburg, Dr. Pittman recommended that I continue my education.

"Whatever will be, will be," he said.

As I continued my education and returned weekly to the doctor for checkups, he felt positive that intrauterine death had taken place. For weeks we did pregnancy tests. I was home waiting for the results of the pregnancy test when my little one moved inside. I laughed and cried at the same time.

I grabbed the phone and dialed Dr. Pitman and excitedly told him, "We can forget about taking the baby."

He said, "Mrs. Harber, I am so relieved."

With great relief, I continued my education and carried my baby until spring break of April 1968. Ralph had taken a week's vacation and Dr. Pitman induced labor.

"Why don't you go on and get a hair cut and something to eat," I suggested to Ralph.

He had been with me for a couple of hours. I thought there was still plenty of time before the baby would come.

He said, "I am tired from driving all night. Maybe I should get out for a while and get something to eat if you think I have time."

"Please go," I said.

I was nervous enough for both of us already without him pacing around the room impatiently. I really was more comfortable by myself. I suppose not having to have someone to hold my hand was part my heritage. Men were not expected to be present at the birthing of their children.

I was wrong about how long it would take for the baby to come. Before Ralph made it back, a beautiful eight pound, nine ounce baby girl was born. The look of surprise on Ralph's face when he walked back in said it all.

"It's your fault that I wasn't here when she came. You told me to leave and I thought I had plenty of time!"

We named her Jacqueline Duvall. Jacqueline was named for my cousin Jack who had died from aplastic anemia. Duvall was from the French sociologist, Evelyn Duvall, who we had been studying in sociology class that semester.

Dr. Goodman had mentioned to the class one day, "Mrs. Harber should name her baby after a sociologist."

So, I did.

Within a week, I was back in school. I graduated in August 1968 after completing a four-year degree in two years and seven months.

The commencement exercises were packed with my husband, daughters, brothers, sisters, cousins, in-laws, and friends. I was the first woman in our family to complete a college degree. It was a proud moment for all of us.

Pauline at the beginning of her teaching career and at the onset of kidney disease

Jacqueline, Ralph, Kimberly, Pauline, and Edwina Harber
- taken at cousin Kelly Smith's house

CHAPTER 12

Ralph had carried the financial burden for our family alone throughout our seven years of marriage. Armed with a college degree, I was eager to contribute to our income and build a life for our family in the valley of Martin's Fork.

A teaching position was waiting for me in Harlan. Ralph was still working in Ohio. I bought a mobile home to park on his grandparents' land and assumed the payments for it.

The first time Ralph came in from Ohio to see our new home, he came loaded with accessories for it... dishes, curtains, bedspreads, silverware. He had picked everything out himself and bought it in Cleveland, Ohio. He had chosen everything to match the colors of our new home. He was so proud that we had a decent and safe place to live. He wasn't about to give up the job in Ohio until he knew there was a job waiting for him in Harlan County, but he was happy to know that his family and home were waiting for him when that day came.

The first year of teaching was really hard. I taught seventh, eighth, and ninth graders at Hall Junior High School. I was responsible for teaching geography, health, language arts, and science. Our school was overcrowded and each class had thirty to thirty-five students on the roll.

Hall Junior High was a huge building that sat in front of the mountains in Grays Knob. A railroad track ran in front of the school. Beyond the track were coal camp houses and then the river with Highway 421 adjacent. The old school had wooden floors and the windows stretched almost from floor to ceiling and our heat was from a coal furnace with steam radiators. We roasted in hot weather, but stayed fairly comfortable in cold weather. The wooden floors bowed up and flattened out depending on the weather. The first year my room faced the mountain, the second year the coal camps.

I had graduated from the very same school when it was known as Hall High School. When the county consolidated high schools into a new facility named for James A. Cawood, Hall became a junior high school.

As the year went on, my entire body began to feel terribly exhausted. I credited it to having worked very hard during my college years in which I often carried as much as twenty-one hours a semester and attended summer classes as well. I pushed myself to the limits because I wanted to finish as soon as possible so that our family could be together. On top of that, I had become pregnant and had a baby during my senior year of college. All things considered, I assumed that my exhaustion was a result of those things together.

One of the most difficult things to learn in that first year of teaching was that I had to be loving toward the students, but also firm. I had always loved and trusted young people, to the extent that I was naïve enough to believe that if I was totally sweet, nice, and trusting that there would be no discipline problems. Most students responded to the way I treated them, but the few that didn't made me feel that I had a great deal to learn.

In the spring of my first year of teaching, I developed polyonephritis, a severe kidney infection, which explained my extreme fatigue. Some days were such a struggle with the demands of work and the girls needing my attention at home. I loved my job and my girls, and I had worked so hard for both, but at times it was all I could do to keep going. I was put on an antibiotic called chloremphenocal. After taking this drug for about six months, my body became so exhausted that it was a nightmare to see daylight come. To face a day of teaching and caring for my three children was almost more than I could do. Ralph was still working in Ohio.

I began thinking that something was terribly wrong and I was pleased that Ralph would be returning in the spring. I researched the drug that I had been taking and found that one of the side effects was aplastic anemia which could be fatal. Aplastic anemia had killed my cousin Jack so I was really scared. I knew that I had to discontinue the drug, but there was the fear of what would happen if I didn't take the risk.

During a routine visit to my doctor, I told him, "Dr. Kirch, I have researched the drug and fear the side effects."

"The drug has been prescribed as a last resort. Pauline, you have no other choice."

A routine urinalysis was done. The infection was gone, and I hadn't developed aplastic anemia. I believed a divine intervention had taken place. With the passing of time, I began to feel healthier. Summer break allowed me time to rest and recuperate.

Ralph moved back that summer also. After being apart for about three years, the adjustment wasn't easy. I think it was harder for Ralph since I was the one who cared for the children while we were apart. After four years of living alone, living with four females had to shake him a bit.

I am sorry to say the separation didn't prove to be good for our relationship. We seemed to have lost a connection that truly never returned. Even though we were together, we led separate lives to a great degree. I couldn't let this spoil my happiness so I built my life around our children. Ralph worked and provided for our needs but it seemed we never did things together. The only thing we seemed to enjoy as a family were Kimberly's varsity basketball games the last two years she attended high school.

CHAPTER 13

My third year of teaching, I was transferred to the senior high school, Cawood High, where I taught sociology, psychology, and science. This was exciting for me because I would be teaching juniors and seniors along with a couple of freshman and sophomore classes in general science.

Cawood High School was a huge school sprawled out on what was once Skidmore farm. I was still rather young, looking only a bit older than some of my senior students. Of course, most of my students had their individual concepts of my personal life. Information about the lives of teachers travels quickly. Word circulated that I had done some modeling in California. Suddenly, several girls adopted me as a role model.

I tried to use extreme discretion in handling situations with the boys who often became infatuated with a young, female teacher. I always let them know that I was a teacher who cared for them in a professional capacity. I strived to gain their respect as a lady and a teacher. One of the most positive outcomes stemming from a teacher/student relationship was having them respect my opinion. They saw what my morals and standards for living were and wanted me to think well of them. Hopefully, I became a good role model.

The Department of Education emphasized that we teach the student as a whole - academically and socially. This undertaking wasn't anything new for me since one of my objectives from the onset of my teaching career was to teach the student self-esteem, good morals, and to care for themselves and others. Being a sociology and psychology teacher made it much easier to interweave those objectives. I loved the students and believe they loved and respected me.

Many students asked me about religion. I didn't teach religion, but I told them that the choice to be a Christian would be the greatest commitment they would ever make because there is a heaven and a hell and we have the right to choose the road that we want to take. When we were asked to remove the Bibles from our desks and the Commandments from our walls, mine stayed. If someone came and removed them there was nothing I could do, but I didn't have to be the one to do this.

During my teaching career, it was my goal to help as many students as possible who came from troubled homes or did not believe in themselves. I saw myself in their insecurities and knew where they came from. It was also my desire to reach students from outstanding homes who had suffered emotionally due to traumatic experiences in life.

For instance, Jacob was a senior who played football and was in one of my psychology classes. His grades began to drop and I knew that he could do better.

"Jacob," I said, "We need to talk. I know something is troubling you."

"Mrs. Harber, when my dad retired from his medical practice this summer, we took a trip to South Carolina to buy a boat. My dad was killed in a car wreck on the way back. I saw my dad die right in front of me."

"I'm so sorry, Jacob. I hadn't heard anything about it. I knew something was going on that you weren't telling. I had no idea about your father."

"Thank you for asking, Mrs. Harber."

"Are you okay, Jacob? Were you injured physically in the wreck?"

"I had some head injuries," he said without giving further details.

"Are you working through this emotionally?"

"I am seeing a counselor at the University of Kentucky. I'm working through some things."

Jacob and I built a relationship of trust. Once he realized that my concern was genuine, he began to come to me and talk about the things that were troubling him. His mother told me later that the time I spent with Jacob seemed to do far more good than the time he spent with the counselor at UK.

I had no idea the compassion I had for Jacob would return to me years later when Marie DePreist extended the same grace to my family.

~~~~~

Another young student that lingers in my memory is one that came from the 'other side of the tracks'. He was a relatively small young man and very thin. He never showed any interest in class, and I wasn't able to motivate him. One day when I had my back turned putting something on the board, I was hit between the shoulders by a metal spiral that holds a composition book together. Peripherally, I saw who hit me. Slowly, I turned around.

Very calmly I spoke to the class. "Whoever did this knows who you are and why you did it. If you dislike me so much, you have my permission to express your feelings to me. Nevertheless, I still care about you."

A couple days later, this fellow asked if he could sit in a chair in front of my desk. I allowed him to do so. The other students were working on an assignment, as this student began to talk with me.

He told me "I don't care if I live or die. I don't care if I die and go straight to hell!"

I was stunned. "Why in the world would you say such a thing?"

"You don't know what my life is like. There's nothing but trouble waiting for me when I get home."

"What do you mean?" I asked.

"Nobody in my family gets along. All we ever do is fight. I hate it. I hate going home! I hate living!"

"Well, I care about you and I want you to live! Your thinking is all wrong. You need to be thinking about living instead of dying."

I wasn't able to motivate him in science, but after this he began to pick up the Bible from my desk almost on a daily basis, and read it during class. As time permitted, he would talk to me about his problems.

I saw a change in him. He stopped causing interruptions in class and was reading even though it wasn't science.

Toward the end of the school year, the little fellow had been helping a mechanic work on a car when something ignited and burned his legs. He showed me how his jeans had irritated the burns, they were horrible. School was coming to an end for the year and I knew that I would be spending the next couple of days taking my sociology and psychology students on field trips. A substitute would be there for my other classes and I wasn't sure that I'd ever see this young man again.

I asked him to meet me in front of the principal's office. I brought him some underwear or 'long-johns' to wear so that his jeans wouldn't irritate his leg burns. When I arrived I spotted him among other students. He looked so forlorn. It was my last act of kindness for him.

"Thank you, Mrs. Harber," he said with his voice, but his eyes spoke volumes more. He knew that at least one person truly cared about him. I saw calmness in him that he had never had before and the spark of life that wanted to go on living. He left school and it was the last time I ever saw him.

~~~~~

During my career, I tried to deal with students as individuals. I fought back tears on one occasion when a set of twins came to me in the ninth grade that couldn't read. I was so heart broken, I had to step outside the door to try to control my tears. I had known the twins since their birth. They were thin, kind of tall, with dark skin and brown hair. They were so misplaced, so hurt and lost. I tried to teach my class and work with these two boys on an individual level as time permitted. They always appeared to be uncomfortable.

They were only biding their time until they reached the legal age. Both dropped out of school when they turned sixteen. As fate would have it, one was killed in the coal mines at nineteen years of age, and the other died in an automobile accident in the mid 1980s. Both left behind little boys who bore their fathers' names.

~~~~~

In another science class as students were taking turns reading, I asked a freshman boy, "Would you please read the next paragraph?"

"I can't read," he replied.

I thought he was trying to be cute, assuming that all freshmen would be able to read. I couldn't comprehend otherwise. When I found out that this young lad was serious about his reading disability, I was very hurt for him. He dropped out of school right away. A couple years later, I learned that for some unknown reason he was on the railroad tracks and was run over by a train.

His smiling baby face and blond curls that I saw on that first day in my science class still haunt me. The words, "I can't read" will ring in my ears upon every remembrance of those young people that I cared about and wanted to help so badly.

~~~~~

As a teacher, it is important to feel a bond with all students. But it seems the students who are from your own community or your own family hold a special place in your heart. The students from Martin's Fork were especially dear to me.

I knew Bobby and his family well. His mother was one of my cousins. Phoebe was a lovely mountain woman who had experienced much sorrow back in the mountains beside the Wild River. She had borne a large family and was a kind mother who stayed home and fulfilled the duties of a true mountain woman. Life was not always pleasant, but she never complained. Her children and home were important to her. She had no work experience on a public job, so she had no choice but to continue on as all loving mothers did in those days – putting the needs of her children before all else.

One night after church ended, Bobby witnessed something no child should ever have to see. He and his mother were leaving the building together and she started down the high steps of the little wooden church nestled beneath the trees on a hillside. She was dressed in a lovely cotton flowered dress, and had pretty olive skin. Her long brown hair was braided and wrapped across her head like a crown. She took one step down on the rock steps and fell to her death as a result of a massive heart attack.

The little fair skinned son who loved his mom more than life itself had to be hospitalized due to the shock of witnessing his mother's death. After that, I was very attentive to Bobby. He became very attached to me and came every morning before classes started to talk to me about anything that was bothering him at school or at home.

Years later after I had been transferred to teach in the senior high school, Bobby was in my psychology class. He was a brilliant young man who did an outstanding research paper in the behavioral science category. I worked very hard with Bobby, taking him where he needed to go and supporting him as much as possible. Bobby's father entrusted him completely to my care on every trip we had made out of Harlan County. We had even traveled all the way to the big city of Louisville to enter one of Bobby's science projects at the University of Louisville. On our trips, we laughed and talked of the great talent that came from our hollers.

We went to the regional science fair at University of the Cumberlands where he won, assuring him a trip to the internationals in San Diego, California. Bobby and two other students were very disappointed that I would not be going with them. The superintendent of the Harlan County Board of Education had promised another teacher that if any honors came up for county students involving a major trip, she would be the one allowed to go as the faculty representative. I was greatly disappointed and felt that it really wasn't a fair arrangement. I had been with Bobby and supported him in all of his other projects; yet another teacher was awarded the trip to California.

The Science Fair in San Diego went very well for Bobby. He only won an Honorable Mention, but was offered assistance in getting into pre-medical school in Kentucky. However, he had so many bad memories in Kentucky that he wanted to leave the state. He went to Michigan and entered college. Later, he returned to the University of Kentucky in Lexington to enter college as a pre-med student. I saw him there during some of my visits to the medical center.

Time passed. Even though I was no longer such a significant figure in his life, I was happy and proud of Bobby for following his dreams to become a doctor. I kept informed of his progress through other family members.

When his sister, Carol, called I expected more good news.

"I have some bad news, Pauline. I just got word that Bobby was found dead in his apartment. He would have wanted you to know," she said.

I was speechless. I don't even remember what was said next. It was just too hard to grasp.

The cause of Bobby's death has never been solved, but the suspicion of foul play was strong. This young man who had experienced the life of a mountain boy and eagerly awaited his departure to the big city and another way of life, now forever lies in the quiet mountains of Martin's Fork. Bobby was young and dreamed of what was beyond, just as I had. Our fates were so different. Some people in these parts say the mountains keep us trapped. Others say they protect us from the world outside. For Bobby I guess it was neither.

~~~~~

One of the most devastating experiences of my teaching career came after a restless night when my instincts warned me that something tragic was afoot.

Homer, one of eight children belonging to my cousin Wash Smith, spent his early youth in a little valley on Bradford Branch that lay in a side holler at the foot of the Martin's Fork Mountains. Joyous days were spent playing in the streams and grassy fields, watching for and running to meet his dad upon return from a hard day's work in the shallow coalmines a few miles away.

Homer was seven when his dad was killed in the coal mines. His death was just another statistic of a rock fall for the coal company, but was felt far deeper by all who knew and loved him. Homer's face and eyes continued to portray a hint of sadness regardless of what he was doing or where he was going.

Homer began his freshman year at Cawood High School. He came to school one morning not knowing what awaited him.

The night before, I had an overwhelming dream that something terrible would happen. In my dream there was indescribable chaos and police everywhere. Going to school earlier than usual that day, I talked with my dearest friend, Brenda Henson, in the teacher's lounge. I told her about the dream and my body began to shake with apprehension. Not knowing what the tragedy might be, I was unnerved with anticipation. The teaching day passed as usual, except for the unexplainable tension I felt.

That afternoon, there was a baseball game. The students that wanted to attend were allowed to and the ones who chose not to go stayed at the school. My fifth hour psychology class was in a trailer across a blacktop drive. Trailers had been added as additional classrooms placed near the river because of over crowding in the building. When the bell rang for the evening break, I walked over to the main building to the teacher's lounge. There weren't many people left in the building.

Hearing some commotion, I made my way through the long hallways and walked out back to the driveway in front of the trailers. When I stepped out the back door, the assistant principal, Mr. Smith, and a few students were standing over someone. I nudged my way through the young men who stood in silence.

I looked down to see a handsome fourteen-year-old boy, Homer Smith, lying on the blacktop. As I looked at him I saw no blood, no wounds. My blood turned cold as I saw the essence of life leaving Homer. His color was changing. There was no suffering, no movement, but I knew that he was dying.

When the ambulance came, I immediately made my way through the building to the main office. I ran to call his mom to tell her that there had been an accident and to meet us at the hospital. I situated my students with another teacher and left for the hospital.

When I arrived, Homer had been pronounced dead. His pillow was still on the table with one little spot of blood about the size of a dime. His mother, a very quiet woman who had already endured many hardships, was in too much shock to make a sound. I will never forget the empty look in her eyes. Her husband was gone and now her son. There were no words to say. What could you say to a mother who watched her son get on the bus heading for school feeling that he was in the safest place possible, but finds as the school day ended, that he is gone forever?

A few hours later, I learned that a couple of people were target practicing about half a mile away from the school. A bullet ricocheted in Homer's direction and hit the back of his head as he stood outside during the break drinking a Coke. As he talked with his friends, the bullet struck the back of his head in an area of the brain that proved to be fatal.

I drove Homer's two friends that had been standing with him when the fatality occurred home. I was overcome with grief as we crossed Crummies Mountain, but I held my composure. It was a desolate place and this added to the intensity that I was already feeling. The fading of the sun left the winding mountain highway even lonelier as I drove home.

At school, each time I walked across the "chalked off" area where Homer died, I remembered the helplessness that I felt when I looked down upon him the day that he lay dying - not able to do anything. I remembered passing Homer and his cousin Sam the same day in the school hallway and speaking to them, hoping that my friendliness might encourage them. I understood just how upset Sam was, being Homer's cousin, classmate, and friend. He had been very close to Homer. When you saw one, you saw the other.

In a short time, the grief that I had felt for Homer was also felt for Sam. Sam was also my cousin, and spent many hours around my home. He always had a smile, a cute face framed with dark curly hair and interesting eyes.

One Sunday evening as I was getting ready for church, after previously being troubled about Sam, word came that Sam had been hit on his motorcycle only a few miles above my house. Sam was placed on a respirator for a few days but was clinically dead after the accident.

I remember vividly the night Sam was taken off the respirator. As I walked outside the hospital, I met the young lad who was a party to the accident - a freak accident with no one to fault. He was leaning against a huge oak tree in the parking lot, with the street light being the only light on that dark, lonely night. He was frozen in his position. The only movement was the hand that brushed the tears that were slowly sliding down his face. I tried to offer comfort but to no avail. I will never forget the brokenness that I saw in his young face.

Homer and Sam's deaths were a shadow across Martin's Fork. The two boyish figures that seemed to be out and about on a moped or motorcycle as we traveled Highway 987 were never to be seen again, but memories of them will long remain in our hearts. Stone monuments mark their graves on Britton Graveyard at the foot of Stone Mountain.

~~~~~

Another tragedy involved a student I had originally met the very first year that I taught at Hall Junior High. Clark was an extremely pleasant young fellow in my Language Arts class who was making failing grades on his tests.

One day, he came to my desk, "I get so tired of making F's", he said with such sadness. He explained that he had gotten spankings every day in sixth grade as a result of misspelling words on his test.

Special Education wasn't very prevalent in our area at that time. I thought the situation over and decided that I must teach this young boy according to his ability. I began to choose very common words, maybe four or five a week, for him to study. After a week, I gave his test orally. The smile on his face after getting all five words correct made up for any frustration I may have experienced that day.

I gave him an "A" on his report card after deciding if he could make an "A" on what he was able to do, he deserved it and would feel good about himself. He was so proud to take the report card to the uncle who had only one leg but did his very best with Clark. The little man was always so pleasant and kind.

One night after going to bed, I heard a knock on my door. I made my way downstairs to the kitchen door. There stood seventeen-year-old Clark, bloody and frightened half to death. I brought him in and asked my husband to take him to his relatives. He and another boy were out browsing around (as a lot of youngsters did in our neighborhood) on Halloween night. A couple of boys had chased him through the river and one had beaten him in the head with a chain. It was hard to comprehend how he managed to make the distance that lay between the river and my house.

He was taken to the hospital. Later while visiting him, I was told that parts of his skull were crushed similar to crushing a boiled egg before peeling. His mother came south and took him to Ohio after his dismissal from the hospital. During testing that was performed in Ohio, it was discovered that he was in kidney failure. The news came as a great shock. He eventually went on dialysis, had one transplant, rejected it, and went back on dialysis.

He became very depressed with the ordeal and returned to Martin's Fork to his great aunt's house that lay below the train tunnel that cut through the mountain to Virginia. He died two weeks later. He was buried in his homeland surrounded by the peaceful mountains. It was by choice he had returned to spend his last days.

I didn't know of his problem or that he was in Martin's Fork at the time. My heart was broken, but I did find consolation in knowing that I had helped to make him happy and feel good about himself a few years prior. At age nineteen, his life returned to God who gave it, forever safe.

~~~~~

Through the years, I have met some of my dearest and closest friends because of tragedies. One such friendship is with Elizabeth. I first met Elizabeth when she was fourteen years old.

One morning while in homeroom, a petite young girl with dark hair and skin came to my classroom. I didn't know this young woman let alone anything about the turmoil that was going on in her life. However, I could see the pain and hurt she was feeling by her expression. Her beautiful ebony eyes said it all.

During my planning period immediately after homeroom that first day of our meeting, I was able to talk with this young lady who seemingly didn't want to leave me. As she began to talk, she spoke of a fire. Living in the city of Harlan, she had been a student in Harlan City School. She felt like a stranger to everyone at her new school. As we talked, Elizabeth began to tell me about the fire that resulted in the death of a preschool aged brother and sister. She had loved them so strongly; it was like losing her own babies. Her mother and another sister were also badly burned. A bond formed between us that day that still remains.

A few years later, after the fire tragedy, Elizabeth's mother lost her life in a tragic accident. At the time of her death, I was out of town. After I learned what happened, I went to visit Elizabeth. I wasn't a Christian and I must say that I was at a loss for words. I told her that I believed that if she would go to church she would receive help.

That very Sunday we went to church. I accepted Jesus Christ as my Savior and the following Sunday, Elizabeth made the same commitment.

~~~~~

Another incident that happened in my early teaching career left a permanent mark on me. I had a fourteen-year-old cousin in my class name Lonnie. Lonnie was from a very poor family and the other students made fun of him. He had grown up on Catrons Creek across the mountain from Martin's Fork, and was fairly well groomed and a nice looking boy with very light blonde hair. He delivered newspapers and once told me that one of his customers gave him the blue striped shirt that he was wearing which set off his blue eyes. Lonnie was behind in school and was older than his fellow classmates. My heart ached when I heard Lonnie being ridiculed by the other kids.

I asked this fair-haired youth, who always wore a pleasant smile, about his family, where he lived, etc. I learned that he was a second cousin of mine. His mom was my mom's niece. After telling Lonnie that he was related to me, I overheard him say to some of the other boys, "Mrs. Harber is my cousin."

"We don't believe you, Lonnie!" they said.

One day a group of boys came with Lonnie to my room. They were snickering. One of them asked, "Mrs. Harber, are you Lonnie's cousin?"

"Yes," I replied.

You should have seen the pride on Lonnie's face. That one moment was worth all the hard times that I had gone through to become a teacher. I noticed that the students began to treat Lonnie differently. Lonnie was proud to be the teacher's cousin. There was a new sparkle in his blue eyes.

Lonnie was often absent. He wasn't present the day I did a lesson on drugs and emphasized how important it was not to drink alcohol and take barbiturates. About a week later, I stayed in town to do grocery shopping after school. I was on my way home and turned my radio on to listen to the news.

The newscaster said, "A fourteen year old boy, Lonnie Taylor, has been found dead after being missing for several days."

Tears slid down my face as I drove.

The autopsy showed that he had consumed alcohol and Darvon. It was told that a group of boys had challenged him to see how much beer he could drink with the Darvon. When he died, the other boys became scared and ran away leaving him behind, not telling anyone where he was. Lonnie's dad searched for three days and found his son's rain-soaked body in a pine grove in a secluded area of woods.

For a long time my mind was haunted by the sad picture of his death. I felt that maybe if I had tried harder that Lonnie would have come to school more and might have been present the days that I did a unit on drugs and alcohol and the fatality of the deadly mixture. He was uninformed about what he was doing and hadn't realized the risk he was taking by mixing barbiturates and alcohol. He was starved for attention and no doubt felt this would make him look important to the other boys. If only he could have heard my words: *the mixture of alcohol and barbiturates can cause death.*

~~~~~

At the end of the school year, a very unique freshman and sophomore class expressed their appreciation to me by bringing refreshments and having a party for me the last day of school. I began to speak words of appreciation and say my goodbyes. I was giving final words of advice - telling them to always do their best in academics, but to remember that the most important decision that they would ever make would be to be a Christian. As my eyes fell on Andy's innocent, smiling face I knew those words were taking root in him. Andy was tall, very slender, with brown wavy hair. He was a kind young boy and an A student.

When school ended that year, I was admitted to the University of Kentucky Hospital for specialized tests related to my kidney problems. The day that I returned home, I stopped at a small country store that was not far from my home.

While at this store, I heard someone say, "The rescue squad is in the process of dragging Martin's Fork Lake for a boy's body."

"Who is it?" I asked, but nobody knew.

I went home to try and find out more by telephone. I learned that this accident had happened as a group of young boys were playing tag. One boy went under the water to hide and his clothes caught on some type of debris and he could not free himself. I called the Martin's Fork Lake office to enquire about the identity of the boy, fearing it may have been a family member.

The employee said, "The body has been found and identified as Andy."

As I hung up the telephone, my heart wept. "This can't be!" I cried.

I could still see the seriousness of his expression the last day of school as he sat at the back of the class. I was so thankful I had taken the opportunity to tell them that academics were important, but the most important thing they would ever do was to become a Christian and make a genuine commitment to God.

CHAPTER 14

It was a sunny autumn Sunday with a warm breeze blowing. My three, six, and nine year old daughters played in the glory of the mountains at the mouth of Rockhouse Branch. I stood watching from the porch of the little four room weathered board house we occupied.

I was filled with sadness as I got up from the old straight back chair and opened the screen door. It made a whining sound as the spring pulled and closed it with a little slam. Ralph would be taking care of our girls until I returned from the hospital. I went to the bedroom and picked up my small suitcase and walked outside and explained to the girls that momma had to go away for a few days.

As I kissed them goodbye, Edwina said, "Momma, you look so pretty in your pink dress."

Kimberly added, "And you smell good too."

Jacqueline was only three, but she hugged and kissed me as I held her in my arms. Their little compliments made my heart swell and my leaving that much more difficult.

I slowly walked to my car, smiling as I went. "My attitude will affect the girls after I have gone," I thought

As I headed down Highway 987, I was struggling to be positive. The beauty of the world that surrounded me was enough to make anyone smile, but there are times that tears come regardless of our efforts.

The mountains on either side stood tall, blanketed with the indescribable leaves of luminous gold, mauve, and other autumn colors; to look at it made my chest feel as if it would burst. The wind was warm on my tear-drenched face as I drove the white Limited Buick convertible. There was very little traffic. I hadn't looked or felt ill, but I had known that the last visit to the hospital for tests was different from prior ones. I knew in my spirit that I was facing an uncertain future. Just how uncertain I did not know. There are many things in one's life that are like the mountains, strong and sure. But there are those things that are like the wind, never being told which way to blow or which direction it will take.

As I drove, my long, dark hair blowing in the wind, I felt pretty and very much alive. The route from Martin's Fork to the hospital at Browning Acres was fifteen miles, passing through several small communities: first Cawood, then to Bobs Creek, Mary Helen, Chevrolet, Grays Knob then Browning Acres. Traveling through these small communities, my mind encountered many thoughts. I knew I was blessed; I had three little girls at home, a husband and a career that I loved. Still, deep in my heart, sadness threatened to overwhelm me. I tried to convince myself that perhaps I was sad because I had to take myself to the hospital, or perhaps because I had to leave my beautiful daughters. As I struggled for peace within, I knew there was more to my feelings than I wanted to admit.

I had battled many things alone in my life, but I had never encountered such heaviness as this. Finally I parked in the parking lot, got my suitcase and made my way to admissions and checked myself into the hospital. Testing would begin the next day. The testing was no problem, except that I was thin and didn't like lying on the unpadded x-ray table for so long a time.

I wanted to make the best of my stay at the hospital. Each day I groomed myself and dressed in beautiful pastel gowns that accented my tan and my long dark hair. I wanted to feel good about myself. Two days had passed and I hadn't received any bad news; I thought perhaps the fears I had were only in my mind.

The last afternoon of my stay at the hospital, Dr. Kirch sent someone to bring me to his office in the clinic connected to the hospital. At the time, I didn't know that Dr. Kirch was terminally ill with liver cancer. He had been my doctor for the last fourteen years, ever since I was seventeen years old. I think he wanted to be the one to tell me the test results.

The moment I walked into his office I knew something was terribly wrong. He had medical books opened and spread out on his desk. There was only seriousness in his expression as he lifted his eyes toward me. Pictures, along with information, lay in front of him.

"Pauline," he said, "I want to explain your condition to you." He proceeded to talk. "I know that you are an educated person, and you will not be the type who will go home and worry yourself to death."

With such a greeting, I knew the news could not be good.

Now he was looking directly at me while he spoke. "You have polycystic kidneys. The cysts will gradually destroy the nephrons in your kidneys. The nephrons are the filters that filter poison out of your blood; therefore, when the cysts destroy the nephrons, renal failure is inevitable." I looked out the west facing window across the river into the tall colorful mountains and for a moment did not choose to believe what I was hearing. Shortly I returned to reality.

I had known nothing about kidney disease, kidney failure, dialysis, or transplants. I had not been confronted with the problem, at least not renal failure. Kidney infections had always been prevalent in my body, but I had never anticipated kidney failure.

I wasn't ready to digest this kind of information, but I tried to be very noble and handle the news gracefully. I couldn't let Dr. Kirch down. I knew he really believed I was intelligent, strong, and able to deal with the news.

I tried to respond pleasantly enough and, for the moment, I convinced myself that I wouldn't worry. I left the hospital feeling fine and in a good frame of mind.

When I arrived home, there sat my baby girls - two little blondes with blue eyes and one little brunette with hazel eyes - happy that their Momma was home and totally depending upon me to take care of them. My chest began to tighten.

The tears began to swell but I knew I had to remain in control of myself and not let the fear control me.

At this point, I wasn't worried about myself, but I couldn't help thinking, *"Oh, God, my little girls! What is going to happen to them?"*

My thoughts raced frantically. I asked myself how long it would be before I became very ill, and what about my little ones? Who would love them and take care of them as I did? I loved them so much; the very pit of my stomach tightened in agony. I feared I could not raise them with the patience and energy that a normally healthy person would. Only God knew how much I loved them. Our lives hadn't exactly been easy but I had done the best I could, and at least I'd had the benefit of good health on our side. My confidence was shaken to my foundation.

The news of my condition brought on a severe depression that I had never experienced before. I wandered in total darkness, but I was able to put up a front. No one in my family sensed the depth of my feelings, except my nine-year-old daughter, Edwina. She had always been a perceptive and sensitive child.

A few days after my return home, while we were alone in our little four-room house, Edwina came into the bathroom, looked up at me so sadly with her beautiful, deep blue eyes and said, "Mommy, is there something wrong? Do you want to talk about it?"

My heart sank. I began to think, as I gazed into her loving eyes, *How much do you tell a child, especially a sensitive child?*

Of course, I told her only enough to relieve her worry. "Mommy has a problem, but everything is going to be all right."

The depression began to lift within a couple of weeks after researching renal disease and learning there were possibilities for a transplant, which could mean prolonged life. The need to know as much as possible about this vicious illness threatening my life and to make plans for the well-being of my children became a coping mechanism for me. I may not have had the tools to fight the disease in my body, but my mind would be armed with knowledge. I also knew that fatalities still occurred regardless of transplants.

As the years passed, I tried to prevent the illness from interfering with the upbringing of my three daughters. Regardless of my physical condition, I tried to appear cheerful for them. I desperately wanted their years of growing up to be happy ones that they could look back on as joyful and peaceful.

I wanted so much for them. I hoped for them things I had never experienced. I could not bear to think they would have to shoulder the responsibilities I had as a child. I hoped there would never be hunger or lack of clothing. My desire was to stay able to work and supplement our income so that we could build a larger house to live in and enjoy together.

I knew the hardships of completing a formal education after taking on the responsibilities of a family. I wanted my girls to be able to complete their secondary educations before they might have to deal with the same hereditary health issues as mine.

~~~~~

Ralph's Grandfather Pace owned several acres of mountain land above the valley of Martin's Fork. He allowed Ralph to cut pine trees from the land. Grandfather and Grandmother Pace deeded several acres to us and there was already a barn on the land. Katie and Pee had raised Ralph from the time he came home from the hospital. They were mother and father to him.

Ralph cut hemlock pine from his grandfather's property and hired our neighbor, John Middleton, to haul them to the sawmill on his flat bed truck. There was enough timber to frame the entire house.

Our plan was to pay for the house as we built it in order to prevent the interest charges of a loan. At the time we were still in the little twenty-four by twenty-four foot, four-room house that was near our new house seat.

As I looked at the site, the rolling pasture stretched all the way to the foot of the mountains, and the bottomland ran adjacent to the Wild River. I knew this would be the place where we would bring up our three daughters. I hoped we would spend the rest of our lives on that piece of ground lying at the mountain's base beside the beautiful Wild River.

I was extremely busy taking care of the children, teaching, and working on my master's degree, and left everything to Ralph concerning the house. We lived on my income alone. Ralph poured his checks into the house he was building with the strength of his own hands and the mental ability that God had blessed him with. He had drawn the house plans himself. He worked on the house every day after he got home from work and all day on Saturdays. Ralph would set himself a goal of one little thing at a time and work steadily on that until it was done.

First came the foundation, then the floors were framed. Next, he put the walls up to divide the rooms. When the trusses and the roof were on, he stopped worrying as much. Once the house was under a roof, he could take his time doing the rest without fearing changes in the weather. Ralph's grandfather, even though he was in his early seventies, was Ralph's constant companion doing the work. He worked like a young man. I couldn't believe it when I looked out and saw him up on the roof, right beside Ralph, hammering away. He was always happy and singing old time songs like "Rank Stranger". Working with Ralph made him happy.

Our plump little Granny Katie was as proud of the big house we were building as if it was her own. I'd catch her looking up at the house site, watching the progress with a big grin on her face.

"I don't know what in the world would have ever become of Ralph if it hadn't been for you…" She believed with all her heart that I rescued him from taking the wrong road in life.

The first level had a family room with a cathedral ceiling that measured twenty-four by twenty-eight feet. Beyond lay the foyer that led upstairs, with an adjacent utility room. On the other side of that was a bedroom, bathroom, closet combination. On the second level was another foyer where the piano would sit. Adjacent to that was a dining room and on the same floor, there was a big kitchen, and a small conversation room where I could talk quietly with company. On the third level were three bedrooms and one bathroom.

Ralph knew how much I loved to look at the mountains, especially Table Rock and Chimney Rock. He filled the house with huge windows to allow me look out and to let the sunshine in. Every side of the house had a special view looking out over horses and pastureland, the mountains, the valley, or the creek.

It truly was our dream house. To wealthy people it would have been a very common house. However, beauty was in the eyes of the beholders. The five Harbers who had traveled from city to city for survival would now be settled in our beautiful mountains.

Our daughters were so excited to have their very own rooms. The spacious 3,360 square foot home with 1,720 square feet of porches and decks seemed so large in comparison to the 576 square feet that we had occupied over the previous five years.

We all certainly enjoyed the new house. The girls continually brought friends home. I preferred other children visiting our house so I didn't have to worry about letting mine visit away from home.

God gave me much patience. I truly enjoyed my children and their friends. We sleighed down the hillsides in the winter and swam in the Wild River in the summer. My children were my life. I couldn't allow a precious moment to be lost. Life was all the more fragile since I didn't know how soon mine might be changing, or possibly ending.

I took my children to church every Sunday. If their friends came and didn't bring church clothes when they spent the night on Saturday, they knew they might as well start looking for something of Edwina, Kimberly, or Jacqueline's to wear. Staying home from church was not an option. Julie, Robin, and Anita were always anxious to go with us.

"Get up, sleepy heads!" I'd call to whoever was there. "Breakfast is on the table and it's time to get ready for church! Rise and shine!"

Ralph was like my dad in church matters. He was a good, moral man, but he did not go to church with the rest of us. After breakfast, he spent Sundays working on his Mack coal trucks and making sure they were ready to get back on the road Monday morning. The girls would wash them after he finished. They loved to see the red, blue and yellow colors shine. They didn't mind washing the huge vehicles. They looked like a bunch of squirrels hanging all over the trucks.

~~~~~

The years passed swiftly. We laughed and cried together and lived life to the fullest. The girls and I had a simple but fulfilling life, even though Ralph was seldom there to share it with us. He was more into TV, watching ballgames and things of that nature during his spare time.

Ralph worked all the time from as early as four in the morning to nine at night or even until midnight when work was plentiful. There were times when it was scarce. He wanted to provide the best life for us that he possibly could.

There were many animals on the grounds such as horses, cows, dogs, cats and our bull, John Henry. He was a scrawny little calf that was born on the farm, and the children teased that poor calf all the time. They chased and played with him as if he were a dog instead of a bull.

The original plan was to raise him for beef that would provide fresh meat for the winter. He grew fat and sassy. He would let the children chase him across the field, then suddenly turn on them and chase back. This would send the children and me running for the barn loft. On occasion, John Henry chased us into the barn when we least expected it. He would sneak up close, then run at us. We laughed, yelled, and felt half stricken with fear as we ran and thankfully made it to the barn, yet were thrilled that it happened. He eventually became such a pet that no one could bear taking him to the packinghouse to be slaughtered for beef. He could relax and be mean.

We had simple chores that had to be taken care of daily, like gathering eggs. Sometimes we couldn't resist an egg fight, throwing fresh eggs at each other. It definitely was a fun chore feeding John Henry and the horses - Cocoa, Lady, Prince, and Susie the pony. Susie was just as important as any of the other animals, even though she was only a pony. Caring for the animals was a calming therapy.

One evening, the girls and I decided to settle down and watch television. While turning through the channels, I was stunned when Jim Ed Brown appeared on the screen. He had made it as a singer. The girls were fascinated when I told them Jim Ed and I had been friends when I lived in Nashville.

As my kidney disease progressed, our lifestyle began to change. Jacqueline was twelve, Kimberly fifteen, and Edwina eighteen. Teaching became too hard for me. My days were long and miserable. Many evenings when I pulled into my driveway and parked, I fell over in my seat from exhaustion and just lay there until I had the strength to walk into the house. By the time the children came home, I had recovered a little strength and pretended to be okay.

For the next few years, I kept my physical problems to myself.

Eventually, I had to face reality. I could no longer handle the mental and physical stress of teaching as the kidney disease worsened. With greatly mixed emotions, I found it very difficult to tell my principal, Josh Hensley, that I had to retire. I had worked extremely hard to get a degree in teaching and had been able to teach only twelve years. Still, a part of me was glad to leave it all behind. The last two years had been an indescribable struggle. My career had come to an early end.

The year the kidney disease finally forced me to retire from teaching, Edwina graduated and would be planning for her first year of college. Kimberly was a high school junior, and Jacqueline was in the seventh grade. I tried to be optimistic by reminding myself that I could be home and not be so tired when they arrived.

~~~~~

When the 1979-80 school year ended in June, Edwina and I headed to the University of Kentucky Medical Center at Lexington. There was no way around it. The time had come to deal with the reality of the disease. A fistula had to be done in my arm to get me ready for the dialysis machine. As a result we were at the University of Kentucky hospital for ten days. Edwina, by choice, was by my side. She was eighteen and beautiful both inside and out. I will always remember her dragging in her lawn chair, setting it behind my bed, and piling it with her quilt and pillow.

The nurse later exclaimed, "You can't stay here!"

She slept in the nearby lobby the first night. Somehow, no one ever seemed to notice that she spent the other nine nights on the lawn chair behind my bed.

The hospital stay was very depressing. I was weak from the surgery as well as from the other tests. A few times my blood pressure dropped to zero. When I fell down in a faint, my blood pressure came back to normal.

One doctor on the transplant team was very tactful about my situation. He felt that I should walk down to see the dialysis unit but I couldn't bring myself to go. I was secretly thinking, *I'll see it soon enough.*

As I lay on the hospital bed night after night, everything seemed foreign. I missed my rolling hills, the tall mountains, the ground covered by velvety green grass, and the Wild River. Only the hustle of cars and buses darting here and there could be seen and heard through the hospital windows. I felt trapped. If I could only get to Martin's Fork and be surrounded by the peace and serenity in the center of that quiet, blessed, God given place, I might feel better. If I could be there, I might be able to forget my fears of future pain and the struggle of dialysis that was necessary for my survival.

I almost convinced myself that if I could be at the 'earthly heaven' on Martin's Fork, nothing bad would happen to me. Then, I realized that no matter where I was, I had a cup of bitterness to drink from. Nothing would change what awaited me as the little life supports inside my kidneys were being systematically destroyed in clusters.

I thought of my little blonde, blue-eyed, twelve-year-old daughter. I thought, "Oh, God! Please spare me another year before complete failure. Let me be there for her until she is thirteen!"

I deceived myself into believing everything would be okay if she was thirteen. I was a fool to believe that. I thought she would be old enough to handle problems in her life at that age. Deep down, I knew leaving my little girl alone would be devastating. Mothers that love know such things.

As I left the hospital after testing was finished and the surgical procedure complete, the sick feeling that rumbled slowly in the pit of my stomach began to calm. Returning home to the place where I had found peace in the past years would be, in part, a cure for my mental state. I had to dismiss fears of future pain from my mind if I had any hope of enjoying the present.

The following week Edwina and I were off to enroll her in college. She would be commuting in the fall. It was only a two-hour drive there and back.

Edwina worked hard and made almost straight As. In spite of her outstanding performance in school, I was always aware that she worried about me too much. I knew her far too well and my pretence of being well never fooled her.

The 1980-81 school year was very busy for the girls. Kimberly and Jacqueline were both on basketball teams. Jacqueline was in middle school and Kimberly in high school. I tried very hard to keep up with their activities. For the most part, I hid the physical agony resulting from symptoms of kidney failure, the extreme fatigue, and nausea.

My car was usually packed when we attended the ball game. I offered rides to other children in Martin's Fork who did not have transportation. It was all fun for the children. I enjoyed their chattering about how the coach reacted to their performance during the game. Everything was comical to them, especially when they were in their early teens. One young man, Larry Hensley, told stories of how his coach had pulled his hair. Then he would mimic the coach's mountain language, which brought more laughter from the group.

There were times that I was overcome by tiredness and had to stop the car. My way of not worrying the children was to say that I was sleepy and needed to rest my eyes for a few minutes. Exhaustion along with the other symptoms did make me very sleepy.

Our daughters were so young and full of life. I couldn't cheat them. As long as I could, I would be there for them. I couldn't bear the thought of them someday being all grown up and looking back on memories of Momma complaining and being sick all the time. I wanted their memories to be ones that let them know I enjoyed bringing them up.

The school year seemed to fly by and suddenly was over.

My health declined just as abruptly. In February, I became ill with a chest cold. The girls were all in school and Ralph was at work. When the children came home, I couldn't bring myself to tell them how ill I was. My creatnine was around 12.0 which meant I was near complete renal failure.

While my family was gone, I stayed downstairs in the family room where the Buck stove kept the room warm and cozy. My thin frame chilled from the least puff of air. I became so ill during that month that I couldn't make it upstairs to prepare myself something to eat. I lay on the couch day after day. As I looked through the glass doors, I could see the Martin's Fork highway and the driveways of our neighbors. As I watched people coming and going, I hoped that maybe someone would stop by. February was a long month - one I have never forgotten.

When March came, the nausea and weakness worsened. The nausea bothered me more than anything. My diet was a tasteless, renal diet, which didn't amount to much food. However, I knew that if I wanted to live, I had to adjust to the change. I found it strange that when first starting the diet, my body screamed for the sodium, potassium and other chemicals that it was used to getting. For one time in my life, I could sympathize with an alcoholic, particularly if every nerve in his body screamed for alcohol when it was taken away. As time passed, I wasn't hungry anymore. I ate only to stay alive.

Frank and Ruby Twinam, Pauline Harber - one month before first transplant

Pauline, shortly after dialysis

CHAPTER 15

In April 1981, I entered the University of Kentucky Medical Center to begin dialysis. For such a long time, I had feared the unknown. I was admitted the day before the procedure started. When morning came, I was taken to a room that contained only a couple of machines. I was the only patient occupying the room since it was my first time to dialyze. A technician went through the entire procedure with each patient individually, answering any questions they might have. Fear took over as I sat there alone waiting for the technician to come in. My friend, Isabelle, who had taken me to U.K. so many times before, was waiting outside the hospital door in the hallway, whispering a prayer for me.

The technician came with syringes and other necessities. Everything was ready. She began sticking the needles into my arm.

"I'll try not to make you too uncomfortable," she said.

One needle went into the artery that carries blood to the machine, and the other into the vein, which returns the blood to the body. As the blood began to flow from my body, the sensation I felt from a sudden drop in blood pressure frightened me. The technician tilted the chair in a position that seemed to almost turn me upside down. She allowed saline to go into the blood, and my blood pressure came up a little, which eased my fear considerably.

As I watched the blood flow thru the long clear tubes then into the artificial kidney, I felt quite sick to my stomach. "How long am I going to have to do this before I get a transplant," I wondered. "How can I stand a life hooked to a machine?"

The procedure continued with a blood thinner called Heprin being added. My blood pressure was taken often. We did our own clotting time by turning a tube of our blood back and forth, which saved time for the technician.

After my first four hours of dialysis, the machine was disconnected. When my arm ceased bleeding, I tried to stand on my feet, but couldn't make it. I remained seated until my blood pressure stabilized again. Back in my room, as I lay lifelessly on the bed, my mind was crowded with thoughts. I knew I was going to have to be a fighter and have a lot of faith in order to survive.

I was released from the hospital on a Saturday to go home, but was scheduled for a return visit to Lexington the following Monday. The drive was approximately two hundred miles one way. The dialysis rule was that all patients had to dialyze at least one time at the Lexington Dialysis Center before going to the Corbin Center, which was only one hour and forty-five minutes from home. Monday seemed to come much too quickly when we had to make another trip to Lexington.

Isabelle and I chatted as she drove. The petite blonde with a heart of gold was not only my cousin but a true friend.

"You can do this, Pauline. It won't be long until you will get a transplant. This is only temporary."

I didn't feel overly anxious. However, I couldn't stop the thoughts of what life was going to be like in the days, weeks, and months to come.

Since it was my first visit to a dialysis center that was occupied with so many renal patients, I didn't want to go in. I wanted to turn back, but there was no turning back. This was a life or death decision. I slowly opened the door. The room was small, but packed with many people. My courage faltered as I looked at the faces of some who were younger than I. Others were older and probably had been dialyzing for years. Some could hardly hold up their heads, and all had skin that looked light yellow.

I thought, "This is how I will be in a few weeks or months." My faith seemed to be far off at that moment.

The waiting room was so filled with patients that there was no place to sit. I so much wanted to turn back, but I knew I would only be running from life. No matter how unpleasant the machines, they were life supporters. I should have been more optimistic and thoughtful of how the machines would keep me alive until I could receive a transplant. Under the circumstances, I found it impossible.

Finally a technician called my name. "Pauline Harber."

The door was opened and I entered the unit. As I looked down the long, narrow room that accommodated machine after machine, patient after patient, my heart dropped. Everyone looked so sad and lifeless. This was quite different from the dialysis unit in the hospital where there were only one or two machines to a room. The technician led me to the very end of the unit where I was connected to a dialysis machine.

Nausea swept over me. My legs and arms began to cramp. I couldn't hold back the tears slowly flowing down my face both from physical and mental discomfort. I felt so trapped and helpless, but this was a time of no alternatives.

I pleaded with the technician to let Isabelle come and stay with me and was relieved when she agreed. Isabelle looked at me with tearful, compassionate eyes as if she could feel the terror and pain that had consumed me. She had never seen my emotions surface as they did that day.

I was hooked to the machine for five long hours. After leaving the center, sickness and depression lingered with me as I rested against a pillow in the back seat of the car. With the fading of the sun, dusty darkness began to hover over the city as we drove out onto the interstate that cut across the farm fields. The sunshine within me faded just as it faded beyond the green fields.

The four-hour drive seemed endless. Surely it must have been a long drive for Isabelle. I didn't say ten words on our way home, nor did she. The depression had taken over my soul. All I could think of was, "If this is what life is going to be like, I don't want to continue living."

Nearing home and looking up to see the familiar mountains partially lit by the moon allowed my spirit to embrace hope again. Coming home to the mountains always gave me a sense of protection, as if everything really would be all right.

From the time we left home in the early morning to make the return trip to Lexington, until the time we returned that night, fifteen exhausting hours had passed. I went to my room and lay lifeless with my mind in too much turmoil to sleep. The next day, I rested to gain enough strength to make the trip to Corbin to dialyze.

While getting dressed before my trip to Corbin, I glanced into the bedroom mirror. I saw an image of a forty-year-old woman who looked very young, with long, dark, shiny hair and not a wrinkle to be seen. I put on a touch of make-up to give myself a little extra color, and wore a white, three-quarter length sleeved blouse with an a-line skirt of soft cotton in pastel blue and pink with white eyelet lace along the bottom. I was thin and felt very feminine in the outfit.

Nervously, I arrived at the center in Corbin for the first time. I entered the waiting room and was instructed to go through the door in the center room, which led into the unit. When I entered, I was reprimanded by an unfriendly technician who wanted to know what I was doing coming through the door into the dialysis unit. I introduced myself and explained that I had come to dialyze. She was terribly embarrassed and apologized. She repeatedly told me during my stay there that she had read my chart and was expecting a forty year old teacher with short hair, glasses, and a short, plump stature.

The center was extremely clean, decorated with soft colors that seemed to soothe and reduce anxiety. The unit dialyzed only ten or twelve people at a time, the technicians were very attentive and the ratio of patients per technician was small. This change of dialysis center was very uplifting.

After dialyzing on Monday in Lexington and Wednesday in Corbin, my blood had been cleansed, I was feeling much stronger physically and emotionally and was encouraged about the process. As the days passed, however, when I awoke each morning before going to dialysis an all too familiar sick feeling hit the very pit of my stomach and depression seemed to overshadow me. The entire dialysis episode including travel time took eight to nine hours each time. Each time after dialysis, my body was in such a weakened state that I could only rest in bed all the next day, struggling to gain enough strength to return to dialysis the following day.

My sister, Wilhelmina, only twenty-eight years old, was willing to lay her life on the line by donating a kidney to me. She was willing to make this sacrifice in spite of the knowledge that for a short period of time she would be unable to take care of her young son. I accepted her gift of life, but it was required that I be on dialysis for three months before the surgery could be performed.

"I guess you're worth it," she'd say with a grin. "I'm paying you back for being my little momma when I was a baby."

Realizing the excruciating pain she would be in after the surgery allowed feelings of guilt to creep into my mind. No greater example of a sister's love could be experienced, nor could the sisterly bond have been strengthened tighter.

CHAPTER 16

The day I had long awaited finally arrived and I was off to the University of Kentucky Medical Center to receive a kidney from my sister, Wilhelmina. By God's grace, I was happy that I wouldn't have to be on dialysis anymore. I was so happy that I had very little thought about the actual surgery. The four-hour drive from Martin's Fork to Lexington passed quickly that day. As we drove I kept thinking, *'I am going to get my life back.'*

As the last step before surgery, I was sent down for an ultrasound.

The doctor doing the ultrasound said, "Honey, I have bad news for you. Your kidney is huge. It will have to be removed before the transplant can be done."

I told the doctor who had been seeing me in the clinic weeks prior to the transplant that I really believed my kidney was so large that there couldn't possibly be room for another kidney. I knew my own body. I could feel the kidney from the front beside my hipbone. I couldn't see the protrusion but I could feel it. She stated that the diseased kidney could be removed when the transplant was being done; I wanted to believe her but doubted that it could be done. Even though I had suspected as much, I found myself very disappointed with what the ultrasound revealed.

I was later brought back to my room. My children, husband, mother, and sister, Morine, and brother-in-law Bob, were there for moral support. Wilhelmina had been released and joined the others. Dr. Lucas, head of the transplant team, entered the room and broke the news that instead of a transplant, I would be receiving a nephrectomy and would then go back to dialysis.

The thought of going back to dialysis after major surgery was a nightmare. I tried so hard to fight back the tears as I looked around the room. My daughters were trying to be cheerful. So were my mother and sisters. I looked over the foot of the bed to see Ralph squatting on the floor. Tears streamed down his face, but they were silent streams. My husband had never been able to express his feelings verbally but those tears spoke volumes.

That night was perhaps one of the longest nights of my life. I had too many lonely, quiet hours to think. I imagined every horrible thing that could possibly happen.

The night finally passed and I was taken to the operating room for the huge kidney to be removed. Hours after the surgery the fistula in my arm that was used for dialysis was not functioning properly. Dr. Casaul was called in and I was taken back to surgery. The fistula was declotted and working efficiently again. At about 3:00 a.m. Dr. Casaul called from his home telling the nurse to put a pillow under my arm to keep it elevated.

Very early the next morning he came to see me. He sat on the side of my bed. He was a young man, probably in his mid-thirties with dark hair and a kind face. As he sat there he picked at the paint on his fingernails.

"I've been painting my porch swing," he explained. I realized he was on his own personal time and was worried that my fistula would stop. He wanted to keep a close check.

"I appreciate your concern," I said. "It means a lot."

He said, "You have been through enough for one night."

Months later I asked Nancy, my transplant nurse, "Where is Dr. Casaul?"

She said, "He has moved to another state. He has been diagnosed with lymphoma. He already had the diagnosis when he was treating you."

I can still see his face and wonder what his fate has been. I never asked again. If it was not good, I don't want to know.

The following days were rough, not only healing from the surgery, but also having to go through dialysis on the same schedule as before when I was already in so much misery.

Nine days passed before I was released from the hospital. I returned home and began my trips again to Corbin Dialysis Center. The traveling was very uncomfortable. The surgery had been more difficult than usual because of the size of the kidney. It weighed over four pounds - about the size of a football.

Week after week passed with no word from Lexington about the date for the transplant. Then early one morning, while getting ready for dialysis, the phone rang. Discouraged and downhearted, I answered it. I was surprised to hear the voice on the end of the line. It was the head nurse, Nancy, of the transplant team. I froze with anticipation, almost afraid to breathe.

"We have an opening in our surgical schedule and we'd like to move the date up for your kidney transplant..."

A surge of adrenaline raced through my weakened body. I barely heard the rest.

She said, "Your sister and you have been rescheduled for an earlier date and will be admitted next week for the transplant."

My spirit soared.

~~~~~

We arrived at the hospital on Tuesday evening. The transplant was done early the next morning. As I lay on the table before going to sleep, I knew my precious sister was lying on another table just beyond the door that joined our rooms, risking her life so that I could regain mine.

A host of family members nervously awaited the news of how the surgery was progressing. It was especially hard for Mother. She was extremely concerned, having two daughters in major surgery at the same time. She didn't stay in the waiting room with the others all the time, but hid away in the chapel, because she had to be alone to pray.

After approximately three hours, Dr. McRoberts, a jolly doctor who had a talk show on Lexington TV, entered the waiting room and informed the family that the kidney was already functioning and had put out several cubic centimeters of urine, and my sister was fine. Our family was overcome with joy and relief. What a glorious day it had turned out to be!

After recovery I was taken to a private room. When I opened my eyes, the walls looked beautiful. Everything looked beautiful. The toxins were out of my system, and the creatnine and BUN, which measures the function of the kidney, were moving toward normal at a fast rate. In spite of the pain and discomfort, I could feel myself coming alive.

The words rushed over and over through my mind, "*Thank you, God. Thank you, God.*"

Each day I continued to improve, even though my body had to adjust to the anti-rejection medication, which would have many negative side effects. Just being alive was such a great joy that I tried not to think negatively in any way. A second chance at life strongly motivated me to appreciate things, both tangible and intangible, that I had taken for granted for so many years.

After thirty days, I returned home with rosy cheeks, looking lively and well. At last, I could be a good mother. I could make up for precious time that had been lost. My husband was running for magistrate and I could help him in his campaign. I could go to church. There was so much I wanted to do and how wonderful it would be to be able to celebrate Thanksgiving and Christmas as I once did.

~~~~~

As the months passed, my good health seemed almost unreal. I was so alive and wanted to live life to the fullest. I even looked pretty again instead of frail and white. I enjoyed my daughters like never before. It was very exciting to be able to have supper cooked when they arrived home from school and to be able to attend their ballgames and help them with their homework. I even entertained the thought of going back to teaching the next year.

Thanksgiving came. Family members began arriving at our home to celebrate one of the holidays I love most. We had always been thankful, but this year we felt more blessed than ever, so each and everyone seemed to enjoy themselves immensely. We celebrated the gift of life, love, and family in our house snuggled in the Martin's Fork Mountains.

When night came, I didn't feel very well. I became concerned and brought it to the attention of my sister, Morine. The next morning my brother, Harold, and

Morine, drove me to the University of Kentucky Medical Center. I explained to the transplant nurse that I didn't feel normal. I was ill, but found it hard to describe just how I felt. The nurse called the doctor that was on call, and he instructed her to do lab work immediately.

The lab tests revealed that my creatnine was 1.4, which was a low normal; however, mine was usually 0.9, which was a high normal. The nurse assumed I was within a normal range and released me to return home. I tried hard to suppress my humiliation because I had allowed my family to drive such a long distance for nothing. I found myself almost embarrassed to tell Ralph that there were no problems.

As the days passed and Christmas neared, I grew worse and worse but kept it to myself. I wanted my family to enjoy the holiday without worry. The snow fell and the atmosphere was perfect. We walked and visited with neighbors and enjoyed our loved ones who shared our big room downstairs with the festively lighted live spruce tree. I had a wonderful Christmas with my family, but knew something was going wrong in my body and I wondered if I might not be present or able to enjoy Christmas the next year. I had an unusually sad feeling as I stored my Christmas decorations.

My next appointment at UK was in January. When the date came, I rode down with my cousin, Justin, and his wife, Linda. Justin had also had a transplant two years prior to mine and was having his usual lab test run. I wanted to spend time with them as I very seldom had the opportunity. He didn't wait for lab results and because I had ridden with him, I didn't either. The transplant nurse said she would call if there should be a problem. I had a horrible headache as we traveled I-75 toward Harlan.

I returned in time for Jacqueline and Kimberly's ballgames. Ralph attended Kimberly's at Cawood High School in the huge domed gym. I attended Jacqueline's game at the same old rock gym that had accommodated me in high school.

The transplant nurse finally succeeded in tracking me down. She reported that my labs were not normal. This news brought the most awful feeling to my soul. She instructed me to go to the local hospital and have the tests repeated the next day. The results showed a higher abnormality than the ones at UK had shown. I called UK back with the results from the Harlan lab and a conference was held with the transplant team. Their decision was that I report to the University of Kentucky Medical Center immediately.

It was a cold January evening and the snow had just begun to fall. Edwina volunteered to drive me to Lexington but had to make arrangements with the department head at the college to miss her classes. So we drove to the college to get assignments. In her field of study, to become a laboratory technician, getting behind could be detrimental, the department head was concerned about Edwina leaving, but there was no stopping my girl.

When we left the campus that sat above the little city of Cumberland nestled deep in the Appalachian Mountains, snow had already covered the grounds and was falling fast. Such beauty momentarily let me forget where I was headed and why. With everything covered in white I felt that the earth was pure and cleansed. The highways were covered and two hundred miles of snowy road lay ahead of us. We journeyed through the deep snow with the flakes flying toward us. The drive would have been pleasant under different circumstances.

Kimberly had packed our car with blankets, food, flashlights, water; everything needed if we became stranded.

We battled the deep snow with only one lane open at a time. Our world was white as far as we could see, but we slowly made headway. Occasionally I looked toward my beautiful Edwina and marveled at the grace and bravery she possessed.

We arrived in Lexington very late. I was hospitalized and new lab tests were done. The results showed that I was in rejection. Dr. Lucas ordered Solu Medrol intravenously. Unfortunately, the medication did not reverse the rejection. I grieved for the possible loss of the kidney and for the fact that it might prove to be a useless sacrifice by my sister. I had known something was wrong for weeks, and wondered if the rejection had gone too far.

The doctor chose to keep me in the hospital for a few days. A friend picked Edwina up and she returned home and back to school, leaving the car for me to keep in Lexington.

A couple of days later, a biopsy was done on the kidney. The results were very clear. It was too late to save the kidney. Regardless of my previous feelings, at that moment I blocked the possibility of rejection out of my mind. Dr. Russell, a very young man with blonde wavy hair and compassionate blue eyes, clearly stated to me that I was in kidney failure before he released me. He said the function of the kidney would gradually dribble out or, in plain words, cease to function. My mind failed to accept what it had been told. I not only refused to believe it, but totally shut it out of my mind. Gail Daniels from Martin's Fork, who now lived in Lexington, had come to visit. When Dr. Russell left the room I continued chatting as if I had had no news at all.

After dismissal from the hospital, I got into my car and drove to my home in Martin's Fork. The evening I returned was parent night at Kimberly's school. Parents were to walk out onto the basketball court after the game with their daughters. I made it in time to get dressed and groomed for the event, and enjoy every moment of the game.

I was in total denial of what I had heard only a few hours earlier. I chose not to tell my family anything except that they had done the usual lab work at the hospital and released me. I suppose, in part, I chose not to tell them because I was in denial myself.

CHAPTER 17

The days passed without a major physical episode. I was doing my household chores as usual, keeping the horrible news to myself; possibly hoping the results were wrong, or that a miracle would happen. One morning as I cleaned downstairs, for no obvious reason, I didn't feel well. My body felt so tired and I couldn't shake it off. The nagging sensation that something was wrong caught up with me. I got myself ready and left a note for Ralph and my daughters that I was ill and had gone to UK.

As I drove north on I-75 in March of 1982, the weather was cold, but the sun shone through the car windows making me feel warm and comfortable. I was able to relax and put aside my worries. I had programmed my mind to think good thoughts when I didn't want to think of what was really happening to me. I was daydreaming of times when I was home with the girls, the sun sparkling through the windows on the south side of the house as we enjoyed just being blessed with so much serenity and beauty.

I became so relaxed that I fell asleep while driving. I was awakened when a sudden, loud horn jolted me awake. I saw a truck driver staring down into my car, blasting away at the horn. He knew that I was asleep and didn't stop blowing until I woke up. I had been a disaster waiting to happen.

The interstate was very straight. My arms were fixed at the wheel in straight alignment. It would have been only a matter of time until I would have swerved into the flow of traffic in the next lane. I never met the trucker, but I certainly thanked God for him. Perhaps God uses people on earth as guardian angels at given times. The unknown trucker was certainly my guardian angel that day. I wish I could have seen his face more clearly.

The irony of it all did not escape me. In the midst of fighting for my life against kidney disease, I sometimes thought that it would be easier to have it all behind me. But with almost certain death waiting for me on the interstate, God had allowed someone to see me and wake me in time to prevent a car wreck. I clung to the hope that this was an indication that I would recover and that my life still had a purpose that had not yet been completed.

I arrived at the hospital and slowly crept through the revolving glass doors. I walked through the chair filled entrance area passing many people both sick and well. I passed employees and visitors on my way to the elevator. As I stood in silence in the elevator, I felt numb. Entering the fifth floor of the clinic, I saw Linda, the transplant nurse, and Dr. Russell from a distance.

"Pauline Harber..." I was paged to come to their examining room.

There were no labs done; no examination; only words. Linda sat in front of me, Dr. Russell stood. They tried tactfully to make me understand that the kidney was in rejection and there was nothing that could turn it around. My mind still refused to accept what was being said and apparently it showed. I stared at them, giving no response - just an empty look and no emotions.

Dr. Russell left and brought Dr. Lucas back with him. Dr. Lucas, without his usual friendly smile, looked straight into my eyes and said, "Pauline, there is nothing we can do."

It seemed as if I had suddenly awakened from a deep sleep, just as I had in that startling moment of the trucker's horn blast. For the first time, I really heard what the doctor was saying. The tears begin to swell in my eyes and a tightness form in my chest.

I very calmly stood and said, "Is this all that you can do?"

They stared silently at me.

I turned and left the room without another word spoken between any of us.

I made it to the car with no memory of the corridors, elevator, or waiting rooms. Sobbing uncontrollably and nearly blinded by tears, I drove out of Lexington. I longed to go home and I didn't want to go all at the same time. I had never had such a strong feeling of indecisiveness.

I considered going east of Lexington to Morehead where my sister, Wilhelmina lived. In my heart I knew that wouldn't change anything, but only prolong the inevitable. I knew I had to go home. My heart would not let me cast this burden upon my family.

For four hours I sobbed in the solitude of my car. At times I cried out loud. Occasionally I talked to God and asked for His guidance. I realized I had to get myself together before I reached home. I couldn't bear my family seeing me out of control.

When I finally arrived home, I allowed my family to believe that I was doing okay. At the time, I convinced myself I was doing the best for all of us. I had to be able to accept the reality of the doctors' prognosis before I could expect my family to accept it.

My mother and daughters wanted me to be well again. I just couldn't find the words to tell them. I couldn't bear their disappointment. My daughters needed a mother that was well.

My mother had made plans for the following year for quilting, gardening, and visiting her children... all the things she enjoyed doing. I hated to take that away from her.

"*Am I cheating everyone?*" I asked myself.

CHAPTER 18

There are times when the wounds of life go too deep for words. I wasn't able to talk to anyone about the awful emotional defeat. My mind was bombarded with thoughts of the kidney that was supposed to have changed our lives and brought back sunshine and laughter. All that was shattered by the illness that was visiting again.

I had no control over the catastrophic sickness that would lead us again to an unknown destiny. I was only forty-two, yet I wondered if I would see another birthday. Emotional struggles overshadowed my entire being with darkness as black as Brush Mountain when the moon was new.

My mind raced frantically, *My children need me. Will I see them complete their education? Will I ever hold a grandchild, or will I simply cease to be?*

Oh my God! How I wanted to live for my children. I wept often in private. I knew they needed me so.

My mind continued to focus on my family. Only my frail body and uncontrollable thoughts occupied our home. The girls were at school and Ralph was running load after load of shiny black coal to see that we survived financially. Sweet Momma was in her little white house with its tin roof sitting on the hill above Martin's Fork River in her state of contentment. She loved her peaceful home.

When Momma felt the dark clouds gathering around her, she sat in her rocking chair looking through the big window with a view across the river over the acreage of green fields that reached the foot of Stone Mountain. Although it was called Stone Mountain because of the rocky cliffs that covered the summit, it was rich in beautiful green foliage. She loved to look out on the huge oak, walnut, poplar, beech, hickory, and maple trees that stood plentiful. Most of all the dogwood, redbud, and sarvis in bloom made her joyful. Many times she would sit there and sing the old time songs like *"Wonderful Peace"* and *"When I Walk up the Streets of Gold"* letting the joy of the Lord strengthen her and drive the clouds away.

I couldn't help but feel guilty in knowing that I would soon have to tell her that we were facing another mountain without the hope we previously held. This time I did not have a donor. Even if someone had given me a kidney I don't know if I could have accepted it. I bore too much guilt from losing the kidney Wilhelmina gave me. I couldn't even think of putting someone else through that kind of pain.

I had many emotional issues to deal with before I could tell my three little girls and my momma what lay before us. No matter how I handled the situation, all our lives would be affected by this unwanted repetition of what had taken place only two years prior. I continued for some time to tread this path alone.

In the beauty of the morning I walked to the kitchen door and opened it wide. I didn't want to look through the glass. I wanted to feel the coolness of the early spring air that was blowing my way. Oh, how I had loved springtime for as long as I could remember. I longed to see the apple blossoms blowing from the apple trees and covering the ground like snow.

Spring represented new life coming back into the mountains after a long, freezing winter. Even as a child I was joyful when spring came to the mountains. I ran, jumped, and put my feet in the clear water that ran by our house. I chased the hummingbirds that drank from the pink touch-me-nots and the bleeding hearts. I was so full of joy and life inside and wanted the whole world to know what I was feeling. How I wished I could have done the same that very moment.

As I looked over the grounds and into the mountains, I cried, "Oh God, why can't I have one beautiful spring season? It has been so long, why can't I be well enough to enjoy the new life that spring brings?"

The years of not being able to enjoy my mountains, my valleys, my rivers and streams had left emptiness inside.

When closing the door slowly behind me, I was overwhelmed by a flood of grief. I could see no light that sparked the human spirit to go on. The inner ray of light that had always shone outside in peace as I walked through renal failure before, at this moment would not surface. I could not block the hopelessness that was slowly ripping my life apart.

As I stood in the small formal living room, my place to sit and look at the outside world, I knew I had to talk to God. He was the One that would listen to my cry for help. I walked into the small room across the hallway that was so pleasant, decorated in light yellow and green with cream colored walls. Just beyond the windows the oak trees were displaying new life; the leaves were tender and green. This restored my peace when I was tired.

I knelt slowly to my knees and cried, "Please, God, don't let me lose the kidney that Wilhelmina gave me."

I still had not accepted that the kidney was failing. I entered that room day after day and talked to God. Friday came. Again I fell to my knees in agony.

Suddenly I began to pray in a different way. I said, "Please God, if Your will is not to heal this kidney, give me the inner strength and courage to live one day at a time."

I knew in my heart this was something I had to deal with in the spiritual realm. I had been in denial for days. The thoughts of dialysis, another nephrectomy and the fact that I might never get another kidney were more than I could humanly accept. I could feel my whole world caving in. There was so much in my life that was unfinished.

As I told God all these matters, a weight lifted from my spirit that would physically equal a mountain being moved or lifted from the earth that lay beneath it.

My final prayer was, *Please God, give me the strength to face tomorrow. Let me enjoy every day that I have left*

This was my miracle. The endless darkness and gloom that hovered over me was gone. It was as if I saw light that I had not seen in such a long time. This supernatural event did not occur in my physical being but in my spirit.

I knew the kidney was failing, but it would not happen instantly. It would be a few months before the kidney would completely shut down and I would have to go back on dialysis.

CHAPTER 19

It was two months into the spring season and time for Edwina to graduate college. Momma, Ralph, Kimberly, Jacqueline, and I attended the delightful ceremony at the college in Cumberland, Kentucky among the tall quiet mountains. Edwina gracefully received the honor for the highest grades of her class. I knew that Edwina would go forward with confidence of steel. She had far outgrown the lack of security that over shadowed her during her younger years.

Not many days later, we attended Kimberly's high school graduation at James A Cawood. She marched down the Trojan's gym, which was different to the other schools in the county, with its distinctive dome shaped roof. Kimberly's dreams lay ahead of her. She entertained the possibility of someday returning to James A Cawood High School as a teacher. However, being the high-spirited girl that Kimberly was, she tossed around many ideas of what her future held.

The following week, Jacqueline's eighth grade graduation was in the same auditorium I had walked down so many years earlier, located in a remote area in the striking mountains of Gray's Knob. The school was constructed of rock, which had been laid one by one by local laborers. As we waited outside before the ceremony began, the bright sun tried to warm us as the spring breeze blew through the trees, sending chills through our bodies.

I was blessed to be there for my girls and see doors close behind them only to open new ones that would secure their futures. Meanwhile my prayer was to be there to support their efforts.

As the summer heat sizzled and the fresh mountain air abounded, the girls and I were able to enjoy every glorious day by going to the crystal clear Wild River that flowed softly toward the valley. We were able to find a hole of water that had not been contaminated because there was nothing beyond it but mountains that were off limits to strip miners and loggers. We called this place the Narrows because the huge boulders that lay on each side had narrowed the river. The water was extremely clear and frigidly cold; it would almost take your breath away.

After sunning on the big rock for a while, I yelled, "Girls, I'm comin' in!"

Together they would yell, "Mom, it's as cold as ice in here!" Somehow they always found it hilarious when I first jumped into any hole of water.

As the leaves began to show their many colors and the air began to feel nippy, my body was weakening. Lab work showed that my renal failure was progressing rapidly. I had to realize that I would be returning to that dreadful miracle machine that hopefully would sustain my life again until a kidney came my way.

~~~~~

We knew the coal business could bring feast or famine. Ralph's work depended on coal and coal was in slow demand. Edwina was motivated to venture into a different setting. Since there were no jobs in Harlan, she felt that it was time to walk away from our little paradise and enter the working world. However, she still did not want to leave the mountains that were such a part of her life. She had not been secluded from the rest of the world as I had as a young girl and did not crave to venture beyond the mountains of Appalachia.

Edwina said, "Mom, I know where I am going to find work."

"Where," I replied.

She said, "In Norton, Virginia. They say the mountains are so beautiful and are as close to the little city of Norton as the Brush and Stone Mountains are to Martin's Fork. I have already set up an interview at Norton Community Hospital."

I pondered and worried a little because our finances weren't very good at present, but I knew I could find a way to help her get established in a new setting.

Edwina asked, "Mom, will you ride to Norton with me? I want to be with you as much as possible."

"I will be happy to," I answered in an enthusiastic voice. We lit out for Norton, laughing and talking as we drove.

We drove through the mountains over the winding roads, passing through two or three small Virginia towns. Upon entering Norton we located the small hospital that sat right in the middle of the tidy little town. We felt right at home with familiar scenery in every direction. All we had to do was look slightly above the city and find the same beauty that we had driven away from. I waited in the hospital lobby while Edwina interviewed.

"I got the job!" she said as she came rushing down the hall.

"Honey, I am so proud for you," I said.

Regardless of how happy I was for Edwina, my mind swirled with thoughts of finances for an apartment and other necessities. Before I could worry too much, the administrator sent his secretary to us.

"Edwina, the administrator owns a couple of apartments behind the hospital and one of them is empty. Will you come with me and see what you think?"

As Edwina and I followed, we glanced at each other thinking, *this is too good to be true*.

I should have known that God was taking care of my little girl just as he does the lilies of the fields. As we entered, our eyes filled with excitement to see a cozy apartment with a living room, kitchen, dining room, bedroom and bath. It had shiny hard wood floors and clean antique white walls, but no furniture.

Edwina whispered, "What will I do for furniture?"

Before I could say anything, the secretary turned to us saying, "What kind of furniture do you like?"

"Any type will be fine," Edwina answered, trying not to show excitement.

Immediately this wonderful, tall dark-haired lady ordered elegant new furniture by phone, and then called security to make sure the windows on the balcony were secure and to check the locks on the doors.

The administrator had learned from Edwina that I was with her and later asked me to come to his office. To say the least, I was puzzled.

He said, "Mrs. Harber, I know that you are uneasy with your young daughter moving away from home; I want you to know we are one big family here and we will take care of her."

"Thank you, sir," were the only words that would come.

He continued, "Edwina will not have to pay rent until she gets paid."

I was relieved in so many ways; I could have jumped ten feet in the air. At that moment I did not feel the tiredness or oppression that kidney failure was imposing upon me. I knew someone was walking before us; someone who was not manifested in the flesh and was preparing the way for our needs.

Edwina

CHAPTER 20

I had bouts of sadness and happiness about Edwina's leaving. She was all grown up and I had to accept that she was not a little girl anymore. At twenty years old she would be on her own working as a medical lab technician. It was hard for Ralph to accept Edwina being old enough to make her own decisions. Had she remained at home, this probably would have bred conflict. He had somewhat of a control problem over our girls, regardless of their age. At this time in her life, it was good that Edwina would be independent.

As Edwina and I drove back to Martin's Fork, she seemed very sad.

"Edwina, please smile," I said. She had so much wanted to get a job in Harlan and be near me because of the trauma I was facing.

Sunday afternoon arrived. The sun was shining and the cool breeze gently blew on us as we packed the gold and white Buick that she would be driving until she could afford to buy her own.

I told myself over and over, *Pauline, you will not break into tears when she leaves.*

When every thing was in place, we stood by the car parked in front of the porch with the big columns. As she pulled the car onto the lawn to load her things, our eyes met. Tears spilled over on our faces, but we were silent. We embraced lightly. She gracefully slipped into the car.

I sat in the white wicker swing and watched her move down the drive adjacent to the flat green pastures. Even her horse raised his head and gazed as she crossed the bridge that stood over the Martin's Fork River. When she disappeared from my view while rounding the last curve visible to me, my heart was saddened. I sat there for along time and just stared at the bend of the road.

'What will her destiny be?' I wondered

Edwina's insecurities had changed as she grew into a young lady. She was independent, strong willed, and confident in everything she had learned in general life and in school. This knowledge of her gave me the greatest feeling. I knew she was like the mountain laurels that grew just beyond our home in the mountains by the cool fresh stream with their shiny green leaves and delicate light pink clusters of flowers surviving nature's forces. My innermost being was telling me that this lovely young woman will survive the same way during her storms of life.

"She will be a beautiful flower among the suffering," I thought. "Her inner beauty will spill over on them. Perhaps this will be, in part, her destiny."

Edwina called me often. She was touched by the distress and pain of others, yet strong, loving, and supportive.

I was nearing the end stages of renal failure. Because of her medical training, she was acutely aware of this and very protective of me. She usually kept her own problems to herself, but when Edwina called one evening, I recognized her spirit was broken. I encouraged her to talk to me about what was casting this heaviness upon her.

She began to speak in a broken tone. "Mom, this patient just died and I had to tell his wife, children, and relatives that he was gone." She began to sob, "Mom, this man died from kidney failure."

I knew then Edwina was finding herself in a situation that had hit home. Edwina was more than just a lab tech. She found herself in diverse situations, especially when on call for weekends. Being in a small hospital she learned far more about human suffering than she expected. I will never forget how she grieved over the coal miner who was injured and still covered with dust when he was brought into the emergency room.

She walked in to X-ray him and he said, "You are 'bout the prettiest doctor I have ever seen." Then he took a deep breath and died.

All the death that surrounded her seemed to breed more worry for her over my condition. She began to take on a maternal role toward me. Her love and concerns were too great.

I begged her, "Please, Edwina, do not relate every unpleasant situation you experience to what you fear will happen to me."

She replied, "Mom, I love you so much. I can't help the fear that grips me."

I told her, "We have to live one day at a time. We can't lose the good times. Let's not think of the tomorrows."

"I will try, Mom. Honestly, I will try," she said.

CHAPTER 21

As time swiftly passed, we tried not to think of the tomorrows that would bring struggle and pain. This darkness did not overtake me. My spirit continued to win over this awful combat I was facing - the fight for life.

I continuously tried to believe that it wasn't going to happen, but the day finally arrived for a check up at the University of Kentucky Medical Center in Lexington that would determine my fate relative to dialysis.

I drove out of the center of Martin's Fork leaving the comforts of home, my loving daughters and my husband. Edwina was at work in Norton, Virginia. Kimberly was attending Lincoln Memorial University in Tennessee, and my little Jacqueline was just a freshman at James A. Cawood High School. Ralph was high in the mountains hauling coal among the beauty of the autumn trees. Their spectacular colors of mauve and luminous gold were so bright that the trees looked as if they were lit up. My heart longed to be with them.

I wondered when driving by the wild river running down from the mountains, "Will I ride through or climb these mountains again? Will I be able to wade up the river?"

I remembered other walks in the clear water as it rippled over slick rocks. One false move would literally sit you in the ice cold water when your feet flew up. You were sitting before you realized you had fallen. I thought of the good laughs we had.

As I looked at that familiar scene I began to think of the time when I took eleven children up the Wild River to the waterfalls in July of 1974 shortly after my Dad died. I recalled how I wept inside for my hero. Even without him, life had to go on for those children.

What a happy time that was when we rounded the bend to see the clear water sliding steadily and peacefully over the huge rock formation that had an unimaginable space between the rock and the river below it. I watched the children jumping off, holding their noses as they went down before landing in the big water hole that almost took their breathe away. I thought of Cheryl Ann, Lectie, Jacqueline, Edwina, Stevie, Alice, Kitty Ann, Larry Jr., Warren Lee, Sam and Kimberly Lynn and wondered if we would ever do this again.

Memories carried me on my journey for hours. Coming back to reality, I realized it wouldn't be long before I would be on the big highway leaving my thoughts behind. It was almost like going into another world. After crossing the flat farmland by I-75, I saw the familiar signs leading to UK.

Upon my arrival, labs were drawn that would determine if the kidney that Wilhelmina gave to me had shut down. I sat in the hallway instead of the waiting room. I wanted to be alone as I waited. A young Dr. Smith would read my labs and make the decision. Not much time lapsed before the pleasant doctor walked into the short hallway that lay between the examining rooms.

He placed my hand in his so gently and asked, "How do you feel?"

"I feel pretty good," I responded.

He very kindly and considerately said, "You don't feel as well as you think. Mrs. Harber, let's go to the dialysis unit."

He saw through my false hope. Everything happened so swiftly that there was no time to dread what was coming. The next thing I knew he was leading me down the hallway and I was sitting in a dialysis chair. The empty room was filled with silence.

It was late and dark. The other patients had finished for the day and were gone. No one occupied the room except Wendell, the dialysis technician, who was an extremely pleasant young man. He had been my technician several times before during my first episode of renal failure. Wendell began to prepare needles to hook me to the kidney machine. Suddenly my composure and bravery were gone. I began to sob softly. The tears were sliding in a steady flow, falling to my lap. My head pounded in endless pain.

Every emotion in my being was screaming, *"What is there to look forward to but dreadful hours, days, months, years, or will it be forever? Who knows how long it will be."*

All that I could think was that I wasn't ready to face this again. I sobbed audibly. Wendell became very concerned when he finished getting the needles into the veins and arteries that would transport the blood through the artificial kidney and back into my body for four hours to cleanse it. He realized that I wasn't doing so well. I gently raised my head and looked through the tears to see that he had disappeared from the unit, but immediately returned with Dr. Smith.

He paused there for a second with a look of compassion and then said, "You have the right to scream, cry, stand on your head or whatever you like."

His words were strong and shocking. The tears began to subside, but my head still pounded with pain. As the blood flowed through the lines into the artificial kidney and returning to my body by way of the veins, I suddenly began to feel better. The pounding pain in my head began to disappear.

I began to tell myself, *that wasn't so bad. You can't think beyond this night. You can't think of your daughters at home.* I knew I could only deal with the present.

After about four hours Wendell asked, "Are you ready to go to a room?"

"More than ready," I replied. I hadn't comprehended how ill I was until after the dialysis process. The four hours of blood cleansing had taken away many symptoms of discomfort for the time being. My blood was cleansed. The nausea and pain were gone. I slept through till daybreak.

CHAPTER 22

As I lay in the hospital, I couldn't help wondering what was going on back in Martin's Fork. I was wishing for a normal life, thinking of how I would like to be home cleaning my house, having supper cooked when Jacqueline returned home from school and Ralph from work. I knew that Jacqueline must have felt very lonely when she entered the big silent house that had once held laughter, sunshine, and a mother that made this house a home. As the hours led into mid-morning I began to realize I must get out of this room and let my mind settle from thinking of how I wanted life to be.

While taking a walk I discovered that Janet Bruce, a young, intelligent, and beautiful girl I had taught in high school as a freshman was now twenty-eight years old and a patient on the west wing. She was suffering from leukemia but was currently in remission. After hearing the sad news, I slowly made my way down the corridor, looking out big windows at the buildings, concrete, and traffic. Oh, how I yearned for the peace of God's mountains where He so graciously allowed me to be born and to live. As I continued my journey to the west wing, I began to feel a little uneasy about seeing Janet. I really didn't know what to expect.

My heart and spirit were broken when I entered Janet's room. Her long, lustrous blonde hair was gone as a result of chemotherapy. Her lips that had once been full and beautifully contoured were now covered with blisters. They were touched by a wet wash cloth occasionally to soothe them. The inside of her mouth and throat were the same as her lips.

Looking at me with sorrowful eyes she said, "Don't you wish we could go back to the time when I was fourteen and you were twenty-eight when we were student and teacher?" She didn't give me time to answer. "We both would have too much pain and hurt to experience if we could go back in time."

After dialyzing the last day of my stay at the hospital, I slowly headed for the west wing. This would be the day that Janet would receive a bone marrow transplant. At that very moment her brother was downstairs having the bone marrow extracted to be transplanted into her.

As Janet was out of remission, her chances of survival were very slim. Her sister, Karen, and sister-in-law, Ettafaye, were with her. I was compelled to ask that we pray before I left for home. As we quietly prayed, there was a presence of God's spirit that was unexplainable. I could feel the manifestation in the very air that peacefully circulated in the room. There was a calmness that soothed the storm in my life as well as it soothed the trauma that Janet was feeling. I believed that Janet would live to raise her three small children that awaited her in the mountains of Harlan County. I knew that Janet had tremendous faith regardless of how dim her chances were at that moment.

After spending time in Janet's room, I no longer had feelings of desperation because of the trauma that lay ahead of me. My body was in a weakened state, but the strength of my heart, soul, and mind soared like the phoenix of old when he regenerated and flew again. I felt a much needed hope. At that moment it seemed there was not an obstacle that I could not conquer. I didn't dare think that I would ever have to face reality again. I was living in a moment where I could look beyond my own suffering and have hope for others.

Lela, my sister-in-law, and Momma had come to take me home. They entered my room. "This is not what I expected," Lela said. "You look so happy."

I softly replied, "I am happy for Janet; I know she will live."

~~~~~

As we drove down the interstate the grass was still green on the farmland, but in the distance, where the mountains bordered the fields, the trees were many colors, fire yellow, crimson, and dark mauve. The delicate colors calmly swayed with the gentle autumn wind. Even though I was in a time of burden, I rejoiced because I knew that sweet Janet would live. She, too, could return to nature's gift only ten miles east of mine. She could be with her children when the blanket of autumn leaves fell to cover the ground before the winter snow came. She could sit by the fire in her house that sat in the mountains at Bob's Creek, with her family once again and treasure life that was restored to her.

CHAPTER 23

When I entered Martin's Fork my spirit spoke hope to me. The mountains were clothed in fall colors that glowed, when looking to my right I could see the Wild River was somewhat still, as the rain had been a little scarce.

I said, "Momma, I would like to walk down the Wild River all the way home, just to feel the coolness and the quiet peace that it would bring."

Looking very saddened, Momma said, "One day we will be able to take autumn walks and wade the clear still water together."

So many times the two of us had enjoyed our mountain and river adventures. We were best friends. She was my momma, my confidante, and my spiritual mentor.

The weekend flew by. It was time to start the dreadful dialysis once again. It had been a little over two years since I had spent what seemed long, lonely, and miserable hours on the machine. My thoughts were, "Live one day at a time, and don't think of the tomorrows."

Edwina was away at Norton working, Kimberly at the University, and Jacqueline at James A. Cawood High School and not old enough to drive. I was so worried. I didn't want to take away one minute of my children's precious time as they were doing what they needed to be doing. I loved them too much to deprive them of a normal life.

The following day, I lay on the bed upstairs, not another soul in the house, in the room that was adorned in soft blue and white colors. This room overlooked the big pond and the little house that once sat on the hill above Momma and Daddy's house. When we were young we occupied that little house to give more room to accommodate ten children. The little house fell because the supporting posts rotted away, but the wood of the house was almost petrified. Just when I went into kidney failure with my sister's kidney, Ralph and our girls brought my little house from the hill and restored it. They placed it just above the pond among the many trees.

I lay looking out the window through tear dimmed eyes, watching the leaves floating in a slow rhythm resting on top of the little house or beside it on the brown soil or the blue water. I began to think of how I would be able to get to dialysis, an hour and a half drive away. I entertained the thought that I could drive myself, but knowing how lifeless I would feel after the machine had filtered my blood for four hours, and dropping my blood pressure to induce a physically dysfunctional state for my body, told me that driving back would be impossible. I lay there looking at my beautiful environment trying to figure out a way without robbing my children of their time. Suddenly, I heard soft steps on the stairs making their way to my room. It was Kimberly's friend, Wanda. She had moved down from the north with Ralph's cousin, Jimmy Pace. She was as pretty as any model.

Many of the young men in the county wished they had met her before Jimmy had married her.

As I turned toward her she saw tears in my eyes. "Are you having an unpleasant day?" she asked.

I paused for a moment to prevent speaking broken words. "I am concerned about how I am going to make it to dialysis in Corbin three days a week. Each visit will take at least eight hours." I replied.

Wanda looked at me ever so pleasantly. "I will take you! Jimmy will be at work and he mentioned that he wanted us to spend time together anyways."

When Wanda left, I felt that an angel of mercy had paid me a visit. It turned out that Jimmy was delighted that Wanda wanted to drive me.

CHAPTER 24

After dialysis the following day, I sat upstairs looking out the window almost mesmerized by the October skies and trees full of autumn colors. The scene brought peace to my heart and soul as the warm blue and peach autumn skies slowly floated over the mountains. Only a few days ago the wild geese had flown over the Wild River and the Martin's Fork valley, their destination unknown to me. I only knew they were survivors. I almost wished I could have followed their flight to escape the storm that I was in.

Winter was upon us before I realized the change. It was time to bring out my pretty suits, long plaid skirts, blouses, and split corduroy skirts. The navy blue, mauve, different shades of rose, soft shades of gray and brown were my favorite winter colors. Matching suede boots of brown, gray, navy, and black accommodated my entire wardrobe.

I told myself, "You must keep that hair silky, take care of your skin and do those nails." They were long and pretty because I could do no work. I tried with every ounce of life within me to be positive.

There was still a battle to fight. A part of me wanted to curl up and escape this awful warfare, but perhaps again, I would walk across this great gulf in my life. I knew there was a source of strength within that would fight, win or lose. There was also a higher power that would take two steps if I took one.

I could not forget the teachings of my mother. She always said, "You must do your part."

As we were returning from dialysis on the wintry days, Wanda plowed through the snow that covered Highways 119 and 25-E that lay between the high mountains. The trees were bare of leaves with the exception of the many pines that always stayed green. The soft, white snow hung to the branches as though it was permanently placed. As far as I could see, the mountains portrayed a work of art. The scenery made my heart feel as if it was so filled with joy that it would burst right out of my chest. Wanda wasn't slowing down for anything. We weren't far from home so I recognized the landscape we were passing. The snow was flying by both sides of the yellow and brown pick-up truck. Big flakes peppered toward us from the sky. I so much wanted to be out in the open space looking upward with the snow softly landing on my face.

I said, "Wanda Pace, you must have had a lot of experience in the northern snow. I would say that you are a number one driver in this treacherous weather."

Wanda turned slightly toward me making her huge blue eyes and long eyelashes visible. Her big smile showed the most beautiful teeth one would ever see.

She looked very devious, almost sneaky, and replied; "I didn't drive before I moved to Kentucky."

I nearly fell out of the seat just thinking about how fast she had driven over the snow-covered highway. I knew my guardian angel was right there in that truck with us.

My dialysis was going fairly well, but I knew the time was nearing when I would have to have the huge diseased kidney taken out. I also knew how painful it would be because my frail body had been through all this before. There were no alternatives. This had to be done before I could get on the transplant list for a cadaver kidney.

The kidney was removed and weighed. It was as large as the other one had been. A normal kidney was about six to eight ounces. I couldn't resist thinking what a horrible way to lose four pounds.

The next day I was shifted back to the dialysis unit in almost unbearable pain. Feeling deathly ill, I watched the blood flow through the artificial kidney and back into my body. I wanted to weep, but to what avail? I had one more cup of bitterness to drink from and knew there was only one thing to do. That was to face the truth and do the very best that I could. I spent the following nine days in the UK Medical Center.

The night before I left the hospital, a girl probably in her early thirties, very thin, short brown hair, blue eyes, and pale skin was put in the room with me. She looked so forlorn and at times so jittery that she could not be still. Her husband did not seem very concerned. It was hard not to overhear them argue, and it was beyond my comprehension how unbearable it would be to have someone be so thoughtless at a time of such hardship.

I found myself trying to comfort her as the night slowly passed. Seeing someone in so much distress stirred compassion within my heart and seemed to resolve any self-pity that I may have had.

She was getting a transplant the next morning, with her brother being the donor. The young woman, Ann, had rejected her first transplant after seven years. Her marriage was in a mess and her finances were at rock bottom, so I shared with her the money that I had. Ann was unusually nervous as the night progressed. I could see her thin, weak body just pacing back and fourth in the dim room, shadowed by the trees from the parking lot. She continued to walk the floor bound by fear and shuffling ice in a Styrofoam cup throughout the long hours.

As I lay in my bed at the opposite end of the large room, I wondered how one copes with being in poverty, rejected by her spouse, and suffering both physical and mental pain. While observing her situation, I realized just how thankful I should be. Morning came and Ann was taken down to the operating room, there she met her handsome, curly headed, dark skinned brother. Just as Wilhelmina had risked her life for me, he chose to risk his in order to prolong hers.

A few hours passed. Ann's procedure was constantly in my thoughts. I prayed throughout the procedure, hoping everything would be all right.

Nancy, my transplant nurse, knew I was concerned about Ann. She felt the need to talk to me.

"Ann experienced hyper-rejection. Her brother's kidney was fed by three arteries. One of the arteries did not show on the scan. Two is normal. The kidney had to be removed immediately."

When Ann came back to our room I could see the carotid artery in her neck throbbing excessively. It looked as though it could explode, but her mood had changed. She no longer seemed nervous or scared, even though the kidney her brother had given her was in vain. She had been through the ultimate trauma. I was at a loss for words. She and I were headed in the same direction. I had lost my sister's kidney, and she had lost her brother's. We were both back on dialysis and hoping for a kidney.

I struggled for words that would give just a tiny ray of hope to her but had not gotten a word out of my mouth before Ann began to relate to me the experience she had encountered during the removal of the kidney that was hyper-rejected.

Ann said to me in a very calm voice, "Even though I was in a medically induced state of sleep I had a vision of being in a beautiful land. It extended as far as I could see. The grass was the prettiest green and the sun glistened down illuminating it even more. The greatest picture of all was the man standing amidst all this beauty with outstretched arms of rescue and rays of sun surrounding him."

I saw at that moment Ann was no longer frightened. She said, "I will go on the list and wait for another kidney."

I was elated to see that Ann's emotional state had improved. I could not think of anything else.

~~~~~

I was anxious to head southeast to the mountains.

My Uncle Cliff called. "I will be picking you up, and will drive you to cousin Jasper and Mary's home in Corbin. You can go to dialysis from there the next day."

I waited and waited, but Uncle Cliff didn't show up. Since my family was told not to pick me up until after dialysis the next day in Corbin, I didn't call them.

I called Mary, "Do you know where my Uncle Cliff is?"

"I think I know what happened and I will pick you up in about ninety minutes," she said.

After about an hour I went down stairs to the huge lobby. Many people were stirring around but I spotted Uncle Cliff making his way through the crowd heading in my direction. He was walking a bit stiffly. I realized that he was three sheets to the wind. He had stopped at a club in Richmond, Kentucky and had one too many drinks. It would be in my best interest to ride with Mary.

My uncle was a good and intelligent man but after his retirement from Cape Kennedy he began to indulge a little too much. After a couple of drinks he must have felt he was in hog heaven and forgot about the good deed he was about to do. I still loved him. His intentions were genuine. He just couldn't resist the temptation to drink.

Mary and I got in her little Chevette and headed for Richmond Road. It was my favorite road because it passed by the Henry Clay Estate, which was an enormous house with grassy land and big beautiful trees spaced just the right way to show its beauty. I became aware of much discomfort in my side and pulled the lever to let the seat slightly back. It didn't work as I had planned. The seat vigorously slapped flat back as level as the road we were traveling. My finger had gotten caught between the lever and metal next to it, which brought terrible pain. I couldn't feel the pain where staples bound the twelve inch incision together. I just lay flat on my back not knowing how to release the lever. Suddenly the whole situation seemed hilarious. I lay there and laughed so hard that there wasn't any way I could raise up. Finally Mary pulled off the road, stopped and released my cut and bruised finger. The good laugh was better than medicine.

The next day wasn't so much fun as I sat for hours hooked to a dialysis machine with another two hours lying ahead of me before I could return to the refuge that always seemed to soothe anything that was wrong in my life. Late in the evening I returned to Martin's Fork. It was the place I had loved since the day I was born.

I realized my condition had not changed by changing places. It helped mentally, to be home, but certainly not physically. I fell on my bed totally drained.

As the sun peeped into my bedroom the next morning, I smiled when looking out my window at the familiar grounds, but knew then that I had to face reality. I looked to the blue sky and asked myself, "Is this the beginning of the end? Will I get another transplant or will I die?"

As time passed, God gave me the grace not to think of death. I knew I had to feel hope or not feel at all. Without hope I would not be able to face what lay ahead. I had already tasted of what the future held for me and the taste was bitter. I began to think back to the spring day that I accepted that I was losing my sister's kidney; I remember the vow to myself that to live only one day at a time would be my way of survival.

Dialysis was a trying time.

The redheaded technician, Velma, was so wonderful; she made a difference in what was going on in my life. On one occasion she brought tomato seeds that she had dried from her harvest of tomatoes. I kept them till spring and I planted them in little cups of potting soil and sat them inside the big glass door where they could drink in the sun. I watched them grow green and lively, the opposite of what was happening to me. As they grew, I was slowly dwindling away.

Every time I sat facing the other patients at the center I worried over them, especially the young woman that had five children and had kidney failure due to toxic poisoning during her last pregnancy. Listening to her, I realized that she was living a life of total discouragement and abuse. Her body was frail and her pale face and semi-transparent blue eyes looked so sad, her dark hair enhanced the paleness of her face which left a picture in my mind not to be forgotten. Many times I looked at other patients and prayed silently for them.

Robert was doing pretty well. He was a big man who had a pleasant smile. He wouldn't consent to be on the transplant list because of fear of the operation. "Those surgery tables are awfully narrow," he said.

"Robert, are you afraid they don't have a pan big enough to hold your guts." Velma replied. We had a good laugh.

"Robert!" I said "You are too young to be a quitter; I have been through multiple surgeries and am still surviving."

"I will ponder on it," he said. He did just that and went on the list. He received a kidney within three weeks. The last report I received, he was doing well.

One day Carol and I were in the unit receiving our treatment when the technician came to her with an excited look on her face. "You have been asked to go to the University of Kentucky for a cadaver kidney."

Carol's face lit up like a Christmas tree. I was so happy for Carol, but inside I wept for myself. I had become so ill that my name had been removed from the transplant list. I felt all hope departing from me. I was so happy for the others, but felt left behind. I wondered if a joyous day would ever come for me.

Even though I wasn't on the list I still daydreamed about how I would react if I were told that I had a call to come to UK to be tested for a cadaver kidney. I knew without a vision I would perish. I was off the list from January until April. Those months were spent without hope and the days became longer and harder. I can truly say that God blocked the worry of death from my mind. I continued to live one day at a time. Dialysis was one day and I lay in bed the next, only to gain enough strength to go back the following day.

CHAPTER 25

As I continued my treatments I worried about my beautiful fourteen year old daughter, Jacqueline Duvall. She had grown into a lovely young woman – tall, thin with big blue eyes and long blonde hair. She was graceful and quiet, going to school and taking on too much responsibility at home. Oh how I grieved. It seemed when I sat hooked to the machine I thought of her more. I wept silently because I could not be there for her as I had been for Edwina and Kimberly. My heart was so heavy; my situation deprived her of so much. She could no longer play basketball because I was occupied with just trying to stay alive. She needed me in so many ways.

With Edwina and Kimberly Lynn away at work and college and Ralph working long hours, Jacqueline Duvall must have felt alone in the world. Ralph's relationship with her must have been blotted out by all the stress. I could plainly feel in my spirit that my illness was going to change the course of my daughter's life. I could feel her slipping away. My heart hurt, but there was nothing I could do when I could hardly walk across a room. I was growing more helplessly ill.

During this time, Jacqueline met a boy that was older than her. In overhearing her talk to him on the phone, I pleaded for her not to get involved. I could tell right then that Ben was going to manipulate and play on what was missing in her life. It made me sick to my stomach to think about it.

This handsome young man knew how to play head games. When Ralph came against him, he became more determined than ever. Ben could not let go of the confrontation he had with Ralph. He continued in his devious ways. His twisted way of thinking made winning Jacqueline a challenge for him.

Jacqueline was barely turning fifteen and the boy used every lie he could dream up to turn her against her dad. He convinced her that I was dying and that her dad really didn't love her or want her to be happy. He met her at the skating rink and saw her there every Saturday. His mind was made up to win her.

Ralph did not have a communicating relationship with Jacqueline and demanded too much responsibility from a girl her age. This blinded her to the bad relationship she was getting into with Ben. There were things missing in Jacqueline's life and Ben convinced her that he could fill them. It wasn't long before he had control over her thoughts and emotions.

I progressively grew worse. Due to no longer having my original kidneys, a very vital substance that stimulates the bone marrow to reproduce blood cells, wasn't being released. Normally, blood cells die over a period of months and new ones are reproduced. My bone marrow could not stimulate the reproduction of new cells, so my blood levels became very low. I began to receive transfusions periodically just to stay alive.

I asked myself, "What kind of a mother can I be for a daughter while in this condition? How can I fight against someone who is out to steal my daughter?"

My little girl was so alone in the world. I tried to tell Ralph how to handle the situation but he felt that force was the only answer and resented my input. In my heart I knew there were more effective ways to handle what was happening.

Ben hired someone to follow Jacqueline at school to make sure that she talked to no one and that she no longer associated with her best friend, Anita. He had taken her mind into captivity and had nearly brainwashed her.

When a mother is flat on her back and gone half the time, what does she do?

Jacqueline was kind and sweet to me, but in her heart, I knew she was convinced I was leaving her. She didn't want to be left alone with her dad if I was going to die. There was no other relative close enough for her to turn to for advice and moral support. With an underdeveloped father-daughter relationship, there was only fear that she couldn't please him if she had to take on all the responsibilities at home if I was gone.

Over a period of two years while my illness kept me away from her much of the time, the stress on Jacqueline's young, tender mind prevented her from looking beyond that moment of time. Ben convinced her that he was the solution to her problems.

I sat in my recliner at dialysis choking back the tears with a lump in my throat, wondering what was going to happen in my daughter's life. My husband's relatives lived very near, but never took time for her, no one did. She was a timid young girl, vulnerable enough for someone who had no morals to attack and destroy her life. I was haunted by guilt for years because I wasn't physically able to protect her from what she was going through. The months continued to pass, I grew more and more ill. My heart was heavy for my daughter and I knew the outcome would be bad.

~~~~~

May 1983 came. I wanted all of my sisters and brothers to come home for a reunion. Secretly I must have thought this would be our last time together.

Everyone came and we had a wonderful reunion. In spite of all the discomfort, I tried to be pleasant. At one point I went to my bedroom and sobbed because I didn't think I could make it through the day. Memorial Day weekend passed. My family returned to the cities where they had been forced to move after finishing high school. None of them expected to see me alive again.

June came. The weather had begun to warm. I continued the long trips to Corbin for dialysis, growing more fragile all the time. On June 14, 1983, Kimberly drove me to dialysis and back. I sat in the truck too weak to carry on a conversation, but my thoughts seemed to be traveling faster than our automobile.

The warmer weather made me feel worse. My body was becoming weaker and I wasn't sure I could make it through the summer.

I was silent all the way home. During the long stretch of silence, my mind blocked out my experience of only the day before as I stood in the kitchen. The wind softly blew the sheer curtains over the sink. The white gauze skirt and blouse that I was wearing were brightened by the sun. I was strong thanks to a blood transfusion the day before.

During this moment of serenity a still voice spoke to my spirit saying, "You are going to get a young person's kidney."

I shivered, thinking, "I don't want a young person to die."

During my teaching career and rearing my children young folk were of great importance to me. As much as I hoped for a kidney, I had never considered that it might come from a young person.

Upon returning home, I lay down as usual, drained and exhausted. That night I lay in my room sort of blank. I was too lifeless to think. Suddenly the phone rang; it was Zelma, a cousin who had left Martin's Fork many years ago.

"Pauline, how are you?"

"I am okay," I said.

"I needed a friend to talk to. I am really distressed and don't know just how to handle a situation."

I counseled Zelma as best I could and felt at peace knowing I was able to comfort someone else and was still needed.

CHAPTER 26

The date was June 14, 1983. The time was 11 p.m. After talking to Zelma, I lay in bed. Dialysis had been exceptionally uncomfortable that day, my frail body began to relax and my mind was filled with the old time hymn *'Precious Lord, take my hand, lead me on let me stand, I am tired I am weak I am worn...'* In the darkness I lifted my arms and believed that Jesus was holding my hands. While in this warm comforting moment, I heard the phone ring again.

Slowly I moved from my bed, through the hallway, dining room and into the kitchen. The phone continued to ring until I took the receiver from the wall. With the moonlight shining through the doors and windows, no light was needed.

"Hello..."

A pleasant voice spoke words to me that will never be forgotten; "Pauline, this is Linda, the transplant nurse. We want you to come to the University Hospital and be matched for a kidney. There will be two other possible recipients coming."

My adrenaline began pumping vigorously. I hadn't experienced a surge of energy like that in a long time. As soon as I hung up the telephone, I began yelling for Ralph, Kimberly, and Jacqueline.

"I am going to UK to be tested for a kidney!" It was wonderful news for all of us.

I called Edwina at work and told her the happy news. She was so excited she could hardly contain herself. "I will head that way as soon as my shift is finished."

I decided to allow Ralph the privilege of calling Momma. Knowing how my mother wept and prayed for this moment, I could not have told her through my tears.

My brother, Frank, and his wife, Ruby, were spending their vacation with Momma. They preferred leaving the north and spending every moment of their two weeks in the mountains that they so sadly left years ago to find work. The three of them arrived at our house, faces grinning as I moved about in the house, my arms filled with housecoats and gowns. I must have had a feeling that I was going to be gone for a while.

My excitement was comical to the rest of the family.

Momma, Frank, and Ruby went home to get some sleep since we would be leaving around four the next morning.

I was still in a state of elation and tossing around in the bed when Ralph said, "Please try to sleep, Pauline. It is two in the morning. Let's try and get a little sleep."

I said, "My mind will not slow down, you go to sleep!"

At four we all headed through our little valley down the winding road. Everything seemed to be lit up by the moon. The moonlight reflected on my thin frame that was adorned in a pale yellow dress, double breasted, a white wide belt. My hair was dark and curly and hung just below the shoulder. I was a bit pale, but this was one morning that I did not feel the overshadowing darkness as I had so many mornings as I traveled to dialysis. I actually felt normal, even radiant, and pretty.

On our way I prayed silently, "God, give this kidney to the person who needs it the most."

Later in the day Momma told me she had prayed the same way. I wanted to rid myself of all greed even if it meant no kidney.

Looking out at the big city, even though it was a happy time for me, I got that same old sensation in my chest that I experienced the first time I neared Nashville, Tennessee at age nineteen. It was a fear of the unknown.

We parked in the big paved parking lot with several huge trees standing here and there. I began to relax. We made our way to the UK Medical Center lobby and headed towards the elevators. I was like a child at Christmas as I stepped out onto the fifth floor and was immediately called back to the examining room.

It seemed as though Dr. Jones was especially waiting for me. He was young, friendly, and had a big smile along with his good looks. His bedside manner put me at ease. I still wondered where all my strength was coming from when only the day before I had to hold to something just to walk.

The doctor said to me, "Pauline, if there is the slightest chance that this kidney will work for you, you will be the recipient, because you may never get another call. The others are somewhat younger and healthier."

I knew then just how grave my condition really was. His meaning was clear.

Without the miracle of a transplant I wouldn't be around to respond to another call. Back in the waiting area, my family and I chatted and laughed. In a short time the doctor called for me again. He really had some unexpected news this time.

He said, "The cadaver kidney has been left on the plane by accident, flown to Pennsylvania and is to be flown back to Lexington, which will delay the matching process another four hours."

I was speechless but not upset.

He said, "You and your family should go for lunch. There will be plenty of time."

I maintained an endless level of energy that was surprising, as we sat at the table of a nice restaurant on Richmond Road. I could not calm down enough to eat. I had eaten very little for so long that food meant nothing to me.

After my family ate, we returned to the hospital where routine tests would begin. My potassium was high so I was taken to a small examining room. The process to lower my potassium was horrible, but Momma was right by my side.

Ralph was in the main lobby and saw the kidney being carried through in a small cooler. He found us and let us know that which might determine my fate had made its way back to UK.

Tissue matching began, but the uncomfortable process of lowering my potassium eventually broke my spirit. At midnight I said, "Mom, the balloon that is forcing the kaline to stay in the intestines has to go." I detached myself from the apparatus and headed to the shower. As I showered I began to worry that maybe the kidney wasn't a match for me. My thoughts were becoming negative, but my will to fight till the very end returned to me. I knew then that I would battle this illness until my dying day.

Just when I had brought myself to accept that I probably wasn't compatible to the kidney, I heard the door open. A happy voice rang through the room and into the shower stall. "Mrs. Harber, you get the kidney."

"Thank you!" I called in a more meaningful way than could ever be expressed. My voice almost carried a melody.

As I finished my shower I only thought positive thoughts. *"Dialysis is going to end for me."* I had no fear of the surgery, and could hardly wait to be whisked away to the operating room.

In the exam area, I was asked to get on the bed, and then handed a phone. Ralph was on the other side of the curtains and was given a phone. Some gracious person had already dialed my daughters at home. Each was on a separate phone.

I said, "Girls! I am getting a transplant!"

Everyone was silent. There was a presence of peace, joy, and hope that we felt had been slipping away as we had walked through our months of despair. It was as if we were all thinking, "Is this really happening?" None of us said goodbye.

Edwina said, "We're on our way."

I could imagine them smiling as they grabbed their things and made a dash for Edwina's little blue sports car. I knew they would be taking the shortcut through the mountains on the narrow road.

Since time was of the essence, I was taken to surgery as quickly as possible. While waiting to be put to sleep, I looked up to see Dr. Lucas, head of the transplant team standing beside my bed.

He said, "Are you surprised to be here?"

I announced, "Yes."

He said, "I am surprised, too! I will be doing the surgery."

He was a tall pleasant man whose smile seemed to say that he cared and everything would be okay. He had a daughter the same age as Kimberly Lynn who also played basketball. He treated my family with utmost respect and my children as special.

The last thing I remembered as the IV entered my vein was my prayer.

"*Dear God, Dr. Lucas has a brilliant mind, but please direct his hands during my surgery.*"

Pauline and Junior Ginter - one week before the transplant

Momma and all the kids - one week before the transplant

CHAPTER 27

Edwina, Kimberly, and Jacqueline arrived at UK to find Ralph crouched in a chair with his face buried in his hands, waiting for just a word as to how my surgery was going. They all knew that such major surgery was a risk when my health was in such a desperately weakened state. He had mixed emotions when he greeted the girls. While I was in surgery, my family made the best of the endless hours.

After the transplant was finished I was in ICU receiving dialysis. In spite of the excruciating pain I was enduring, a brief feeling of excitement flowed through my mind; I believed the transplant would work. Even in my agony I could not let myself think that this organ would be rejected.

My first transplant had begun working properly in surgery. I had no concept of how the second transplant could be so different and how I would have to battle to live. I wanted so much to walk out of the hospital with hope. I knew that God's grace was sufficient and I would do my part. I couldn't give up.

Ralph allowed my mom to come first when visitors were allowed in to see me. He must have realized that no other earthly love could surpass a good mother's love. Kimberly came with her. I barely remember trying to smile as I looked into their eyes.

"Please pray," I said.

Mom touched my side with her soft hand. Relief came as she touched the transplanted area. In seeing the pain that I was in, tears fell from Kimberly's big beautiful eyes, slid over her high cheekbones, and splashed on the floor.

I drifted into a peaceful sleep and later awakened to see the rest of my loved ones. They were allowed in two by two. I vaguely remembered how to smile as I looked into their eyes. I could see the love and compassion that they had for me. No words were needed. This support strengthened my will to live.

I was removed from the ICU unit, but the new kidney had not yet begun to function. A new drug called ATG was inserted into a vein in my chest just below the collarbone. For fourteen days, a pint of ATG was to be allowed to drip into my system with the hope of preventing kidney rejection.

The doctors and nurses warned me, "Occasionally a patient will have at least one reaction to the drug. If you do, please, don't think you are dying."

This scared me somewhat. The drug began to drip into my veins around four p.m. and the process took six hours. The first couple of hours everything felt normal. Then my teeth began to chatter from body chills, and my temperature began to rise. By midnight my temperature was around 105 degrees, and I was extremely nauseated. The nurse insisted that I throw the covers back and bathe in ice water. After that I had to have chest x-rays, urine analysis, and blood work just to make sure I wasn't in rejection or getting pneumonia. Every day that I received the treatment I experienced indescribable discomfort.

After nine treatments the line clotted which stopped the flow of the medication. So Dr. Lucas decided to discontinue the treatment. Even after the treatments were over, a type of rash formed from the top of my head to the bottom of my feet. The itching was almost unbearable. The itching of my eyes was the most uncomfortable, but nothing eased the many days of pain. My face peeled, along with the palms of my hands and the bottom of my feet. I wasn't able to eat and my nervous system was shattered. At times I was delirious because the misery was so great, and it seemed it would never end.

After discontinuing the ATG, the kidney began to slowly kick in. I was still going through dialysis every other day. The reactions to the previous treatment had left me in a poor state. I had nothing left to fight with physically or mentally. As I sat in my dialysis chair early one morning, I simply couldn't fight anymore. In pain, I watched the other patients, the technicians, and social workers as they moved about the area. Dark thoughts came that I had never had before.

I talked to God and told him, "I can't take any more."

At this moment, the Lord took my load. A miracle was born. I asked the technician to supply me with a bedpan. This may sound strange, but something spectacular took place. I was able to pee for the first time since my kidney failure began eight months prior. My new kidney was functioning!

Again, my pain and discomfort was behind me, along with nineteen extra pounds of fluid, the itching, vomiting, and rash.

Each day the kidney came closer and closer to becoming normal.

As I lay on my bed a couple of nights before being dismissed from the hospital, my second transplant was working perfectly. With the passing of time, I knew that my strength would return. I was very thin and weak from the entire ordeal. Surely my appetite would return and then my strength would increase.

I could hear the mountains calling me home. I began to picture the green trees, the rocks, and the clear river again. I couldn't wait to look up at Chimney Rocks and Table Rock that were still weathering the storms.

Most importantly, Jacqueline would be at home waiting for me. She was my fifteen-year-old baby who had suffered the most because of my illness. I wanted us to be able to make up for lost time. I hoped she could become involved in school activities and I would be there to drive her. We would have a wonderful life.

CHAPTER 28

Edwina's boyfriend, Wayne, was on vacation and volunteered to pick me up at UK so that my family wouldn't have to miss work or school. He had a charming personality that complimented his good looks. He reminded me of the good looks of the stars from the 50s. He had dark hair, brown eyes, a healthy complexion, and a smile that accentuated his perfectly white teeth.

Momma was really fond of Wayne. He had always treated her as special. Momma's house was before mine, so we stopped there first.

When walking in, the kitchen was pleasant and cozy as the sun glowed through the sparkling clean windows. It made the cream colored linoleum shine more than ordinary as it reflected the soft, fresh apricot curtains. There Momma stood at the stove making sure the beef stew, cornbread, and baked apple pies were perfect. It had been a long time since I had smelled food that sparked my appetite to the point of really wanting to eat. When she sensed we were in the room, she turned.

Looking at us with loving eyes, a sweet smile and out stretched arms, she said, "Paulie, you deserve to be free of suffering. It's been far too long… too long for your loving family and you."

At last I felt that a new beginning was about to take place. We had a short but heartwarming visit then Wayne and I headed home. Walking into my house after thirty days made my heart so full of joy.

Wayne said, "I am leaving so that you can be alone."

"Thanks." I said. I walked through the house smiling with tears flowing down my face, thinking of the unforgettable years my girls and I spent together. I sat in front of the window in the upstairs living room and looked over the fields of green grass. My heart filled with joy as I saw my trim little blonde haired, blue eyed Jacqueline walk across the field from the pasture that held the horses. I was so thankful that I was going to be there every day for her to lighten her responsibilities.

I said, when embracing her at the door, "Jacqueline, we are going to make up for all the precious time that has been lost."

As the evening progressed, though she did seem a little distant at times, we had an extremely pleasant talk.

Before she left my room, I said, "Jacqueline, we do have wonderful days ahead. You will be able to play sports and enjoy school to the fullest."

"I'm going downstairs to sleep," she said as she walked out of the room.

I fell asleep thinking of the days of joy that would come, and how I wanted to make up to Jacqueline all that she had missed. I drifted into a peaceful state of sleep silently rejoicing in my soul and thinking of how we would all be together at the dawning of the new day.

Little did I know that I would awaken to one of the most heart wrenching experiences my spirit had ever encountered. The bliss of returning to the mountains and to my family was about to be consumed. The night would not pass before my emotions would be crushed. We had not had a chance to reunite our little family before disappointment gripped us.

Our celebration of life and love was on hold.

Around midnight, Edwina, Kimberly, and my niece, Lectie Ruth, came from Norton, Virginia after Edwina had finished a second shift at the hospital. Their low voices woke me up. Being a light sleeper, I could hear them from upstairs. I listened for a moment then felt compelled to get up.

I got out of bed and walked very slowly down the hallway, down the stairs, through the dining room and into the kitchen. My eyes were on all of them when they noticed me and became silent. The emptiness in their faces told me that something wasn't right.

Frantically I asked them, "What's wrong?"

They just looked at each other and no one responded.

I saw that Jacqueline wasn't standing with them. I knew they would have awakened her when they came in before coming upstairs to the kitchen.

I begged them to tell me what was going on as we all stood in the kitchen. "Please tell me. What's the matter?"

Moments of silence passed. Ralph spoke in a low tone and broken words, managing to say, "She's gone."

It was obvious how bad the three girls felt when they saw the pain that manifested in my eyes.

Desperation seized me, like never before.

Jacqueline had left a note, which was only read by the girls. That July night was the saddest night I had ever experienced. My glorious homecoming turned into a nightmare.

Ben had manipulated her to believing anything he said. She had been a little lost lamb being led to the slaughter while I was away, a mere child when he came into her life. I could not blame her.

I could only stare into the looking-glass and say, *What if I had been thrust into her situation when I was thirteen?* That was Jacqueline's age when I had started dialysis. I couldn't imagine being without my mother at that age.

After my thoughts began to settle in I could only say to myself, "She is gone and in such unstable company."

I had hoped for her life and mine to be better after my illness ended. I wanted to make up for the many days that were lost while I was forced to only be a small part of my daughter's life. I grieved until I thought I couldn't grieve any more.

Ralph, Wayne Creech, and Warren Lee, Ralph's brother, were searching for Jacqueline. I was in the big house alone as a horrible storm raged outside with thunder that would shake the earth and lightening that momentarily turned the darkness into total light.

The phone rang. It was Ben. He said, "Your daughter will be in danger if you don't back off. We are together and I have won!" His voice sounded evil.

I pleaded, "Please bring my little girl home to me," but the phone disconnected.

I sank to the cool floor and wept for what seemed an eternity. The thunder still roared and the lightening flashed. It was a night that wouldn't be forgotten.

I had to let the torment go and pray that my daughter would be safe. Time would pass and all the weeping and feelings of guilt for being away from her during my illness would resurface.

I prayed, *"God, send an angel to watch over Jacqueline."*

I believed with all my heart that my daughter was going through hell on Earth. Ben had literally brainwashed her.

I told myself she would be a survivor just like Momma who raised five children of her own and five nieces and nephews; Grandmother Emily who survived with the bare necessities of life; Aunt Fannie who raised five boys alone after the death of her husband; and Aunt Liddie, a widow with five children, who fought for survival till her dying day; Momma's niece, Mary Jane, who left the mountains and went north to Indiana, working in a factory shoveling sand into a blazing fire to raise her three children as well as her sister Martha's two children because of tragedy in her life that caused an emotional break down; and my sister Morine who walked through fire physically and mentally. They were women who survived in a cruel world.

I believed that Jacqueline had the same bloodline, the same heritage and strength, and the same will. I knew that one day she would walk out of her world of intimidation. Jacqueline, too, was one among the mountain laurels.

Wilhelmina and Pauline - after the transplant

CHAPTER 29

Autumn was in the air and I had gained back my weight while getting much stronger. Everyone I saw said, "Pauline, you are a picture of health."

I worked very hard to get my life back on track, trying not to let myself be unhappy because of everything that had taken place when I returned from the hospital.

Kimberly had just begun her second year of college on a basketball scholarship and made the A team her freshman year. When reading in the Knoxville, Tennessee newspaper about her sports achievements, my heart swelled with pride. I was so proud of my girl.

More than once that past year I had said, "Kimberly, I wish with all my heart I could attend your games."

She always replied, "Mom, it's okay. I understand." It seemed that at her high school games my presence intensified her performance.

~~~~~

I enjoyed the brisk, late September evenings. This one was nippy, but the house felt cozy and warm. I was physically well and emotionally coping in spite of what I had been through the previous three years.

I was relaxed and peaceful so I said, "Ralph, I am going to bed early."

Just as I slid between the light yellow sheets in my warm bed the telephone rang. I picked up the phone on the nightstand.

Kimberly was on the line and very pleasantly asked, "Mom, can I talk to Dad?"

I yelled, "Ralph, pick up the phone in the kitchen."

I knew something was wrong! I slipped out of bed and crept to the kitchen, observing Ralph's reaction and listening to his end of the conversation. I could see by his expression that all was not well.

After he hung up the phone I demanded, "Tell me what's going on!"

Knowing that I would not let it rest and how much I loved my children he calmly responded, "Kimberly is in the hospital in Tazewell, Tennessee. They don't know what's wrong yet, but she doesn't want you to come to the hospital."

Even though it wasn't easy, I respected her wishes and went back to bed. I awakened as daylight began to filter through the light yellow curtains. I said to myself, *How can I stay here? I must go see her.*

She had been by my side and knew how I had suffered. My conclusion was that she wanted to spare me from suffering with her and whatever she was going through.

I got out of bed, showered hurriedly, did my hair and makeup, slipped into a white peasant blouse and a straight denim skirt. Only three months since the transplant, but I could hardly believe how radiant and healthy I felt.

I drove through the valley feeling uneasy, although the beautiful autumn sun seemed to boost my spirit. I cut through the mountains that were barely beginning to display their beautiful fall colors and headed towards 25E, to Harrogate, Tennessee. I found the doctor's office near the university. The receptionist was very pleasant.

"I need to see Kimberly's doctor," I said. "I am her mother."

There was no waiting.

"Please follow me, Mrs. Harber."

I followed her to his office.

"Dr. Wilson, this is Kimberly Harber's mother."

Kimberly had told Dr. Wilson that I had under gone a transplant three months prior. The doctor had a surprised look on his face and said, "I am amazed at how healthy you look, Mrs. Harber."

After a brief conversation about my transplant, I asked, "What is going on with Kimberly?"

"I am sorry, I can not tell you. I must respect Kimberly's privacy."

Of course I asked, "Has she inherited my kidney disease?"

Dr. Wilson replied, "Kimberly asked that I not discuss her test results with anyone." Then he looked at me and said, "I am very worried about her state of mind and the fact that the blood work showed that she may have leukemia, however she doesn't know about the abnormal blood cells."

I stood in trepidation, thinking. *This can't be.*

I was so distraught, I wanted to run; I wanted to cry, but did neither. I shook the doctor's hand, thanked him, and said, "I am going to Claiborne County Hospital to see my daughter."

I drove on through the beauty of the cool, breezy, sunny morning. I located the hospital on a hill at the edge of the Tennessee mountains in Tazewell. I parked my car and got out slowly. When nearing the entry of the hospital I felt a little unstable but realized that I must be strong for my eighteen-year-old daughter. Outside her room I composed myself trying as much as possible to look normal. When entering Kimberly's room I saw youth, innocence, and beauty.

She began to question me, "Mom, what were your symptoms with kidney disease?"

Her questions confirmed what I suspected. She knew that she too had kidney disease. As I looked at her with the white sheet pulled close to her chin showing only her beautiful face and hair, I saw fear and sadness in her eyes. I began to comprehend that she might have leukemia and kidney disease that could not be treated.

I lightly embraced her and said, "Kimberly, I've got to go to the powder room."

Hidden in the ladies restroom, I wept in silence. At that moment I would have bargained my life for my daughter to be disease free. When leaving the bathroom I walked down the corridor to be alone. I couldn't bear Kimberly seeing me giving in to my emotions.

I stared through the window into the mountains and began to think about my young vivacious outdoors girl. She lived every moment of her childhood and adolescent years to the fullest, always bursting with energy and joy. At that moment, I recalled seeing her trail down the road, her jeans rolled up to her knees, her fishing pole in one hand, and the minnow bucket in the other and remembered how Ronnie and Bailey Middleton said, "We are giving your girl a new name. She is the female version of Huck Finn."

Besides spending so much time fishing, I thought of how she loved sports and was my basketball player, who had scored over one thousand points during her high school years and was the best rebounder in the region. She was an excellent athlete, but looked like a model with her long dark hair and hazel eyes enhanced with those long eyelashes.

With Kimberly being only eighteen, I couldn't help wondering, "Will this ill fate change her youthful outlook on life?"

I tried to put away all self-pity and tried not to think that the timing of Kimberly Lynn's illness was wrong because time belongs to God. It was really difficult not to question God. I composed myself and went back into the hospital room.

Tests were repeated the next two days, and the leukemia cells were still present. The entire weekend all I could think about was, "Abnormal blood cells, leukemia, chemotherapy, and death." I was devastated.

Kimberly was discharged from the hospital on Sunday and I took her home with me. Sleep would not come on Sunday night. I eased upstairs to her room. The light blue and white décor was softly lit by the moonlight as I stood in silence and watched her peacefully sleeping. I knelt by her bed and prayed.

Now I know that we shouldn't bargain with God, but I did. I prayed, *"God, if you will make the abnormal cells become normal, I will accept the kidney disease and not spend my life grieving, and worrying."*

From Sunday until Tuesday, I prayed a fervent prayer. We returned to the clinic on Tuesday for more blood tests. As the blood was drawn form her arm, she knew nothing about the abnormal cells. Two days later, as the doctor talked with me in private, I could hardly wait for him to tell me the results of the most recent tests.

"Her blood count has returned to normal and the escentiphill cells are no longer a threat," he said.

I stood teary eyed, "Thank you, thank you, Dr. Wilson."

I knew that a divine intervention had taken place. Because of what happened to Kimberly, I learned anew that God is truly the Master Teacher. For a long time I did not worry or grieve because of her polycystic disease, and hoped never again to engulf myself in pity. No matter what state of mind we find ourselves in we must realize that divine help will come.

After Kimberly Lynn had gone through the trauma of such devastating news about her kidneys, she dropped out of school for the semester. I noticed her personality began to change. She was not as outgoing and vivacious as she used to be.

I tried in my own way to prepare her for the future always pointing out, "Kimberly time belongs to God, not us."

I will always regret that she learned of her kidney disease at such a young age because of the dread it put on her. I prayed continuously, *"Please, Jesus, ask your Father not to let the fear dwelling in Kimberly's mind keep her from enjoying the fruitful days ahead."*

After all, strides in medical science and perfections were being made with family donor transplants, more than one could ever imagine. I knew she too had the strength of a mountain woman and this gave me hope.

Kimberly related to me later, "Mom, I'll be back at the University for the spring semester. I will do well. I will fight my battle and continue my education. But, I will be resigning from the basketball team."

At that moment I saw hope returning to my girl. Her free spirit eventually resurfaced, along with her passion for life.

CHAPTER 30

Until my physical condition had improved, I hadn't realized the effect that my illness had on my girls, and still hadn't learned the effect it had on Ralph. One Sunday morning as I made my way to the little white church, I was filled with loneliness because of the absence of my daughters and my heart was heavy because of the continual bleak, distressed mood that Ralph had been in. As the Sunday service ended, I felt better until I pulled into my driveway.

Ralph was working on one of his Mack trucks. I opened my car door and tried to be cheerful in hopes that things would be better. His mood had worsened.

He began complaining, "I am so tired of all these problems. Seems like nothing is ever going to change."

I walked as if on eggshells. As I looked into the November sky I asked God to please help me because I didn't feel that I could tolerate his moodiness much longer.

That same evening a good friend of ours, John Shows, paid us an unexpected visit. He was very distraught because he was going through a divorce and seeking refuge. Through his desperation, he turned to the church for help.

I heard John say to Ralph, "Will you go to the Sunday service with me?"

The fact that Ralph accepted this invitation almost put me in a state of shock. In twenty-one years he had gone to church with me only one time. That night he went with John to Pastor Will Howard's church. Pastor Will preached loudly, walking briskly up and down the aisle, once in a while he would yell out, "Praise God for old time, heartfelt, soul-saving salvation."

When the familiar hymn, *Softly and Tenderly, Jesus is Calling*, was sung and the invitation to accept Christ as a personal savior was given, I looked up from a bowed position and saw Ralph kneeling at the altar. I couldn't believe it. I was really quiet and stood there to watch what would happen. In a matter of minutes Ralph stood making a confession that he had accepted Jesus Christ as his savior. He was so elated that he hugged the reverend and literally picked him up off the floor. I actually saw his feet dangling about six inches in the air. It was a happy time. Almost everyone was either shedding tears or grinning.

In the coming days, I felt that heaven had come down to our house. I did not feel as fearful as I had the preceding months. I asked myself more than once if everything was really happening, and I wondered if I could enjoy my life again, but there was something stirring inside my heart that made me afraid to believe there could be life without a battle.

As Ralph's life began to undergo a change, he allowed the boy that our youngest daughter had married to visit in our home. This proved to be both good and bad. I was glad that all was forgiven with Ralph. However, the more that I was around Jacqueline and her husband, the more I began to realize that she was being mentally abused. I encouraged them to move their mobile home to our property, so I could watch after her. After they moved, the mental cruelty became more evident. Her self-esteem and confidence were destroyed. Talking with both of them, I encouraged them to try to get their GEDs since neither graduated from high school. It took awhile for decisions to be made because he didn't want Jacqueline to better herself. They took their GED and Jacqueline passed with an excellent score.

Previously, I had spoken with them about going to college after getting their GED, but didn't want to cause more problems than already existed. Jacqueline took on a more determined attitude and made a very important decision. She was now seventeen years old, and decided that she would go to college in order to secure her future. Although she was emotionally battered, she realized that she didn't have to spend the rest of her life feeling inadequate. Thus, she decided to do something for herself.

Jacqueline applied for admission to college and was accepted at Lincoln Memorial University in Harrogate, Tennessee. Since she didn't own a car, she found a ride with our friend, Claudine Hensley, for the first semester. After Jacqueline began college it seemed that her life was getting back on track. She began college the same year that her high school classmates were eligible to start. However, she received no financial or emotional support from her husband. At least her college enrollment didn't seem to create any more problems.

After each school day, Claudine dropped Jacqueline off at our house. One evening I observed her coming up the stairs looking weak and tired as if she was ready to collapse. Her yellow blouse complimented her long blonde hair, her creamy complexion, huge blue eyes, and long eyelashes. Even though she was drained, she was still beautiful.

Upon closer examination I noticed that the whites of her eyes were yellow. I said, "Jacqueline, I am making a doctor's appointment for you."

As a lab technician, Edwina was able to do Jacqueline's lab work without charge as a courtesy. We took the results to the doctor with her initial visit. After examining Jacqueline Duvall, the doctor ordered further tests, one of which was an ultrasound to check her gallbladder.

During this time, I ran errands. When I returned, one look into Jacqueline's big blue eyes let me know something was wrong. Her eyes were filled with tears, which was not normal for her because she didn't usually give in to emotions.

As we walked down the corridor of the hospital she said, "Mom, I have your same polycystic kidney disease as well as a chance of my liver being polycystic, too."

"Jacqueline, let's go back to Dr. Simmons' office. I have to talk to him."

In disbelief, I asked, "Doctor, this is not true, is it?"

His expression said everything. My tears began to flow.

He replied," You're a mother, you have the right to cry." Dr. Simmons was of middle age and had the kindest face you could ever see. His eyes were filled with compassion.

We drove home in silence. I was feeling the same pain and disappointment that I had felt so many times before.

After getting home I sat for hours in silence staring out the window, feeling so weary and devoid of understanding. According to statistics, I had learned, only one child in five would inherit polycystic kidney disease. I had convinced myself that Kimberly would be the only one to inherit the disease. It was so painful to think about what my daughters would have to go through because of their genetic inheritance. A torturing guilt overtook me.

I asked myself a question, *"Did I bear them only to suffer?"* My feelings were beyond explanation.

Nevertheless I encouraged Jacqueline to try to live a fulfilling life, to be a fighter and try not to give in to her feelings. I asked her especially not to look into the future because only today is ours.

Jacqueline worked hard to finish college, emotionally and financially. She tried very hard to make her marriage successful. However, during her last year in college, her husband began dating other women, and moved in out and of their home a couple of times. The last time he returned home she was less than a year from graduation and had a part-time job with the Army Corp of Engineers at Martin's Fork Lake.

Jacqueline came by unexpectedly one evening. As we sat at the kitchen table, she smiled softly and said, "Mom, I want to discuss something with you." I was surprised because she was always reluctant when it came to discussing her personal life. She asked, "Mom, will you call a lawyer and inquire about divorce proceedings."

Only God could realize my relief in her decision, knowing that she had almost been destroyed by this marriage. The divorce became final at the end of June.

CHAPTER 31

July fourth, I awakened to a beautiful sunny, breezy day. Flowers were blooming everywhere; even the wild flowers displayed themselves here and there. The fields and mountains were green and alive from the moisture and the richness of the earth. Our community picnic was to take place in a huge field on the "Old Lloyd Smith place," where the river rippled as it flowed by, the sound soothing every living creature anywhere near. The mountains stood in majesty protecting the bottomlands.

I cooked enough broccoli casserole to feed at least one hundred people and headed for the big celebration of independence. Women, some in long dresses with their hair piled on top of their heads, some in more contemporary attire, were making the tables and displays ready for the day's activities.

Children were running, laughing, playing, and having the time of their lives. Some were playing tug of war in the unpolluted river while others talked, laughed, and enjoyed each other's company.

Handmade quilts were displayed for a contest. Homemade cakes were sampled and judged; every old fashioned recipe of country cooking you could think of was spread on the wood picnic tables brought from numerous homes. A platform was set up for the Doorways, a family that sang country gospel that would make the hair on your head rise, as chills ran from head to toe.

I was carried away with enjoying the heart-warming event when I looked to my right and saw Kimberly Lynn entering the field. She was so beautiful with her long dark curly hair, tanned skin, a big smile that covered her whole face, and her eyes spoke what her soul was feeling. She was wearing a modest outfit, muted red shorts just above the knee and a cotton blouse with tiny flowers of many colors including red. Beside her walked a tall, masculine brown haired, tanned, good-looking man with facial features that would rival any statue of a Greek god. This fellow was a stranger to all of us.

Kimberly had gone to Martin's Fork Lake to see friends, before coming to the event. While there she asked, "Would anyone like to go to the community picnic with me? The food is out of this world."

Immediately the tall, dark stranger, William Jeffries replied, "I would love some good home cooking. GI food will keep a person alive, but it sure isn't like homemade."

William was from Oklahoma visiting with a Harlan county marine he was stationed with in Jackson, North Carolina near Top Sail Beach.

Kimberly and William dated during his leave. He returned to Camp Lajune Marine base. The following Monday, while Kimberly was still sleeping, the phone rang.

"Is Kimberly there?"

"Kimberly," I called, "Pick up the phone."

Later Kimberly exclaimed, "Mom, I really like this fellow; we have so much in common! We have similar religious beliefs and educational ambitions. He's the right age, and neither one of us are dating anyone seriously." Kimberly's face glowed with a fresh, happy look.

Shortly after William returned to North Carolina, Kimberly went to Top Sail Beach to vacation near the base. As the white caps gently rolled in, two beautiful people confessed their love while walking on the white sand along the ocean, caressed by the ocean breeze.

They corresponded by mail and phone after she returned home. When September came, William again was granted leave before he was scheduled to depart for Japan. He visited the area for a few days and came to Martin's Fork to see Kimberly.

On Friday evening in the upstairs living room, Kimberly said, "Mom, we have something to discuss with you and Dad. We plan to be married before William leaves for Japan. If everyone agrees, we will be married Monday, September sixteenth."

The entire situation took me by storm with everything happening so quickly. I told myself, *"You must be positive."*

Saturday morning came. We were up early heading for the Belk store. They carried a beautiful line of wedding dresses and accessories and a great line of men's suits. Kimberly shopped the ladies department as William shopped the men's department. The store had everything they needed. Kimberly's white wedding dress and veil couldn't have been more beautiful. The fullness was perfect for her tall, thin body and long dark hair.

In our mountain community, news spreads extremely fast by word of mouth. By Sunday most people knew that Kimberly and William would be married at the Riverside Baptist Church, and they were welcome to attend.

I had friends, Gary and Brenda Henson, who owned a floral shop. Brenda and her sister-in-law, Doris, decorated the church with all white flowers and white candles.

In spite of all the hustle and bustle, the wedding was beautiful. Kimberly looked stunning as she walked down the aisle in her long, flowing white wedding dress. The bridesmaids and maid of honor wore long full dresses that swept the floor as they walked, each a different rainbow color. William looked handsome in his light gray double- breasted suit. Raymond Smith and Barb Saylor sang solos that would have humbled Nashville stars. The church was packed.

Following the wedding, the reception was in the great room at our home. Never had a wedding of this size been planned so quickly in our community. Since

Jacqueline's marriage to Ben had been an elopement and my marriage to Ralph had been a very simple affair at the preacher's house, I was determined that at least one of my daughters would have a beautiful wedding and reception. Everything had fallen together perfectly. It was hard to believe that it had all turned out so beautifully with such a short time for planning and preparation.

Kimberly and William's wedding

~~~~~

In a few weeks, William left for Japan and Kimberly continued with college. I always felt, however, those six months of separation just after a marriage wasn't for the best. The months passed and William returned to the states at which time Kimberly decided to drop out of college for the summer. She met William at the airport in North Carolina. They rented an apartment at Top Sail Beach near the marine base. They hoped a beautiful summer at the beach would make up for lost time. In August, William's four years in the marines were completed.

When talking with him, I found him to be very apprehensive as to his future plans. He said, "I have been on my own since I was thirteen years old. I managed to complete high school and spent four years in the marines. Now I would like to go to college."

With the passing of time William and Kimberly decided to move to Martin's Fork and continue their education, which was difficult for William because he felt that every eye in the community would be upon him. Being self-sufficient during his youth, he felt insecure about not having a job waiting for him after his military career.

Since our house was large, Ralph and I asked William and Kimberly, "Would you like to live in our downstairs area, look for part-time work, and go to college?"

They talked about the situation. Kimberly said, "Mom, we accept the offer and are grateful to both of you."

William was an ambitious man. I was pleased that he had decided to get a college degree and he found part time work that winter working for a lumberjack, Jack Stevens. Later, he was lucky enough to get a part time job at the Corps of Engineers at the Martin's Fork Lake, which was complimentary to the wild life management program that he had been studying.

Within a year, Kimberly said, "Mom, William and I are planning to purchase our own mobile home. We would love having our own place."

When Kimberly set her mind to something, it wasn't long before she made it happen. She found a used home that needed a lot of repair. She never got bogged in the repairs, but pictured in her mind exactly what she wanted it to look like when she was finished. Kimberly worked hard cleaning and decorating after the needed repairs were completed. Decorated in colors of blue, peach, and antique white, the small mobile home became a little dream house.

As Christmas approached, we made our usual preparations. Christmas Eve was spent at home, and Christmas day we drove to Virginia to be with Ralph's grandparents. When returning home in the afternoon, William received a phone call from his family in Oklahoma; a phone call that would involve all our lives.

After the conversation William, stunned, said, "My sister has been arrested for murder. She has three small children – ages three, four, and six. The children were immediately placed in a foster home after seeing their mother arrested and taken into custody, and the children's father can't be located."

Needless to say, our whole family began to worry intensely about the children, although we had never seen them. We soon realized that there would be no rest for Kimberly until she could bring the children to Martin's Fork. Thus, we began calling the District Attorney and anyone else that we knew that could be of assistance. At first, we were told that the two older ones couldn't leave the state of Oklahoma because they were old enough to be witnesses. For about five weeks, we called almost every day to some place in Oklahoma trying to work out something so the children could be released into William and Kimberly's care.

In late January of 1989, I made a telephone call to the Social Services as well as to other authorities. They replied, "A decision has been made. The girls, Corey Danielle and Ashley Morgan, can come to Kentucky, but the boy, Milford Lee, will have to stay until the trial in June."

William's mother was allowed to take the children from the foster care facility and keep them with her until William and Kimberly arrived. Because she was a nurse and self-supporting, she couldn't keep them indefinitely. Kimberly couldn't bear the thought of going to Oklahoma and driving away with Corey Danielle and Ashley Morgan and leaving Milford Lee behind.

She said, "Mom separating them will be devastating, with all they've been through. They need to be together."

"Kimberly, I will not stop until I convince the authorities to let Milford Lee come to Kentucky."

I made several telephone calls that day, and the time was nearing for William and Kimberly to come home from school before beginning their journey to Oklahoma. I had one last brainstorm. I began calling to locate the District Attorney who was in charge of the case. I found that he was in another county that day.

My persistence paid off. I was able to trace his whereabouts, and talked with him while he was on break from the courtroom.

I begged, pleaded, and promised, "If you will allow Milford Lee to come to Kentucky I will be responsible for seeing that he returns to Oklahoma for the trial in June."

He then said, "Ma'am, Milford Lee will be coming with the girls."

When Kimberly and William came from school, I said, "Guys, I have good news, Lee can come with the girls to Kentucky."

We were all so excited. The money was ready for their journey. Kimberly finished packing. Meanwhile, William was like an expectant father, walking the floor and making several trips to the bathroom.

At this time I was forty-eight years old and had no grandchildren, and suddenly I was getting three. Needless to say, I was so excited I hardly knew what to do. Kimberly and William were twenty-two and twenty-three years old and were getting three children after two years of marriage. William lacked three years of college and Kimberly one.

I said, "Kimberly, William - I am so proud of you and very proud to be a part of your family."

Although I knew that this brave young couple had no idea about the responsibility of rearing children, I believed they could handle it. I knew I would do all I could to help.

After arriving in Oklahoma they did all the legal work, took the children to see their mother one last time, and headed back for Kentucky. They were to return home on Saturday night. Ralph, Jacqueline, and I waited patiently. They arrived around midnight, and I will never forget my first sight of these beautiful children.

Ashley Morgan had short brown hair, big blue eyes, and was just chunky enough to look cute. Milford Lee, who asked to be called Lee, was a thin but muscular little boy with big blue eyes and light hair. Corey Danielle was the youngest, with dark hair, brown eyes, and she was tiny in structure. All three were as cute as could be.

One could tell by their pale little faces that life hadn't been overly kind to them. I decided right away they needed special care because they had already experienced more than most people do in a lifetime. Nevertheless, they walked in with a smile on their face and the two little girls hugged each of us as if they already knew us. Lee was different; he occupied himself about the room ignoring everyone. He remained aloof, not wanting to get close to anyone. Corey, who was three years of age, slept with me the first night; reaching for me during the night just to make sure that I was there. Ashley slept with Kimberly and Lee slept with William as we were all trying to make them feel secure.

When Sunday morning came, the family and neighbors were so anxious to meet the children. Edwina and Jacqueline bathed the girls and dressed them in new clothes, styled and placed bows in their hair, and William saw to Lee's needs. I began preparing dinner early for the great aunts and great grandparents who would be arriving to see our new family. As each guest arrived, the girls met them at the door with smiles and hugs. Lee still didn't get too far from William.

Our huge downstairs family room became rather crowded as everyone socialized, talking about getting to know and love the children. Corey Danielle had already bonded with me. After meeting the company, she came upstairs. As I continued to cook, she crouched her tiny frame on the stairs near the dining room, which led to the upstairs bedrooms and began to talk to me. She couldn't talk plain so I couldn't understand everything she was saying. During Corey Danielle's conversation with me, she must have been asking for something.

When I asked her to repeat herself for about the third time, she became so frustrated that she slapped my face and stuck her index finger up at me, then rested her face with her hands cupped on each side. As her sad little eyes began to fill with tears, I began to realize there were many emotional days ahead.

With the dawning of Monday, the excitement of meeting with relatives was over. William went to school and Kimberly moved the children in to the small mobile home. While trying to get everything situated, she realized that the ten by forty foot trailer was too small. It consisted only of a kitchen, living room, a small room that had been made into a utility room and closet, one bath and one bedroom.

"Kimberly," I said "Since the trailer is so small and isn't any more than one hundred feet from our back door, why don't you share our bedrooms."

"Mom, these children have slept in so many different places, now it is time for them to know where home is, even if it is small."

Today, I can still envision how happy they looked when she sat the three of them at the bar that separated the kitchen and living room. The little rooms were so fresh and clean, filled with windows that brought the beauty of the outdoors inside. They loved the view of the fields, the trees, and open skies that surrounded them. The children seemed happy and enjoyed their breakfast. They knew their manners and were very well behaved.

Rules were set at the very beginning, which included bathing, brushing teeth, and getting dressed to begin their day. However, they seemed to have already been taught the habit of good grooming so this was no problem. We were very busy that day getting everything situated because Kimberly would be going to school the next day.

That February of 1989 was when my lifestyle really began to change. It had been nine years since I retired, and I had done what I wanted to do after the trying years of kidney failure, dialysis and transplants. I awakened with things already planned for me. Realizing that Kimberly needed to finish her education, I knew that I would be taking care of the children since Lee was the only one in school. Kimberly had to drive a good distance to school and was carrying a full load, she didn't return until late in the evening and since William worked after his school day was completed, I would be the major care taker.

Most of the time I felt only minimally well even when I took very good care of myself. I knew that this was going to take strength that could only come with God's help because my strength was far from sufficient. Daily, I prayed for emotional and physical strength and knew that God had added years to my life, because by nature, I would have died in 1981. Perhaps these years had been added to my life for a very special reason. Believe me, God gave me strength and love for these children. I loved them so much that it hurt. I wept when I thought of things they had encountered at such a young age. I really began to realize that God knew that I would fulfill my mission in life.

Our Martin's Fork friends were wonderful. They gave Kimberly money because they knew she and William were struggling in school and there would be immediate needs for the children. Elizabeth, my beautiful little spiritually adopted daughter gave them a shower at her house, sending out invitations with the children's sizes on them. With several people attending, it turned out to be a "social" with lots of good food, and the opportunity to visit and socialize both with neighbors and the children. The children received gifts of clothing, coats, shoes, and toys as well. For days, the gifts kept coming.

It has been said, when the chips are down, the people of Martin's Fork rise to the occasion. This was never more evident than in the way these little ones were accepted into our family and the community. The children had fallen into a nest of love.

~~~~~

With the passing of time, the excitement of the community about the arrival of the children began to wear off and everything began to return to normal. Although I hadn't taken care of small children in about seventeen years, I was the one with whom they spent most of their daylight hours. Kimberly went back to school two days after the children arrived.

The first day Corey cried uncontrollably for her mother. She did this, at intervals, for days. I walked the floor with her and held her close with our faces not meeting so that she couldn't see that I too was crying. I knew nothing to do except hold her. By doing so, she knew I loved her and was protecting her.

Corey constantly picked up the phone asking me to talk to her momma, "My momma needs you."

I went along with her pretense and consoled her momma, "Corey, Momma will be all right," I reassured her.

This went on for what seemed endless days. One day as Corey and I lay across the bed, she had a far away look in her eyes. These were the saddest eyes I had ever seen in a child. She bit her nails as she stared.

I could only think, *"What could it be like to be only three and in such state of mind."*

Suddenly she picked up the little princess play phone, put it to her mouth and said, "Momma, you killed my papaw," and forcefully slammed the phone down.

After that moment it was as though a miracle had taken place; there were no more false pretenses. A healing had begun. She began to be more like Ashley Morgan, although Ashley had many emotions to work through as well.

Every morning I went to their home as William and Kimberly left for school, jumped in bed with the girls. I told endless stories, my own stories; making them up as I went. I watched cartoons with them and entertained them as best I could.

Before leaving Kimberly saw that Lee looked his best for school. He adjusted well to school and totally adored Kimberly. She made sure that he was well dressed, fussed with his hair and told him, "Milford Lee, you're about the handsomest boy I have ever seen."

As he walked across the yard to the driveway that led to the bus stop, he seemed self-confident and secure. He was an extremely bright child and excelled in school. With the ratio of adults per child, neither of them felt left out in the beginning of their new existence.

The trailer was lacking in bedroom space. Kimberly said, "William, we will put a full bed in the living room and give the bedroom to the children."

William agreed. Their bedroom was cozy. It was decorated in soft colors of peach, cream, and green.

When spending the night in our house, as Lee and I lay in our twin beds talking he said, "We used to sleep in a van. The floors were bumpy. Corey lay on the seat crying most of the time."

"Lee," I said, "you will never have to sleep in a van again. I promise!"

Often Ashley would sing as we took our walks. Her favorite was "Don't Worry, Be Happy!" This brought peace to my heart; but in my soul I felt that Ashley suppressed her feelings. Her heart was very sad, I was sure.

With the passing of time, I became very tired physically, but tried not to let it show. I tried to be strong for the children despite my physical and emotional condition. One morning I felt so low, I went into the bathroom and closed the door.

As I looked in the mirror, I sobbed silently telling myself, *"Girl, you only think you can do this, but you really can't."*

After releasing my emotions, I was much better, and my old determination returned. Just after I straightened up my act, Ashley entered the bathroom and said, "Grandmom, here is a dollar for babysitting."

My heart told me *"This is your assignment from God. You will find strength."*

Kimberly and William were struggling. Finances were not good, which caused much pressure on the two of them. Although they had bad times, they always managed to bounce back. With the passing of time, they decided that they had to find a larger mobile home. Living in such small quarters caused conflict. However, money was still too big a problem. Kimberly Lynn looked in the paper for mobile home sales, and responded to an ad for a privately owned mobile home with three bedrooms, like new with nice furniture. The fellow who was trying to sell the home said that he could wait for a few days, at least three or four, for them to get the money.

Kimberly and William were able to borrow the money on a personal note. Everyone was excited about getting the money for a new home; however, this excitement didn't last long. The owner, who had agreed to wait for a few days, didn't wait. He sold the home to the person who came along with cash in hand. I burst into tears when I heard the news, because I knew they couldn't find anything affordable that would be as nice.

Kimberly said, "Mom, I don't understand. He gave us his word."

"Honey," I said, "People aren't always true to their word."

So, the search began again. Finally they found something suitable and the children had separate bedrooms at last. We worked very hard painting and redecorating as much as could be afforded. In the end, the trailer looked very cozy. They were very happy.

Both Ashley and Lee were in school now. I kept Corey with me so that Kimberly could finish college and be a substitute teacher on her days off. The children seemed to be situated and well disciplined. The family relationship appeared to be very good.

However, what seemed so right didn't last long. One November day we received word that William's sister, Brenda, the children's mother, had been acquitted and would be released from jail soon. She planned to come to Kentucky immediately.

Suddenly, my heart felt so heavy and my emotions soared out of control. Of course, my first thought was, *"Will she take the children away?"*

We had tried so hard to provide security for them I couldn't stand the idea of them having to go back to a life of uncertainty.

Kimberly had to leave early for classes, before leaving she asked William, "Would you be comfortable taking Corey to class with you and to the airport to pick up her mother?"

"I think that would be a good thing," he answered.

I dressed Corey in a long white cotton dress. Her long dark hair enhanced her outfit. She was four years old, and about as cute and adorable as they come. The two of them headed for Lincoln Memorial University where William had to attend his scheduled classes, then to the Knoxville airport to pick up his sister.

Late in the evening when the three of them made it home, dinner was waiting for everyone. All of our family treated the children's mother as kindly as we knew how, so the first few weeks went very smoothly. She babysat while Kimberly was in school.

One day when preparing breakfast for the girls, she called saying, "The girls say my eggs aren't like Grandmom's."

I was summoned to pop over and cook their eggs.

William's sister and Kimberly seemed to get along very well. Actually I was somewhat surprised as to how well they bonded. We had one of the nicest Christmases ever. It was the first Christmas since our girls were small that we had young children to enjoy on the holidays. The children's mother walked into the family room after the huge tree was decorated, and glowing with bright white lights.

"That is the prettiest tree I have ever seen!" she exclaimed.

My mom, Kimberly, and I bought her a beautiful black and gray coat, black boots and gloves. She loved them and looked beautiful in them. She and Kimberly would have passed for sisters since they were both tall with dark hair. The children were so happy, to have William, Kimberly, all of our family, and most of all, their mother with them.

All I could say was, "What a beautiful Christmas! It is great to have children in our home again!"

After the holidays, our way of life resumed as usual. Kimberly graduated from Lincoln Memorial University with a teaching degree in business, and would be home until she found a job.

Lee, Ashley, and Corey

CHAPTER 32

I tried very hard to help the children's mother. I had compassion for her, invited her to church, talked and counseled with her.

She related to me, "Pauline, our times of talking give me special insight to my life. I've been so confused. Talking with you seems to help me far more than the professional counseling."

"I realize that you have had a hard time and need to be restored back to a normal life," I said.

I was not sure she had ever had a normal life. After hearing about her life from a child up to that time, I could understand in part why her life had come to be a disaster.

I prayed, *"God, let her have a good life."*

She decided to attend college in the spring semester and was able to get financial aid and began classes in January. She made As and Bs in all subjects and had a great ability to learn. Everything seemed to be going fairly well.

Unexpectedly, she said, "I am bored with this little hick town of Harlan."

I had believed the mountains were appealing to her, but she wasn't looking for the serenity that the mountains, trees, rocks, and streams hold. She preferred the bright lights, hustle and bustle, and never-ending pace that city life held. I could plainly see the restlessness within her mounting as the days passed.

She finished the first semester in college, but didn't plan to stick around very long, which made me worry that she would take the children away.

The children had said, "Grandmom, Mom plans to take us."

They had so many fears from the past. "We don't want to go with her. We love her but don't want to go away."

She had contacted a lawyer, even though she had signed custody papers to Kimberly and William while she was incarcerated. My spirit was extremely burdened. As I lay in bed one night silently praying with tears sliding down my face; suddenly I saw a heart-warming sight. In the vision I saw three small children sitting on the ground in a semi-circle, very peaceful and calm. A man in a long robe standing in front of them with his arms reaching over their small bodies. I knew who this man was – Jesus.

I knew this vision was to reassure me that everything would be all right, but with the passing of time my faith began to weaken. I prayed for God to give me the words to say that would reach their mother and convince her to leave the children with us. I rehearsed over and over what I would say to her.

April came, only a month from her planned departure. She needed money and I needed help, therefore I hired her to help paint Jacqueline's trailer. As we were painting, we were both extremely quiet. Meanwhile I battled in my mind as to how I could get up enough courage to explain to her all of the reasons as to why she should not take the children. As I sat on the floor stirring the creamy colored paint, she was a few feet away from me masking around the window and looking very distant. I was ready to give her all the reasons as to why the children should stay with us.

She suddenly said, "Pauline, I've decided not to try and take the children. I know it wouldn't be fair to them, and I know how much everyone loves them and how much they love all of you," she said. "Not only your family loves them, but the entire community loves them. When the tragedy happened, it seemed as though I lost a part of my life and now I have already lost them even if I take them away from you. I feel like losing my children is my punishment, even though the murder was self-defense."

After she finished I said, "You have stated many of the reasons I had planned to express to you." As we painted throughout the day a peace settled over me, as if an emotional mountain had been lifted.

She completed the semester and left the following day. Ashley, Corey, and Lee were at my house when they said their goodbyes to her. It wasn't easy for anyone. Lee had very mixed emotions; he was only seven and had been through so much. He cried as though he wanted her to stay; not wanting her to go, but was glad not to be going with her. Ashley pretended nothing was going on as she pedaled my stationary bike that sat behind the couch; but inside I knew she was hurting. Four year old Corey, whom I held in my arms, latched her arms around my neck.

She said, "Momma, send diamonds for Grandmom and me for Christmas," and hugged her mother goodbye.

I knew the children were safe as I watched her drive out of sight in the misty rain, heading for Arizona. Now we could get back to normal and the fear of the children being taken away would cease. I couldn't bear the thought of them living a lesser quality of life than they had with us. Their mother had nowhere to take them, no job, and no security. God allowed the situation to be resolved in His own way.

William left for California the next day with the National Guard for a few weeks. Kimberly began to feel very ill and nauseous. I couldn't imagine what could be wrong. She had lab work done which revealed that she was pregnant.

Even though they had three children, William had told me, "For such a long time I have dreamed of having a biological son."

Kimberly called him in California, "William, I'm pregnant!"

He was completely ecstatic. I later spoke to one of the boys in his unit, who related to me, "William didn't come down from the excitement for two weeks."

The children were also very thrilled about the baby.

Kimberly immediately began to have problems. Her doctor warned her that her chances were very great in losing the baby. In spite all the problems she delivered a beautiful baby boy by cesarean. This little boy, William Roy Jefferies III, brought joy to all our lives.

Kimberly and Will

William continued working and going to college full time. He graduated a year later. Kimberly was very ill with the flu when graduation came and wasn't able to go. I took the baby and the other children stayed home with Kimberly. Will was almost a year old. When William received his diploma, I raised baby Will high enough to see over the crowd. We were seated on the back row. When he saw his daddy getting his diploma, he clapped his hands as if he knew what it was all about.

I was so proud of William. He had overcome a hard and unstable childhood. He had struggled for many years to accomplish this night.

When he first started college he told me, "I could never have imagined that such a good thing can happen in my life. It scares me," he said as he looked in his closet, "All these clothes; everything paid for in college; it all makes me fearful, afraid it won't last."

"It is real," I said.

His dream had been to finish four years in the Marines and four years in college by the time he was twenty-six. He was twenty-six in August and his accomplishments were met in December. To those who had help and opportunity this may not seem like much, but to an Oklahoma boy who had experienced so many struggles, this seemed like a dream come true. This reminded me of my own struggles for an education.

Due to William's accomplishments during his lake job with the Corps of Engineers, he was immediately hired after his graduation. He had to leave and work in a larger facility in Nashville, Tennessee for a year. Kimberly kept the children in Martin's Fork because of the great expense of living in the city, especially with a starting salary that would not accommodate their expenses. William was very blessed in that my relatives, George and Gene, invited him to stay in their home in Cross Plains, a short distance from his work place in Nashville.

Shortly after William left for his training in Nashville, Kimberly was very fortunate to find a temporary teaching position with the Southeastern Kentucky Community Technical College System. After Kimberly went to work and William moved to Nashville, I spent a great deal of time with the children. Each morning about 6:30 when I saw those four little faces, a feeling surfaced in my heart that created energy that otherwise wouldn't have existed.

I walked through Kimberly's door each weekday morning to help the children get ready for school and care for Will. There, nine year old Lee stood smiling; so handsome with his clothes so neat. I always told him how handsome he was and that I loved him. When Kimberly was ready, the two of them left for school. Corey and Ashley began to scurry around getting ready. They were always dressed so pretty. Clothes were never a problem, as Kimberly Lynn's friend, Helen Hicks, always brought them her granddaughter's clothes that she had outgrown, but worn very little. They were very good quality and well taken care of which added to the beauty and style of their wardrobe.

When they were ready I stood on the porch with them until the bus arrived, got my goodbye kiss and saw them leave smiling. I wanted them to leave happy in order to bring about a better day at school.

After I saw the bus pull out, I always lay down and rested for awhile until I could hear a beautiful sound coming from the baby's room, which Kimberly had decorated in sea green and white, making it so serene. I could hear the sweet sound of William Roy III as he awoke. Upon entering his room his big brown eyes smiled as he smiled. I thought, *what a blessing God has given to me.* We had beautiful days together. Caring for him was a pleasure.

Around three in the afternoon, I began to prepare supper. The children were always hungry when they returned home from school. While I cooked, Will rumbled about in the cabinets entertaining himself by dragging out the pots and pans. As the children arrived home from school, I greeted them with love, gave them their supper, and hoped that they would have many good memories of their childhood.

They took turns spending the weekend at my home; each of them looked so forward to their turn. I really enjoyed them. My prayer was that in some way the years God had added to my life would be used as an influence that would go on for generations.

Kimberly and William were trying to purchase fifty acres of land located in Martin's Fork adjacent to the river that flowed so beautifully, still had very little pollution, and was part of the land that my sisters, brothers, and I worked when we were growing up. Their dream was to build a huge log house to bring up the four children. My goal was to live to see them accomplish their dream, to see the children playing in the woods, picking wild flowers, with all the memories of their past forever behind them.

Fate took its course a short time later however, William and Kimberly were divorcing.

I questioned, *"Oh dear God, what will become of this little family?"*

~~~~~

With all that was going on in Kimberly's life, I was encouraged by the positive changes for Jacqueline. She continued her education, graduated with honors in four years, and met a wonderful man, Brian Hensley. He was a tall, dark, handsome man who was good-natured as well as caring and intelligent. They dated for almost a year before they married. Brian continued his education toward a Bachelor of Science degree and Jacqueline continued to work for the Corps of Engineers at Martin's Fork Lake.

I often thank God for the way Jacqueline's life worked out so wonderfully. Although I can still see that she suffers somewhat from the emotional abuse of her youth, she is overcoming the trauma of her past. I no longer feel as much guilt for not being there for her when she was young and so desperately needed me. I realize that I wasn't absent from her life by choice, and I know that I did the best that I could at that time.

Brian finished college and went to work as an RN. Jacqueline became pregnant and was blessed with a beautiful black-headed boy she named Brian Codey Hensley who would soon become Will's buddy. Jacqueline resigned from her job with the Corp of Engineers so that she could be the best mother possible. Later she had a beautiful little dark haired girl, Lindsey Ruth, and planned to go back to teaching when Lindsey was through kindergarten.

Before Jacqueline could begin her teaching career, fate would not have it that she would have a normal life. She came to me, "Mom, I have uncomfortable symptoms, my breathing is short, my arm hurts, and I have tremors."

After seeing a cardiologist, we learned that fluid had gathered around her heart, the pericardium sac, and excess fluid had to be removed. The atrium had collapsed due to the pressure of the fluid.

"Mom, I don't want you to come with me for the surgery. I need you to stay home and take care of my children."

"Jacqueline, I will do whatever you want me to do. If keeping the children with me at home will ease your worry, that's exactly what I want to do."

Several weeks later when surgery took place, I stayed in Jacqueline's and Brian's home with their children, Codey and Lindsey, and invited the other grandchildren, Hannah and Will, to spend each day with us. It was important to keep them calm and occupied with other thoughts than the possibility of losing their mother.

"Mammaw, it feels like Momma has gone away for ever," four year old Lindsey confided one day.

Each day was torment to be away from Jacqueline, but I had continuous communication with Brian, Edwina, and Kimberly, who were with her at Central Baptist Hospital in Lexington, Kentucky, where she had the surgery. They described the procedure and Jacqueline's pain as horrible. Brian, being an RN, stayed right by her bedside and did everything in his power to keep her comfortable.

Her chest had to be opened completely for the surgery. Jacqueline seldom, if ever, complained about anything, but the pain was so unbearable right after the surgery that she said repeatedly, "I don't think I can take much more."

Edwina told me that Kimberly often knelt at the side of Jacqueline's bed to pray and weep for her sister's pain to go away.

It was a frightening time for everyone.

Jacqueline recovered and did relatively well. Brian kept watch over her like a guard dog when she got home. He was overly protective of her, tending to all of the procedures related to her recovery from surgery. His biggest concern was that everything that touched her be sterile so she would not be at risk for infection. He also watched to make sure she didn't overexert herself.

Front: Lindsey and Codey
Back: Brian and Jacqueline

Lindsey

Codey

CHAPTER 33

In October of 1992, I sat on the couch and stared out the windows into mountains splashed in bright fall colors. The God-given loveliness of nature brought great joy to my spirit.

Early in November, as I stared into the same leafless mountains, the trees looked as empty as I felt inside. They were so still and bare, just waiting to be covered with the pure white snow or the glistening frost. My mind was in awesome wonder. I knew the seasons would pass and the trees would regenerate. They would stand tall and alive, lightly swaying their pretty green branches and leaves again. They were God's mighty works of art. Every spring the freshness of budding trees let every breathing mountain creature and every human being in the valley beneath know they were restored.

I wondered, *Will our lives ever be the same again, will we ever reach the mountain top, or as we climb will the ledges keep crumbling?"*

After six years of doing everything humanly possible to press forward and lighten burdens so a marriage and a young family could survive; after trying to help hold together such beautiful, loving children who had previously been through hell on earth and experienced ultimate heartbreak; I didn't know what else I could do. I could not force a successful marriage. I could not erase the children's recurring nightmares of tragedy.

My mind was engulfed with so many thoughts of the past years. I pondered on how God had given me strength and compassion to care for these beautiful, precious children while Kimberly and William finished their education. With college degrees, they would be prepared for professional careers and would not have to be burdened with finances as they had been in the past. They could have given a stable home and future to their children.

William would soon be coming home. The dream was shattered of Kimberly, William, and the children moving to the beautiful Martin's Fork Lake which lay so still and clear beneath the mountains that looked as if they were especially formed to accent the lake. The mountains stood tall but yet dipped in a horizontal pattern to form soft contours around the lake. This should have been a refuge for Kimberly and the children.

I recalled one occasion as Kimberly and the children stood at the lake in a circle holding hands, praying, "Jesus, when William returns let us live in this little paradise."

Kimberly's prayer was, "Let us live our youth out and only know love and happiness." Her hope had been to stay home and be a mother, wife, and homemaker until the children were older and then pursue her career as a teacher.

In one telephone call, their dreams were shattered. I was afraid the children's biological family would take them away. I had laughed and cried with these little ones and had entertained them endlessly for months and months after they arrived. We spent hours walking through the fields, the wind blowing our hair back from our faces and the blades of green grass, the yellow Easter flowers, and the white and yellow daisies gently waving with the breeze as though they were sharing our happiness.

Ashley would look up into my eyes from her big blue eyes saying, "We are a happy family," then skip along, swinging her arms and singing "Be Happy."

Little Corey, with her long brown hair and her tiny frame, and eyes that portrayed sadness even when she was enjoying herself, puzzled me. There seemed to be no way to read her eyes. I knew there was a deep longing for something in her past or a deep sadness because of the tragedy or perhaps both.

After Lee arrived from school, it would be many hours before Kimberly and William would be home from the University. The children and I would have our dinner, tidy up the kitchen, and take our walk into the mountains. After climbing the hills and mountains we were tired and rested on the flat lands on the ridges. We lay on our backs, in our blue jeans and flannel shirts, looking up into the blue skies while we rested and I made up stories to entertain them. The main characters were Ashley, Corey, and Lee. There we experienced many hours of happiness. I was at peace in knowing I was, in part, nursing them back to good emotional health.

Just when everything was supposed to be good, fate seemed to be handing out a cup of bitterness that I did not want to drink. I could not believe that the divorce could really be happening. I spent three weeks or more of nights when the sobs and prayers lingered for hours and hours. At times I became so tired that I lay on the floor releasing my heartfelt anguish.

Some nights at three in the morning I walked out of the house in to the dark shadow of the mountains, looking into the big sky and praying, *"Please, God, please! Don't let this happen. Don't let anyone have our children. This has been their refuge for three years. Please restore the marriage. Help William and Kimberly to see the hardest days are behind them."*

After trying to find comfort for my spirit I returned to my bedroom feeling total emptiness within, as if an important part of my life was over. These thoughts were devouring my mind. My desire to fight against this awful monster that had ripped our lives to pieces was slipping away.

Before I lay down to wrestle with the powers of darkness I fell to my knees and talked to God lifting my hands and praying, *"God, make everything good."*

I then sensed that the worst was yet to come. For all things to work out, I knew every individual had to be willing to let God do his work.

Kimberly called. "Mom, I feel that the past six years are lost."

Knowing that she was in a critical state made me feel that at that moment my words to her were fruitless. On my knees I wept to God, *"Please give my daughter the strength to find her way through this nightmare."*

Thanksgiving was only a few weeks away; however we had always felt the pleasure of preparation stirring inside us early on. To our family this was a special celebration. The children looked forward with extreme anticipation, knowing that dinner would be served in the huge room downstairs. The fire would be glowing in the fireplace. The windows that stretched the width of the room would bring in the outside world covered in a blanket of snow.

It would be family time. Tables would be set up to accommodate the turkey, dressing, baked ham covered with brown sugar, pineapples and cherries. Sweet potato casserole browned topping with nuts all over. Broccoli casserole made with Velveeta cheese and buttery Ritz cracker mixture baked to a golden brown, mashed potatoes, gravy, green beans, rolls, macaroni and cheese, and so much more. The children loved to think of all the good food we would be preparing. Ashley and Corey were my little helpers.

They would always ask, "Grandmom, can we stay the night before and help with the dinner?" And they did.

This Thanksgiving would be different.

A few weeks before Thanksgiving, Ashley had looked into my eyes with much disappointment showing in her face as she said, "I don't want to go to my family in North Carolina with William. Let them come here. I want Thanksgiving here."

Holding back the tears I said, "It will be lots of fun. You will be going to Great-grandmother's house."

When she drifted into another room the tears flowed as though they had been bottled for days. Perhaps I was selfish, thinking of how empty our house would be on Thanksgiving Day without them. The little ones would be missing for the first time in four years.

CHAPTER 34

In late autumn, a time of trouble helped me to realize that I could not be consumed by circumstances out of my control. A few days prior I had been asked to entertain the idea of running for election as a school board member. The seat for my district would be vacant.

I sat in our formal living room facing Table Rock and Chimney Rock. The autumn trees lit up my little world with a colorful glow that reflected the late sun. I began to try with every ounce of emotional strength to bring my thoughts together, hoping to occupy my mind with the information in front of me relative to the duties of a School Board Member. I was trying to push the divorce out of my mind. I hoped Kimberly and William's separation was working better for the children, since they would not exposed to all the quarrelling. I didn't want them going through continuous discouragement because of the marital problems. At that point I was almost convinced that I could accept what was destined to happen. I hadn't known of a single divorce in Momma or Daddy's family from their time back, except one.

The phone rang. William was on the line. The hints seemed to be coming. Finally I asked, "Are you and your grandmother contemplating taking the children from Kimberly?"

His reply was, "Yes, we have discussed that possibility."

My voice began to tremble as I fought back the tears. I was able to contain myself until our conversation was over.

The entire day tears poured down my face and my hands shook as a terror pillaged my soul. I silently said to myself, *my body and mind have had about all the stress I can handle.*

I cried to God and thought that I had left the battle in his hands. When I least expected it, dread and emotional pain squeezed my stomach and chest, and then flooded my mind. Every day and night I battled a despondency that seemed hopeless, wondering what the end result would be for Kimberly and the children. I knew Kimberly's mind was so clouded that she had no concept of the trials that lay ahead.

Christmas was nearing. The children would visit with me while Kimberly taught night classes for Southeast Community College at the Harlan campus. This would allow the children to be a part of the festivities they looked forward to like the decorating of the huge live tree and indulging in treats that included fresh fruits, marshmallow fluff and cream cheese dip, nuts, cookies, cheese balls, and about any appetizer you could think of.

I kept telling myself, *the peace from years prior will still remain.* I refused to believe the inevitable fate loomed over our utopia. Fate did win and took its course.

Christmas Eve was not the same without both parents. Ralph's emotional state seemed out of control. He did pretty well, but the air was thick with negativity. The same peace that had been there before seemed to be sabotaged by a dark cloud. Although I am sure I felt it greatest, I covered my emotions as much as possible for the sake of the children.

The children's presents were at my house, so they stayed the night with me. Kimberly and baby Will came early the next morning. The children jumped out of bed, ran down the stairs into the family room. The fire, the tree, and the presents made everything look cozy but the children had a trying time understanding why this Christmas wasn't like all the past ones with their new family.

Being emotionally disturbed as Ralph was, after getting out of bed with the morning far spent, he came to me while I was alone in the kitchen to express his dissatisfactions, "Don't you understand? I don't want anybody here! I don't want company or dinner!"

My silence was the best solution to the situation. I didn't argue.

All day long I forced myself to put on a happy face; I couldn't have the children see our problems, too.

Ralph left the house. I proceeded to cook our dinner, our usual holiday feast, while I shook inside. Instead of being gloomy over all that he had said, I was sure that I was doing a good job at hiding my discouragement. The greatest teacher of all, experience, had taught me well.

Dinner was served. I found myself amazed at the spectacular meal I had prepared. Anyone would never have guessed that there was a problem. The meal was almost identical to the Thanksgiving meal we had enjoyed a month earlier. Everyone ate and seemed happy. I was thankful the children had been downstairs and had not heard Ralph's outburst earlier in the day.

After everyone left, Ralph returned and asked in a sarcastic way, "Did you enjoy Christmas dinner?"

My reply was, "How could I? But I was a good actress. I never let the family know anything was wrong with you."

Letting go of the things that fulfill our hearts and dreams are hard, but somehow we must do what has to be done. I knew that some of the most enjoyable times of my life were with my family. However, I had to comprehend Ralph's emotional problems and accept what I thought was best for all. Deep within, I couldn't stop wondering why everyone doesn't have the desire to be agreeable, considerate, loving, and peaceful. Not having walked a mile in Ralph's shoes, I suppose I was a little judgmental.

~~~~~

In the passing of time, above all disappointments, I still had a peaceful feeling within my heart as I looked at all the beauty God had placed around me. Joy swelled inside as I looked at the beautiful creations, the little children, the tangible and intangible things that were valued in my life. In spite of my times of contentment and inspiration, due to my faith in God and the person that my mother had taught me to be, I still hurt inside.

I knew that William was moving from place to place with the Army Corps of Engineers and that there would be no stability without a mother figure. I knew through hearsay and observation their mother had not changed. I was consumed with fear as to what the outcome would be for those little ones that had experienced more emotional pain than a hundred children put together. I vowed to myself that I would do everything humanly possible to help Kimberly give them a stable environment.

The winter passed as we struggled for a normal life. My tears flowed as if they had come in order to ease the pain that penetrated my heart so deeply. It seemed as though there was one existing power of darkness that followed after us, trying with all its strength to destroy our happiness.

Spring came. I tried to make life as normal as possible by taking the four little ones to the Knoxville Zoo. I hoped they would enjoy doing something special and be encouraged by my effort to please them. Only God knew what a joy it was for me to provide the children with an afternoon that made them so happy.

For an hour I observed Will's actions as he watched the huge animals. I peacefully watched his every expression. I marveled at his big beautiful eyes, extremely long eyelashes, his perfect nose and flawlessly shaped lips. He was fascinated by the mother hippopotamus' behavior while guarding her baby from the other hippos. I never dreamed a two year old could have an interest that could be sustained by anything for such a long time. We prowled through the zoo for hours, no frets, no complaints - not even for food or drink.

This was one of the best days of my life.

Ashley, Corey, and Lee - at six, seven, and nine - were in a world of splendor. After the zoo adventure we stopped at a restaurant and ate. We all laughed and talked during our two hour journey home. Will even chattered to his stuffed lion that he bought at the gift shop.

I know God gave us that day of peace and happiness. Even my herniated disk didn't send pain down my hip and legs. Ten minutes before we arrived home, Will fell asleep. I took him home, laid him in his bed, pulled his favorite shoes off and he melted into the soft mattress, falling into a deep sleep. In the meantime, the others had crawled into their pajamas, into their own beds and fallen asleep.

The phone rang. The voice on the other end of the line shouted hostilely. Even in my silence and calmness my heart reeked with pain. My spirit wilted. My soul became restless. I made my way to an empty bedroom and cried many tears and pleaded to God for help.

When Kimberly arrived home, I left.

The heaviness seemed to dissipate for a while only to return when I arrived home. Again, I knew my night of rest was ruined. That evil power of darkness tried to steal my day of serenity. As I lay on my bed and sobbed and talked to the Great One, my heavy heart lightened and my tears subsided; I stacked my pillows and laid back on them. I thought of the beautiful day that God had granted to us.

I lay there thinking of many other women I had known who had their own burdens to bear. Like them, I was a born fighter, not a born loser. I could always scan the world and know that millions suffered more than me.

The women in our family had survived as widows, raising children without social services. They had struggled through by hoeing corn or taking in laundry. But they were still able to smile. The women in my family turned out fine young women and men. They were an enormous testament to the human spirit of mountain women.

Their actions spoke far louder than words. My Aunt Fannie was one of the greatest examples. She lived to be seventy-two. She worked and scurried around in her little Victorian red house that sat beside the river that ran by the weeping willows until the day she had a heart attack and died. The sons she struggled to bring up had built her comfortable home and saw that she did not want for anything.

CHAPTER 35

One evening as I sat keeping Momma company, a couple of gentlemen came by. I answered the door.

They were right to the point, "Pauline, will you run for the school board seat in your district?"

This visit came as a surprise. I said, "This is something I will have to give a lot of thought."

We talked on for a while. "Will you let us know in a few days?" our state representative asked.

"I will," I replied.

As I sat on Momma's front porch in the late fall air my mind went back to the little one roomed schoolhouse containing eight grades where I had attended school. The odds of my ever having broken out of the poverty cycle that set such low expectations for education were small. For some, to accomplish a Bachelors and Masters degree would seem insignificant, but to a mountain girl born in the 1940s the accomplishment was greatly fulfilling.

The campaign was an unusual experience. Visiting door to door for months brought me in contact with many, many adults that I had taught in the consolidated school as well as their parents.

My opposition was two male candidates. I have to admit that made the situation more interesting, especially when the strongest candidate ran a huge ad in the newspaper stating, "I am in good health." Since most people in my district knew I had undergone two kidney transplants, the obvious was interpreted.

The worst thing that happened during the campaign was that I fell on some rocks and broke my leg. By God's help, the injury didn't slow me down too much. I sent out fliers to everyone in the district outlining my campaign platform. I also knew so many of the voters personally which made contacts by phone a successful method of campaigning that worked in my favor.

On the day of the election, all of the candidates waited anxiously for the outcome. I went to hear the results with the Henson family at Henson's Florist. Each precinct reported the results of the election. A courthouse representative gave us the final results.

I had won by a landslide. It was rewarding to hear the result. Regardless of the monies behind my strongest opponent, he had not defeated me!

~~~~~

When I went on board, the appointing of a new superintendent was the first decision to be made and was truly an important one. I realized I had to put away personal feelings about the candidates who had applied for the position and choose the one that would be best for our system. After all, our children were what it was all about - not politics.

Applications came in from various states, as well as our own county. I read them over and over. I even called candidates in other states trying to gain some insight into their personal philosophy of education before the interviews took place.

The appointed day for interviews finally came. After the interviews were completed that day we voted during the board meeting that night. I have to say, I was extremely uptight. During the interviews I had come to a decision that Michael Eberbough, Ph.D. from West Virginia was who we needed. My mind was made up. However that did not mean that a local candidate could not do the job.

I stuck to my guns, as the old saying goes.

Dr. Eberbough had a mind of his own. He would not be easily swayed by local politics. He was a tall man, with gray hair, a firm voice, and was very knowledgeable in the administration of education. Being from another state would separate him from locals who wanted to control the system.

As it turned out, during our vote at the meeting, two voted for Dr. Eberbough and two against him. Therefore, I was the vote that made the decision. Dr. Eberbough became our superintendent.

When I said, "Yes," needless to say, there were some sad faces and negative remarks whispered around the room.

~~~~~

A couple of years passed. Dr. Eberbough was a good superintendent. There had been much progress in the Harlan County School District.

During my term on the County Board of Education, a teaching position came open in the business department at James A. Cawood High School. Kimberly had been waiting a few years for this opportunity. There was one problem. The Nepotism Law stated clearly that no board member could be the spouse or parent of any teacher currently employed within the school district. I would have to resign before Kimberly could get the job.

I related to Dr. Eberbough how Kimberly so desperately needed a job. "She has four children to care for," I said.

He said, "Mrs. Harber, I understand, but I also understand that when you are gone I will not be reappointed as superintendent."

He needed me to remain on the Board of Education to be the tie breaker when two opposing political sides refused to compromise. In almost every important issue, my vote was the deciding factor. Some people hadn't wanted Dr. Eberbough appointed in the beginning because they considered him to be an outsider. An outsider making decisions for our county's school district didn't sit well with those who were accustomed to being political controllers, because he refused to be controlled.

Dr. Eberbough knew that his contract would not be renewed, so he began looking into other counties in Kentucky for a position. A few months passed while he continued his search.

Dr. Eberbough said, "Mrs. Harber, I have found another position in Western Kentucky and will be turning in my resignation. You are one of the best board members I've ever worked with. I just wish that everyone who is elected to a Board of Education had the same love and concern for the children and kept their best interests at heart. I hate the predicament this puts you in, but I understand and hope that your daughter will be hired."

After Dr. Eberbough left, I was still on board to appoint another superintendent. Again I was the vote that made the final decision. I don't think I'd ever been more pressured in my entire life. There weren't a lot of good applicants to choose from but a choice had to be made. It was July. The fiscal year was ending. Hiring had to be done for the upcoming school year.

I voted for the person I thought would do the best job as superintendent at the time. After much praying to God for the answer, I believed He had guided my steps. It was as if I had fallen from public grace. Many made open remarks about my decision.

Resigning my position was very difficult for me, but Kimberly was young. I couldn't stand in the way of her career and her livelihood. I was ridiculed for stepping down so that Kimberly could have a job. I knew what I had to do and I did it. The school system would go on. I could have helped but couldn't have changed everything that needed to be changed, and after all, I was only one person.

Kimberly and I made the front page of the newspaper:

"Harber Resigns - Daughter Lands Job."

The TV station hounded me for an interview but I declined. I knew what I had to do and I did just that. I also knew that the media has a way of twisting words to sound different from what was intended.

While I was on the board every decision I made was with the six thousand students in mind. I was at peace with myself.

In less than a year, everything changed. None of the people that struggled for control remained. Dr. Musselman, from Alabama, was hired by the Board of Education. That board consisted of two new members and three that remained.

I missed being a board member, but my plate was full. Momma still needed me since her health was deteriorating. Ashley, Corey, William, and Lee needed me more since Kimberly was teaching. There were times I needed to be there for Edwina, Jacqueline, and their children Codey, Lindsey, and Hannah. Ralph still suffered from anxiety and depression. He preferred to be alone, which prevented a multitude of friction that could have occurred had he wanted my undivided attention.

CHAPTER 36

Ruthie Smith Hensley was laid to rest in the Hensley Cemetery on August 15, 1998 at the foot of Brush Mountain, overlooking the Wild River. Ten children - six boys and four girls - gathered at her graveside to grieve. Sunrays began to filter through the giant oak tree, the only one left on the north end of the cemetery. The hard rain had ceased just before the funeral procession left the church.

As Rev. Grant Hamlin did the short graveside service he had few words, but words full of meaning, "Children, please do not look at this box as a casket, look at it as a jewelry box, because your momma truly was a jewel."

As friends and neighbors began to sing *Amazing Grace* I eased out from the small crowd and walked slowly out the path toward my white Cherokee, looking back now and then to see my family scattered about.

I prayed, *"God, I know their feelings go just as deep as mine. We have lost the one who has been our source of strength all these years. Our hearts are so sad. How will we get along without her? Please, God - help my brothers and sisters to see that her work on earth was done. Let them be at peace without her and remember that she is at peace in Heaven."*

As I walked on, I began to think of how only Momma had known the depth of her pain, her inability to feed herself, or to walk. A bright mind lived in a body that did not work. I remembered the times she lifted her weakened arms pointing upward, and muttering, "Home." I felt such loneliness but I knew she was with the Father and the Son.

I stopped for a moment at the edge of the cemetery. I didn't want anyone to see me weep so I turned my back and looked into the mountains that were fresh and green from summer showers. I began to weep silently. Tears ran down my face as I remembered standing alone with her for hours as she slowly but perfectly made her departure. I knew God granted me the hours alone with her to say the unfinished things that needed to be said.

"Momma," I had said, "you have been one of the best. You visited the sick; cleaned their houses, cooked their food, visited the old widows, mothered orphaned children as well as multiple other children in Martin's Fork. Remember, Momma, when you walked three or four miles collecting almost every young person along the way for young people's meeting at Pastor Will Howard's Church? Momma, all the children you became involved with have related to me over the years, 'Our happiest memories were in or around your home with your mother'. Momma, you are truly a legend in Martin's Fork."

When my thoughts ceased I looked back to see Momma being placed beside Daddy beneath the tall oak tree with its branches extending high over their graves.

As I neared my jeep, I knew the greatest friend of my entire life was gone from this earth forever. I rode away with my thoughts focused on the positive, trying not to be selfish. She was now resting and one day we would have a great reunion. She would be as she was when she stood tall and beautiful, patiently fulfilling the callings on her life.

I returned to Momma's house. It seemed to hold her personality. As I stood in the back bedroom that held Mom's old beds and Grandma Emily's old dresser, I heard my brothers and sisters returning. It was time to pick up the broken pieces of my emotions and go on.

We gathered around the table to talk. Frank, Sam, and Mary Ruth said, "If there are any unpaid bills we will take care of them."

"Only about three hundred dollars. Momma put back enough in years past to take care of her funeral." I replied.

If her unpaid bills had been thousands of dollars, they would have paid the cost without hesitation. We discussed business arrangements for a very short time, but sat around the table and talked about happy times and lots of good memories of Momma.

Later, after everybody had gone, I sat under Momma's silver maple that she had set in the ground many years ago. Now it was tall and spread its silver branches to shade her front yard. I lingered there in the moonlight in the cool of the night looking through the shadows to familiar grounds. The sound of the river took me back to memories of the young vivacious "Ruthie" and the days of her youth.

She was one of the strongest women that ever set foot on Martin's Fork. Her name, Ruthie, fit her personality. Some called her "Ruth" which was even more perfect, in my opinion. It was a good, strong Biblical name.

She had been an extremely sociable person. Her life wasn't always just about ministering to the sick, needy, and church. In my mind I could see Momma and her friend, Opal Hensley, as they headed through the field to the swimming hole with us.

When they got to the edge of the field, Opal would say, "Here, Ruth, is you a latch pin."

They pulled their cotton dresses and slips between their legs and pinned them to keep the water from pushing their clothes over their heads. They climbed down the banks to the river, letting out screams as they landed in the fresh mountain water.

One evening as we swam a storm suddenly came up. Momma said, "Children, come! Let's get under the bushes that are hanging over the river."

Then she laughed so hard! "What is wrong with me? We are already wet."

One of the boys yelled out, "This water is so cold it could freeze icicles on an Eskimo's hind end."

Nevertheless, Momma and Opal had hovered over us until the storm passed.

I remembered another time one spring morning when mom said, "We are going to the Lewis Place."

Momma's sister, Fannie went with us.

The Lewis place was up the Curt Smith Hollow past Lottie and George Hensley's place, on the mountain where Momma was born. We climbed the mountain in awe, wondering what it would look like. When we got to the old home place, we saw a few apple trees that were barren, but the rest of the mountain was green and lush. The wild flowers were in bloom. Birds were chirping. We filled our lungs with the cool, fresh breeze. The air felt as pure as refined gold.

Aunt Fannie said, "Ruthie, Maw carried many a pail of water from that spring that used to be over there."

Momma said, "See the rocks from the old chimney? That's where the old house stood. Children, do you see what is left of the path that was cleared years ago? That goes down the other side of the mountain. I walked down the side of the mountain to school. I remember being at Liggett School. One day I got so sick, the teacher wouldn't let me go home, so when I caught her head turned I jumped out the window and no doubt was half way up the mountain before she missed me."

She paused, "My friend had given me a chew of backer and I got sicker 'n a dog trying to chew it."

As we sat on the ground she had continued her story telling. She said, "Another time, I went to school one morning and it was bitter cold. The streams were frozen solid, nothing stirring. My hands frost bit. I stopped at the house of two old sisters living in the coal camp above the school. They bathed my little froze hands in a wash pan of warm water."

"Momma, weren't you afraid to walk off the mountain?" I asked.

"Well a little… One other time when I walked up the mountain on my way home from school, I saw a big man lurking in the trees starring at me. Now that scared me."

"How many years did you go to school?" I asked.

"At the end of the fourth grade I quit school, but that was further than my sisters and brothers ever went, I guess being the youngest of all of us I got a little more schooling."

I was proud that my momma could read and write.

I sat for hours thinking about my momma and her life. She truly is a legend in our little mountain community.

Opal Hensley and Ruthie Smith Hensley

CHAPTER 37

After Momma's death, I continued to take care of Kimberly's children. By this time the three children had reached adolescence. Each had a great yearning to go back home.

"*But where was home?*" I wondered. The states of Oklahoma and Arizona, I supposed. That was the home they knew before they came to us, but they had no real roots there that were grounded.

Ashley moved back to Arizona with her mother for a short time but returned to Kimberly's. She was a troubled teenager. Looking back over her life one could see why her mind was so troubled.

Kimberly remarried, which was a big mistake.

As time passed William spent more and more time with me. Kimberly did a lot for him, but I was his security in many ways because I always babysat while she worked. Kimberly's marriage was up and down. John and his parents had their own concepts of how she should live.

To Kimberly, life was not meant for constant conflict, but to be lived and enjoyed. Tensions grew to an unbearable level for Kimberly and the children. As much as she wanted to be married and have a stable family, she knew she this was not working.

Only a few months after the divorce, John's son was swimming early in the season in Martin's Fork Lake with friends. They were frolicking in the water, as teenagers do. When he called for help everyone thought he was playing. Once they realized he really wasn't playing, and tried to reach him, it was already too late. He had gone under the water and they couldn't find his body at first. His family had been busy with Saturday routines and could not be reached by phone during the search. Perhaps it was better that way. Being at the scene could have been too devastating. The young man's family had truly loved him. He was the apple of their eye. Kimberly, living only two miles above the lake, received the news right away.

She said, "I'm going to the beach."

She had grown somewhat close to her stepson; after all, he had lived in her home. Kimberly had so much love in her heart, there was always room for one more - especially a child. However, she was a disciplinarian. She believed children should be taught and corrected no matter how much she loved them – including her biological son.

As Kimberly stood on the white sand looking over the lake that lay beneath the mountains watching the rescuers, tears streamed from her big eyes. It wasn't long until the tall, handsome, dark haired fifteen year old, with smooth olive skin, lay on the soft sand in front of her. Kimberly fell to her knees and wept bitterly, the sound echoing through the mountains.

~~~~~

For a young woman, Kimberly seemed destined for a troubled life; a life filled with ups and downs. She bore far more than her share of pain, her life seemed so complicated at times.

When her marriage failed she said, "Mom I look at others and their lives seem so much easier than mine. But, Mom, I have your blood I am a strong woman. I will survive."

Kimberly wanted a companion to love her, support her, and to be her friend. She wanted someone to bear her pain with her, fish with her, horseback ride, camp with the children in the mountains, go to church with her, send her a single rose, talk about everything with her, to not only see her outward beauty but her inner beauty as well. She was so strong but had a soul that desired utopia as a child does.

To see a flower bloom in the spring was a miracle to Kimberly. She nurtured it and felt such fulfillment as she touched it. A sunset, a full moon, the wind swaying in the trees, the shining waters of the wild river, or birds drinking from the bluebells, pink wild roses, or the daisies outside the fence in the fields fed joy to her soul. A trip to the Caribbean could not have been more fulfilling. She could absorb God's beauty in nature into her soul more than anyone I have ever known.

Kimberly loved to ride Harley Davidsons. She said, "Mom, I feel a calmness as the wind comes against my face, blowing my hair behind me. I feel like a free spirit!"

In spite of all the hard times she saved enough money to go to the ocean once a year. There she could deep-sea fish. Her catches would surpass everyone on the boat. She parasailed, snorkeled, did everything that she could for a week or two, depending on how long her finances lasted.

I recalled one day when Kimberly had been to Middlesboro, in Bell County; a drive through the mountains took you there in less than an hour. Kimberly and I sat on the porch on the north side of the house in the cool of the evening feeling the nearness of spring after she had returned. The fresh smell after a light shower of rain signaled a whole new world clothed with tender buds that would open up, dressing the mountains in an array of green. With Redbuds and Dogwood trees standing amidst, looking as if an expert arranged them.

"Mom," she said, "as I came through the mountains today I saw an Arabian horse tied to a clothesline in a small yard. It looked starved and infested with lice." She pondered for a while, "Mom, I'm going back to make the lady an offer. I stopped and talked with her and I believe I can get that horse."

Back through the mountains she drove as soon as the sun came up the next day.

Kimberly said, "Ma'am, I will give you this gold necklace, a TV and $350.00 cash for the Arabian."

The lady said, "He's yours."

In the condition the horse was in, this was a high price. It looked as if she may have been buying him to bury.

Kimberly brought him to the barn at the very back of the pasture edging the bottom of the mountains then came to me, "You can't see this horse until I have bathed, deloused him, and he gains a couple hundred pounds, because your heart will break.".

The weeks passed swiftly turning spring to summer. One day when I was standing on the back porch I saw her ride over the small horizon on the most beautiful Arabian I had ever seen.

She hollered, "Mom, this is Heartbeat. I gave him the name because he was only a heartbeat away from death when I found him. And he won't be leaving here till the day he dies."

Since Kimberley was a teacher at James A. Cawood High School and the football team was called The Trojans, Heartbeat became a little famous. Kimberly designed her own outfit suitable for a Trojanette. She sewed together a white T-shirt and red circle tail short skirt, bought brown leather and went to the leather shop and had a leather skirt made. It was solid around the waist and the top of the hips with wide fringed leather reaching the bottom edge of the red skirt. She wore brown Roman sandals that wrapped small straps to the knee, a beautiful red sequined cape and a matching helmet that showed her long dark hair hanging far below.

Kimberly and Heartbeat became the Trojans' mascot. She gallantly rode around the football field at half time or out on the field when the team scored a touchdown.

The young people yelled "Xena!" as she rode, so Kimberly had a new name in and out of school.

On her first adventure at a football game, the local TV station filmed Heartbeat and Kimberly and played it on the eleven o'clock news. I could not watch the TV for watching Kimberly. She didn't say a word but her smile and the look on her face said everything.

Kimberly and Heartbeat

CHAPTER 38

Kimberly continuously struggled financially and emotionally. Regardless of life's struggles she loved it and lived it to the fullest.

As the seasons drifted in and out she would say, "Mom, tell me your symptoms of kidney failure, how did you feel?"

"Mostly tired, Kimberly," I would say.

She would smile and say, "Mom, why did I have to be so much like you, even my kidneys? I am proud to look like you and have your strength. You are such a strong woman, but I wish I didn't have your same disease."

"Kimberly," I would say, "look how well I have done with the transplant. I live more than a normal life. The same will be for you."

"I don't know. Sometimes I feel a deep sadness and wonder what my destiny will be."

Kimberly's health seemed to change somewhat but as her dearest friend Rhonda Long Robinson would laugh and say, "Kimberly sucks every moment out of life, and life sucks every moment out of me. She has taught me more about life than I ever dreamed I could know. She has taught me how to seek out the natural fulfillment of life itself."

Kimberly's life seemed to become more and more of an enduring journey. The kidney disease, the tiredness, and the high blood pressure seemed to have a very negative effect on her. Bringing about more stress, she was laid off from teaching business. One of the junior high schools cut the business classes from their program. The teacher that lost his position there had several years seniority over Kimberly, therefore he bumped her and she was without a job.

"Mom, what will I do? Business teaching positions are hard to come by. I'm single and have four children to raise. Mom, I'm afraid."

"Kimberly," I would say, "we'll make it. Remember, we are from a strong heritage and God is on our side. The women in our family are like the mountain laurels, we survive."

Sure enough a job came open in the Alternative School that did not require a specific major. Kimberly went straight to the Superintendent and asked for the position. She had a very good rapport with Dr. Musselman from the time he first became Superintendent. She had invited him to her business class to participate in a special lesson. She was an excellent teacher and did not feel uncomfortable for anyone to observe or to take part in her class, even the Commissioner of Education.

Dr. Musselman had a daughter Kimberly's age that was also a teacher and had died not long before Kimberly lost her job. From the bottom of her heart and soul, she showed the Superintendent utmost compassion during his time of tragedy.

Kimberly walked into Dr. Mussleman's office one day and said, "Dr. Musselman, will you hire me for the alternative job? I have four children and will loose my home, everything I have, if I don't get a job."

Kimberly was hired and not long afterwards, Dr. Musselman moved to another job.

The Alternative School job was very stressful. Being the type of class it was, Kimberly was confined with her students the entire day. There were no breaks. She even had to accompany them during lunch. The only room available was on the opposite end of the huge school separating the Alternative School students from the other students. There were no windows or air conditioning, only a fan.

In spite of all the discomfort, she loved the students. All of them were deeply troubled; some had very negative behavior. She still did everything in her power to help them. For the most part, they loved her in return.

Some days she would say, "Mom, you will never believe what kind of day I had." Still, Kimberly loved her job. She was proud to be their teacher. Kimberly always had a soft spot for the less fortunate.

Being an alternative teacher seemed to classify her in another category by many of the teachers. On one occasion she said, "Mom, my students had the rights for one hour of Physical Education. I took them for gym and one of the instructors said I needed to get back where I belonged!"

Of course she was pretty spunky and told him, "I'll leave when I'm ready," and let the kids have their gym class.

She was treated as lower class by many teachers because she was in an alternative school position, but was respected by many others. Little did they know, my Kimberly would have gone the last mile with any of them.

~~~~~

One evening after school, Kimberly ran into David Estep, a young man she had taught in school. As they talked he asked her to go by Wampus Creek Farm and doctor his boss's horse. She was with her friend Robin Browning, a local lawyer, and she asked her to go along.

Kimberly was dressed in a soft white pullover with a matching cardigan, which accented her long, dark hair. The Levis she wore accentuate her long thin legs.

While Kimberly was taking care of the horse, the owner, a tall, good looking man with a nice smile, brown hair and eyes, stopped by along with some other folks. Kimberly had already injected the horse. There was another high-spirited horse that everyone was shy of. Kimberly saddled him up, stepped into the first stirrup, lifted her leg over to the other stirrup and rested on the saddle.

As she rode, her long hair blowing behind her, the owner looked at Robin and said, "That girl must know a lot about horses."

Walker told me later, "I never dreamed of meeting a young woman with such confidence. Is she afraid of anything?"

Every evening after school Kimberly continued to go by Wampus Creek Farms to inject Walker's horse and pamper him. Walker began enjoying Kimberly's company and made it a point to be present while she was there. They lingered just to talk as they watched the horses gallop and roust around.

As the days passed, feelings they had for each other emerged. As the evening was cool, they sat in the midnight blue pick-up watching the horses.

Later, Walker told me, "We had our first kiss in the truck at Wampus Creek, watching the horses. I knew then Kimberly was more than I had ever dreamed would enter my life. After my divorce, I had no desire to live until she came along."

On more than one occasion he would say, "Pauline, Kimberly saved my life. The way I see her enjoy the small things of life makes me want to live again."

Kimberly and Walker began horseback riding, going to dinner and to tack shops.

Kimberly said, "Mom, my ideal evening isn't partying. It's going to a nice restaurant and then to a tack shop, or maybe trail riding, just enjoying all God's beauty under the stars or horseback riding in a big snow with the flakes landing on my eyelashes. It's so great that Walker loves the same lifestyle as I do!"

~~~~~

Lee was in the Air Force and Ashley had graduated and moved to Oklahoma. Only Corey and William were in the household with Kimberly. William and Corey came to love and trust Walker completely.

Kimberly and Walker's relationship developed Their love and respect grew for each other. Two young people who had been betrayed by their spouses in the past and believed they would never love again were predestined to meet and fall in love. They dated for nineteen months and decided to get married in the spring of 2004, which was only five or six months away.

Being the romantic that Kimberly was, she talked it over with Walker and they decided that the wedding would be on a mountain that Ralph and I had purchased years earlier. The spot had been reclaimed after strip mining and there were many open fields full of beautiful wild flowers. It was like another world up there.

Many times Kimberly and I walked over the fields and I said, "Kimberly, this will be yours if you prefer to build here instead of on your land."

"Mom," she said, "won't it be nice to be married when the white wild roses run through the trees and on the hillside covering them like snow. Lindsey and Hannah will ride Trotter and Cree, their colts, dropping wild flowers to the ground. Hannah, with her long blonde hair and angelic face, will be wearing a long antique white lace dress. Lindsey Ruth, with her long black hair and big beautiful eyes, will be wearing the same. I will ride my big chestnut brown horse, Dar. I will be wearing a long flowing antique white satin wedding dress covered in lace and a veil that hangs longer than my hair. Walker will wear black and ride his black horse. I have chosen the middle field because the white wild roses will be running up the trees and hillsides. We will make our trail at the bottom of the site. Our guests who come from far and near can occupy the area that overlooks the valley and the mountain south of the shiny waters of the Wild River."

"Oh Kimberly," I said, "that sounds like a fairy tale. This will be the wedding of the century."

~~~~~

September 2003 was in its first week. Fall was in the air and it wouldn't be long until the mountains would be a work of art. The vibrant leaves in all their splendor would color our world for a season.

October would soon come and Kimberly would say as in times past, "Mom, I saw them passing over today."

"Saw what, Kimberly?"

"The wild geese… Not long from now the soft snow will fall and cover the mountains and valleys. I'll take Heartbeat and we'll ride as much as we can. We'll drink in all of God's beauty we can hold!"

Kimberly said to me almost everyday, "Walker loves me and understands my illness. He helps me figure out my finances and is good to my children."

She would say, "I'm so glad that I own the thirty-eight acres of land across the river from where you grew up, the very land you and your brothers and sisters worked. I can imagine what it was like for you as a little girl. I love the ponds of water, especially in the spring when the entire west side of the east pond is laced with mountain laurels. When their green shiny leaves and clusters of pretty pink flowers reflect on the still waters, it's almost an unimaginable picture. When Walker and I are married, we hope to build just above the east pond. Only a log cabin would fit the scene. I think the island in the middle would be the perfect place to build a smaller cabin for William, Codey, Lindsey, and Hannah to play and be real mountain children making memories to never be forgotten."

"I know I'm a dreamer", she would say with a far away look in her eyes, "but dreams do come true."

I responded, "Yes they surely do," knowing the importance of keeping dreams alive.

Kimberly would go on to tell me that through her marriage to Will's father, her dreams were what got her through the long hard times.

"I held them in my hands, Mom, but they slipped through like grains of sand." She would say, "I was really young then…"

"Kimberly, hold on to your dreams. I know that you feel shipwrecked emotionally and physically, but you've got to hold on."

"Mom, I do have visions and dreams. I feel that in spite of all the storms, with Walker in my life, the anchor still holds," she replied.

My heart filled with joy to see the new fresh life emerging in Kimberly. It was something from her very inner being, something unlike anything I had seen in a long, long time.

"Mom," she'd say, "I feel like I have the chance to be all that I can be."

Kimberly

Will

Corey - senior picture

CHAPTER 39

Monday, September 8, 2003, again Kimberly and I sat on her porch talking of how happy she and Walker were, and of her dreams of what a wonderful life they would have together. We spoke of our making sure everything was well with Will in school. Kimberly had fallen and required major surgery on her knee. She was off from work during her recovery.

It was as though an oppression had come over Will; almost a premonition of something hard coming his way.

"Will you help me to motivate Will?" Kimberly asked.

"Yes. We can't let this child's education slip through the cracks. You are somewhat incapacitated at the moment. When you are released from the doctor to return to teaching you will have your hands full. I will visit the school one day a week and conference with each teacher".

She smiled a big smile, then was quiet for a few minutes. I could plainly see by the intensity in Kimberly's eyes that something good was on her mind.

She said, "Walker and I are planning to build a black wood fence around the fields in front and behind your house. You can sit on either porch and watch our horses run. I know the joy you get from their high spirits."

I got up to leave.

"Mom", she said, "you look really tired. Please lie down on the swing and rest awhile."

I laid down on the swing. She smiled and said, "I wish you could stay all evening."

It was as if in her spirit she wanted to be near me. With my nature being "I have to do this or that" I didn't stay very long. I walked on down the steps and turned to look at her one more time.

Kimberly said, "Mom, the light hurts my eyes." She dropped her head, as if to avoid the evening sunlight. Standing up, she added, "I believe I will walk down with you."

She stopped at the bottom of the steps to pamper a white rose that she had planted in July after buying Jacqueline's house. Jacqueline and Brian had built a new home and Kimberly was glad to live there until she could get a bridge across the river to her land where she and Walker planned to build their dream home.

I slowly walked on and turned back to see her bent over the white rose picking off the useless dead leaves. She walked the path after me through the field to my house, taking her time. I already had my hands in dishwater when she came in.

She walked by her Dad and said, "Hi, Pap," and added "Mom, will you fix me a glass of ice water? I feel so sick."

I dried my hands, put the glass under the ice dispenser, added water and handed it to her. Her usual smile was gone and there was pain in her eyes that I didn't understand.

"Mom, I feel sick. I'm going back home."

She made her way slowly back up the path. The ACL replacement in her knee slowed her long gait a bit.

Later, as I stood outside, I looked toward her house. She and Will were securing a chain to the doghouse. The local boys had begun to raise chickens. Will wanted to raise a few chickens as a hobby. Along with the chickens, all the neighborhood boys thought they had to have a Walker Hound to guard their chickens. Kimberly had granted his wish by giving him a Walker Hound, so they had to chain him up until he adapted to life with chickens to make sure he wouldn't eat them.

The evening sun had faded from Kimberly's yard. I continued watching them as I walked toward my car. I had a baby shower to attend. When leaving my driveway, I pondered on how the brace from her ankle to above her knee didn't put a damper on Kimberly and Will's project. She stared my way for a moment then continued helping Will. His friend, Fred, stood by looking on while holding a huge rooster.

After returning from the shower, I called Kimberly. I told her that I would bring Will's supper up shortly.

We chatted for a moment and she said, "You will never know how bad my head hurt today."

I made William a plate of vegetables and meat. It was already dark but I headed up the little path through the field. It was so familiar; I could follow it even in the dark.

"Mom has lain down," Will said. "She's probably asleep by now."

I didn't dare wake her. I knew how bad she had been feeling and she needed her rest. I gave Will's supper to him and said goodnight. Will still seemed distant, as though a dread hung over him.

When I got out of bed Tuesday morning everything was so quiet. Kimberly hadn't called as she always did, and Ralph was still in bed. Usually I went to my church and prayed to start the day in a positive way and to seek God for help for everyone I knew that needed a helping hand. I felt strange. Something didn't feel right in my spirit and soul. I was in a dazed condition, immobile, just sitting on the floor in front of the recliner feeling empty. As I glanced at the clock that told me it was 8:15, the phone rang.

Walker was on the other end and said, "Kimberly's in the emergency room at Appalachian Regional Hospital. Corey took her there around 6:30 this morning. Kimberly wants you to call everyone you know to pray for her."

In slow motion I dialed Elizabeth, Pastor Ernest Hensley and his wife Gladys, and a few others and asked them to pray. I knew the word would spread quickly and everyone contacted would be praying for her.

A little later Walker called again, "Kimberly is very upset with the doctor on call. The doctor refuses to take blood to check about the blood thinner she's been taking after her knee surgery. Her stomach is upset, her vision is blurred, her blood pressure is extremely high."

Corey called shortly after Walker and said that the lady doctor that was treating Kimberly had refused to do anything for her. To everyone's shock, the doctor was releasing her and told her to see her primary care physician in a couple of days.

Corey said, "Mammaw, she's so upset that she told the doctor if she had a stroke and lived that she would sue her."

She was discharged, but knew she had to have help. Walker and Corey put Kimberly in the truck and headed toward Pineville, which was further out of the way than Harlan. She wanted to get to Dr. Combs, her primary care physician. She was a wonderful young lady that truly cared about Kimberly.

Kimberly had great confidence in Dr. Combs. She had told me before, "Mom, Dr. Combs has enlightened me so much in knowing my own body, my illness, and what works for me. She also stressed to me that no matter where I went to the ER that I have patient rights."

Kimberly was fond of Dr. Combs and felt they were truly kindred spirits.

As Corey, Kimberly, and Walker drove down 119 to Pineville in the dark green Dodge diesel king cab, Kimberly was nauseous. Walker pulled off the road edging the mountains. Everything seemed to be getting worse but Kimberly had been able to talk and laugh a little when they first started their journey. The ER doctor in Harlan had given her a Loritab by mouth that had given her a little ease for the headache.

A few miles farther down the long stretch of highway she said, "I am so sick!"

Again they stopped. Kimberly was wracked with nausea. While throwing up, she fell. Corey and Walker helped her back into the truck.

Meantime, I was still home and wasn't really clear about where I should go and still calling people to pray.

As I knelt to pray the phone rang, "Mammaw, we're at the Pineville Community Hospital Emergency Room. The nurse said Mom has probably had too much medication and will sleep it off in a couple of hours."

I thought maybe this was possible and felt a little relieved. I went for a cup of coffee and sat in front of the window looking over the grounds thinking that Kimberly would be okay.

The phone rang again.

"Are you Kimberly Lynn Harber's mother?" came a voice from the other end.

"Yes," I replied.

"I am the Emergency Room nurse at Pineville."

"Did my daughter take too much medication for pain?" I awkwardly asked.

"No," she replied. "She has had a brain hemorrhage. She's on life support and is being flown to the University of Tennessee hospital."

I called Corey's cell phone. Corey answered in a frantic voice, "Mammaw, this is a picture I will never erase from my mind. After we got her back in the truck and were crossing the Cumberland River turning onto 25E, she laid her head on the back of the seat and sighed, "God help me", and those were her last words. Mammaw, I tried to make her open her eyes. I tapped her face; I begged her to wake up. The ER team had to carry her inside. Oh Mammaw, I will never forget her face."

Someone told me that Dr. Combs reached the hospital as they were loading Kimberly into the helicopter. The beautiful young doctor stood weeping beneath the wind from the propellers, feeling totally helpless. She had seen and successfully helped Kimberly so many times before.

~~~~~

"I wasn't there! I should have been there!" My thoughts raged.

I felt a sick, helpless feeling sweep through me. *"Why was I so aloof that morning? Why didn't I run to Harlan as soon as Walker called"* Perhaps I could not have withstood the emotional pain.

After the nurse called I ran to the bathroom, showered and quickly dressed. I was pleading, *"God, please don't let my baby die."* She was thirty eight but still my beautiful baby girl.

When I came out of the bathroom, Elizabeth, my dear friend, was standing there. I had called her immediately after the call from the nurse.

Elizabeth did not say a word for a moment, then said, "Charlie and I will drive on to Pineville."

"Will you take care of Pauline?" Ralph asked Elizabeth. She assured him she would.

He sat silently at the kitchen table, smoking one cigarette after another. He was so distraught that he wasn't even able to talk. He didn't move or show any emotions. Finally he got up and went to the garage where he wept alone.

As my daughter, Edwina, drove to my home, I stood outside waiting for her. I just stood there feeling desolate as the autumn air stirred through the treetops in the sunshine.

Edwina prayed all the way while we were driving the familiar path that had taken us so many times for my dialysis in days long past. I felt so cold, so empty inside. Words would not come. Never had I felt so much like the shell of a person. Nothing seemed real. It was as if life had escaped my body.

After what seemed an eternity we entered the hospital. I wasn't sure if the helicopter had already left. I saw the sad faces of Elizabeth, Charlie Wayne, Mark and Diane Spurlock, and Kimberly's friends, Jack Smith and Tina Lobiando.

I asked, "Is she gone?"

Elizabeth replied, "Yes, they are probably there by now."

My heart would not yield its pain beyond my throat. I could not make a sound but oh, God, how I hurt inside. If someone could have looked through my eyes, into my soul, they would never have been able to comprehend the awful current of pain that surged like an electric bolt through my heart.

It was decided that Edwina, Elizabeth, and I would drive on to Knoxville, to the University of Tennessee Medical Center. As we traveled, the two of them talked constantly during the two-hour drive. I said nothing. Not one tear would surface.

As we drove my heart told me *"when you walk in the trauma center, a pleasant, caring nurse will walk toward you trying to smile. She will say there is no hope."*

I played out the scenario again and again in my mind as we drove. *"Will she live? Please tell me she will live!"*

When I entered the corridor the situation played out very nearly as I had imagined it would.

The nurse said, "Come with me, talk to her, hug her."

I walked in to the Trauma Unit. There she lay on the white sheets, her long black hair spread on the pillow, her skin flushed to a light rose color, her beautiful lips full and colorful and her big eyes closed showing her long, dark, thick lashes that lay gently to touch the top of her cheeks.

I slowly slid my arms under the white sheet and said, "Kimberly, I love you. Now, you think of Jesus."

I knew that my Kimberly was gone. I knew that she had not heard. My spirit told me so.

The doctors walked in. One young doctor looked at me with a look of hopelessness, but also a lot of compassion. Neither of us said a word. His arms were folded. I brushed his arm with my hand lightly. With my eyes I begged for him to help her, or please just to give me a ray of hope.

An accompanying doctor said, "Mrs. Harber, can we discuss organ donation?"

His question was so harsh, so unfeeling. He held out no ray of hope for the situation.

My reply was, "Yes… just give me a little time."

He said, "That will be fine," and left the room.

I was so numb, I don't really remember the lapse of time, but evening came and another scan was done. By that time Jacqueline and Brian had arrived with Will, still unaware of the seriousness of the situation. Before we could explain the neurologist walked in, scan in hand.

Jacqueline and Brian stood just inside the door and Edwina was on the opposite end of the room. Elizabeth, Dave, Rhonda, Jamie, Mark, Diane, Tina, Jack Smith, and Walker McKeiver, Kimberly's fiancé, stood and sat among us.

The tall middle-aged doctor looked in my direction and said, "There is no hope. The bleed was so severe that the brain stem is broken."

I hadn't realized until that moment that I had unconsciously had a spark of hope lying dormant somewhere in my soul. Suddenly and violently I felt a surge of anger as I had never felt before flooding my entire being.

The doctor then informed us that they were leaving her on life support for another twenty-four hours, then left.

As the anger continued to overtake me I hit the leather chair arm, "I am so angry that I could beat the wall down with my bare hands!"

In my moment of despair I looked across the small room to see our Will. He was mine and Kimberly's. We had nurtured and loved him together. By God's help, I contained myself and moved to Will's side. As I looked into the sad face of this twelve year old, I saw blood flowing from his fingertips as he pulled them from his lips; he had bitten the ends of his fingers until they bled. This was his way to avoid shedding tears. I wished we both could have wept, but we were like steel and hurting in a way we had never hurt before.

September 9 was a long night. Early the next morning my beloved friend, Brenda Henson, came to be by my side. I only remember bits and pieces of the day. I went to a private bathroom to be alone at 2:00 p.m.

When I returned a host of family and friends were receiving the final word from the doctor. There would be nothing further done except to test for organ donation. I looked on from a distance.

When Edwina saw me, she said to the doctor, "There's Mom."

"Do you have any questions?" the doctor asked.

In a soft tone, I replied, "No."

The sudden anger that had swept through me when the doctor had said it was over was gone. Now, I could not feel reality at all. It seemed that I was just a bystander. Her time of death was marked as September 10, 2:00 p.m. I called my sister, Wilhelmina, and asked her to let family and friends know of Kimberly's passing.

She said, "I will call from state to state to make sure that everyone knows. Don't you worry about it. I'll take care of it."

Knowing that Kimberly wanted someone else to live, I said yes to the organ donation.

Walker said that only a short time back Kimberly had signed her license and said, "If someone had not been an organ donor my Mom would not be here now."

I looked at her beautiful face on her license and her handwriting on the front of it, listing the organs she thought would be acceptable for donation. I felt peace about saying yes.

Edwina stayed with Kimberly for hours while the organ donation testing was being performed. She was wise and knew what needed to be done so that Kimberly's face and body wouldn't swell. All the testing was done, but no one anywhere would accept Kimberly's organs because of her illness.

When the respirator was unplugged Edwina laid her head on Kimberly's heart until the last beat was gone. Jacqueline silently wept in the waiting area, Brian and David by her side. Walker wept alone. Sorrowful friends lingered in case they were needed. I had gone home to be with Corey, William, and Ralph to try to comfort them while the donor testing procedures were being done. Ashley and Lee were in Oklahoma. That ride home from Knoxville was the saddest ride of my life.

~~~~~

Family came from their homes in the cities to the mountains to mourn the death of one of their favorites. Hundreds of people passed to look at her one last time. I heard someone say she looked like a princess. Mountain friends sang at her service with talent that would humble Nashville stars. Most of the songs they had written themselves. Beautiful words were spoken about her.

Elizabeth, knowing Kimberly's self-confidence and high spirit, stated, "The Hallelujah Choir will never be the same again! Kimberly is probably saying, *'David, let me play that harp! I can play it better than you!'"*

The memorial service brought tears and laughter to the sanctuary. It was truly a celebration of Kimberly's life. Beautiful poems written by friends were read. People from all walks of life paid their respects.

Even I was able to give a eulogy of Kimberly's life.

I vaguely remember the procession from the church to the gravesite. Kimberly was placed beneath the tall oak tree next to Momma and Daddy and their fifteen-month-old granddaughter, Ruby Mae. The sun was shining; trees slightly swayed from the mild wind. Just below us the Wild River ran quietly over the rocks as it glistened in the sunlight dancing across its many ripples.

After we had all sung "*Amazing Grace,*" I walked out the path to my Cherokee. The glory of God's creation, with all its peace, surrounded us. I knew I would never see this beautiful person, whom I loved so dearly, on Earth again. My heart ached and was raw with grief.

Many of our family made their departure immediately; however, some came home with us. As we sat on the back porch I suddenly exclaimed, "Please excuse me, but I've got to be alone for a little while."

I walked to the garage, got in my Cherokee, and drove to a road that ran high into the mountains. As I drove the gravel road that was built to accommodate coal mining companies, I observed the beautiful wildflowers beside the road; yellow and lilac dominated. The blossoms appeared so fragile. After passing them I drove out on a ledge where I could see the valley and the mountains beyond. I opened the door and suddenly every emotion inside me was released. As I wept and wailed, every tree, every mountain, every stream was still. It was my time to weep. It seemed the sound flowed sadly through the mountains and the valley below and echoed beyond. After I released the torrent of emotions, I was ready to face my family without fear of breaking down in front of them.

I returned home to sit on my back porch with my family. There wasn't any sun. The evening brought dimness and a few sprinkles of rain.

My brother, Willard, came around the side of the house; he seemed excited. "Come and see!"

We all ran to see what had gotten his attention. As we looked into the sky we saw a double rainbow over the east end of our house. It was an awesome sight.

I said, "This is a sign that our Kimberly is beyond that rainbow with our Lord, in a land of beauty, peace, and joy."

I have often thought about how hard Kimberly would have laughed had she seen all of us when we started to move so quickly. As we all ran across the porch to the deck we had no idea there was a yellow jacket's nest under the deck. We had disturbed them when we were running to see the rainbow. On the way back, they fiercely swarmed among us, and stung a few of us.

We all laughed at Willard. His main goal was to protect his wife. "Run, Jean! Run!" he yelled wildly.

I laughed and thought, "*That is just like God to add a little humor when we are hurting.*"

After everyone left, I made myself ready for bed. This would be my last night with my grandson because his Dad would be taking him to Oklahoma to live. I couldn't bear to think of him leaving. He had been my shadow for twelve years.

I began to think of the day I brought my little black-headed Kimberly Lynn home from the hospital. I remembered her happy childhood. My thoughts covered a million miles that night. Will slept on the floor on a mat next to my bed. That was the way he wanted it to be. Occasionally I looked down to see his long legs beyond the covers. Will was taken away the next day.

I grieved for the two bright and shining stars of my life.

~~~~~

Kimberly's death affected all of her children.

Will went to live in Oklahoma with his father, but wanted to return to his home place. Ashley moved to Oklahoma, but yearns for the mountains. She feels that she must remain there. Lee excelled in the Air Force. After returning back to the States from England, he was stationed in California. Corey was devastated by Kimberly's death, but still in her suffering she remained strong enough to graduate as Valedictorian and earn enough scholarships to go to college.

The grounds that I looked on each day, where I watched my children and grandchildren enjoying for so many years, still looks beautiful, but empty.

~~~~~

Heartaches never seemed to end.

Edwina and David divorced. The soft blue eyes of little blond haired Hannah Grace showed pain that seemed endless. She too will survive.

Jacqueline is facing kidney failure and I often pray that I will not lose another child.

When I was overwhelmed by so many negative circumstances, I drove to Kimberly's grave beneath the tall oak tree. There my emotions faced the raging sea. I wept for all of us. I knelt to the ground beside her rustic stone with her saying carved on it, "*Never miss an opportunity to tell someone that you love them.*"

I sat on the cool grass looking at a scroll that pictured the ocean at sunset which her friend Rhonda Robinson had placed adjacent to the stone and remembered some of our good times. I tried to put the past behind me, but my heart was not ready. As darkness began to push the daylight away, I stood in silence for a moment then walked to my Cherokee, backed out the grassy path knowing that my beautiful Kimberly would remain in my heart forever.

A day never passes that a tear doesn't fall or that an awful vise squeezes my inner soul because of losing her. My only comfort is when I fall to my knees and say, "*Thank you, God, for letting my beautiful daughter come to your paradise.*"

I feel the pain inside begin to subside only to return the next day.

When I walk outside on my back deck or yard, I hear the echoes of the past.

"Mom, what are you doing?"

"Come up for a while. Will is off to school."

"Come see the bluebells I planted. They open in the morning."

"Let's watch the birds playing and drinking from the flowers in my yard."

Sometimes I said, *"I will be there in a second"*, and sometimes I would say, *"I have things I have to do today."*

I think at times, why did I feel that I had to do everything that I did? Why couldn't I have realized it would be there tomorrow? And if there was no tomorrow, it wouldn't have mattered anyway.

Remembering Kimberly's Life

Kim taking a shot as she towers over the opposition

Edwina and Kim at Edwina's college graduation

Edwina, Kimberly, and Jacqueline

Pauline, Kimberly, and Jacqueline

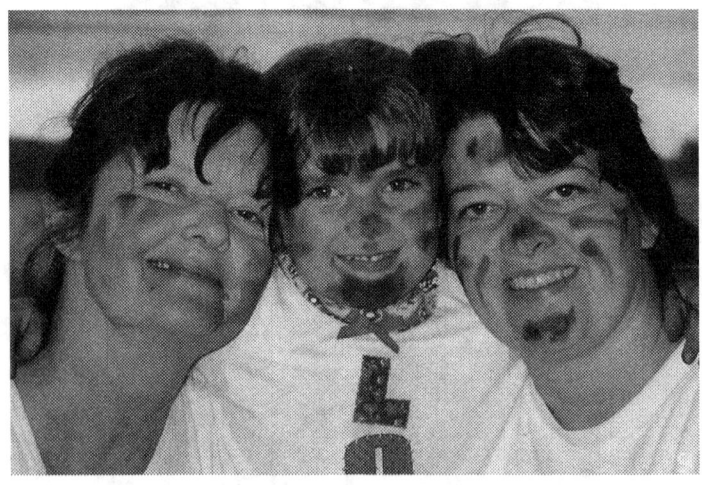

Pauline, Lindsey, and Kimberly

Ashley, Corey, Lee, Travis Daniels, Kimberly, Will - camping

Kimberly - deep sea fishing

Kimberly and Lee

Kimberly and Corey

Kimberly and Codey

Kimberly and Aunt Ruby

Lindsey, Kimberly, and niece Hannah

Kimberly and Rhonda Robinson

Will, Kimberly, and Ashley

William, Will, and Kimberly

Kimberly motorcycling

The day of Kimberly's funeral
Bottom left: Jean Hensley, Bernice Hensley
Standing: Freddy Ginter, Wilhelmina, JR Ginter, Willard Hensley

CHAPTER 40

Kimberly's death made the months following seem like a dream, a bad dream.

June rolled around and Will came for the summer. I was grateful that his dad allowed him to visit. It had been less than a year since his mom died. He had left the day after the funeral and I knew that his return to all the familiar things of the past would stab his heart like a sword. Leaving so suddenly after Kimberly's funeral gave him no time to work through the anger, the grief, and reach the stage of acceptance. It was as though he was in a state of emotions that would not set him free.

How did I know? When you love and nurture someone from the day they are born you feel in your soul what they are feeling, their state of mind, their emotions, their sadness, their anger is sucked right into the heart of your soul. You know when they are happy and when they are sad, and if a healing is taking place.

As Will spent his first summer with us, I saw the sadness in his eyes. He talked very little about his life in Oklahoma and not at all about his mother's death.

At one point when I walked in to the room where he sat in the recliner watching television, he looked slightly toward me, not straight into my eyes and said, "Mammaw, sometimes I forget that I don't live here anymore. It is as though this is my home. Then I remember that I am only visiting."

September 2003 to 2004 was a time of no alternatives for Will. He had to adjust to a new family, new friends, a new home in a strange state, and a new school. His dad worked away during the week and he had no rapport with his stepmother. However, he had a little seven-year-old brother, Joe, who brought a spark of joy to his life.

"Mammaw," he said, "I never go to sleep before four in the morning."

I can't imagine how he succeeded in school the first few months with so little sleep.

Will's dad and mom had divorced when he was eighteen months old. By the time he was twelve he had spent only a few weeks with his father since the separation. When Will went to live with William, there had been a lot of adjustment for both of them. I knew his dad loved him but I also knew that he did not know him. Will had suffered long and hard after the death of his mother. He reacted with anger in school. That was the place his emotions had found a way to escape.

When summer vacation ended, I met Will's dad in Jackson, Tennessee to return with him for another school year. As William loaded Will's dirt bike into the big blue Dodge diesel that sat in the parking lot at the Holiday Inn, I hugged Will, then walked through the parking lot watching as the wind fluttered leaves on the trees that stood around the edges. The sunshine warmed the breeze. I never looked back, but kept walking forward. It would've hurt too much to look back.

I made my way into the huge lobby of the hotel and found the ladies room on the west wing, adjacent to where they were parked. I walked into the empty room. The door closed behind me. I stood in silence trying to choke back tears and swallowed hard. I stared into the mirror, looking back at myself as tears flowed like rain sliding down a windowpane. Giving the tears time to subside, I walked from the powder room and looked through the huge window to see that Will was gone. He was again crossing the country to Oklahoma.

As I traveled home from Jackson, Tennessee, I relived September 14, 2003. Will's dad had pulled a trailer that would haul his chickens and Walker hound to Oklahoma. Just before leaving, the hound broke his chain and ran. No one knew where he was. William came to the family room from where they were loading.

He said, "Mammaw, I will not leave with out my dog."

"Will, you won't have a choice," I replied.

Luckily the hound returned.

As I traveled back to Harlan, I remembered his words on the telephone one day. "Mammaw, the coyotes have killed all my chickens except one. I sat beside it at the chicken lot late in the evening. Its eyes looked so sad. I told it, *"Little chicken, I understand how you feel. You have lost your family, just like me!"*

Not long after, I called and he had even more bad news. There was such sadness in his voice when he said, "Mammaw, my Walker hound is gone."

These words will ring in my ears forever. I wept inside because I knew the dog was the last gift he would ever receive from his mom. A boy and his dog have a special bond and even that had been taken from Will.

My year had also been distorted by more than the loss of my daughter and the absence of Will. It was as though my husband hardly realized that I existed.

When I had returned from the University of Tennessee after Kimberly died, Ralph seemed oblivious to my presence. I knew he hurt and hurt bad, but he wasn't even able to take part in anything related to her death or burial. I walked the trail of tears alone, in the following days, weeks, and months.

As I spent my days sorrowing inside for the loss of our daughter and the absence of our grandson, the land that once held so much liveliness, laughter, and joy was desolate. Corey found an apartment and was off to college. Jacqueline and Brian, Codey, and Lindsey moved to their new house in Hensley Hollow. Edwina and Hannah lived at Three Point a few miles east of Martin's Fork. Kimberly's former fiancé, Walker, continued on with his life. I knew it was the normal thing that everyone's life went on, but that didn't make it easier for me to cope with Kimberly's death.

The biggest shock that came during this time was how Ralph began to spend more and more time away from home. I told myself that perhaps his pain was so great that this was his way of coping. I couldn't help wondering, *"What happened to the forty one years we had spent together? Should we have wept together or should I have wept alone?"*

I thought back to the year, 1989, the month of July, when Ralph suffered his breakdown. I remembered how my instincts at that time told me he would be changed forever. Those changes had played out like the plot in a novel.

The one human thing that helped in my time of hurt was the daily walks with my dearest friend, Mary Lee McArthur. Rain, snow, or sun, we walked and talked as we made our way around Martin's Fork Lake. Mary's knowledge of the mountains, as well as her uncanny resemblance to Laura Bush, never ceased to amaze me.

Mary Lee McArthur, Pauline, and Donna (Mary's daughter)

CHAPTER 41

Less than one year passed until Edwina and David divorced, which brought such sadness to their little blonde haired, blue-eyed Hannah Grace. It seemed tears flowed down her angelic face too often. Her stomach was overwhelmed with nausea every time she came to visit, but she never uttered a word about the source of her problem.

I realized everything had fallen apart when Edwina asked, "Mom, is it okay with you for Hannah and me to move into Kimberly's house?"

Of course I agreed.

Edwina and Hannah moved and everything seemed to be pretty well until September 3, only seven days within a year of Kimberly's death. Edwina was hospitalized for a bile duct procedure.

In the meantime I had been called to Indiana because my sister Morine had been in an automobile accident.

Edwina called, "Mom, I'm very sick. I'm in Knox County Hospital in Barbourville."

By this time Morine was out of danger and I felt the need to be with my daughter.

On September 5, I traveled the three hundred miles back to Barbourville, Kentucky. The sun glowed as if just for me. God knew my spirit needed a boost as I traveled the interstate highways going south. I was apprehensive as to what the destiny of my daughter would be.

In Barbourville, I discovered the small facility in a little town sitting in what was once farmland adjacent to highway 25E, forty-five miles north of Harlan. It was a pleasant looking place. I spent the afternoon sitting beside her hospital bed.

At one point Edwina exclaimed, "Mom, my head is hurting unusually bad."

With her history of migraines I wasn't overly excited, but the flashbacks of Kimberly's headache that ended in death prompted me to call the nurse and ask for the doctor to be called.

Dr. Vora arrived. "I will order a scan for tomorrow morning and will prescribe something for the pain."

A couple of hours passed. Edwina said, "Mom, you look tired, please go to the Best Western and spend the night. I'm fine now."

It was within walking distance and probably not a two-minute drive from the hospital. I *was* exhausted.

"If you need me please call or have the nurse to call," I told her.

Upon returning the following morning, Edwina was doing well. She was experiencing no pain and in good spirits.

Around 2:00 p.m. she said, "Mom, will you drive to Martin's Fork and bring Hannah down? I want so much to see her face."

I drove as far as Pineville and noticed the light was on that indicated that the Ford Explorer was overheating.

I pulled off the highway at a little white house. The front porch was almost enclosed with white lattice. An elderly man of small stature came out.

"What can I do for you, Ma'am?" he asked.

"My car is overheating," I said.

"I will tell you what…" he said as he glanced down. "There is a little garage in downtown Pineville." He looked back toward me, "It's pretty cheap on labor. I'll get you some water to put in the radiator."

He came back with a gallon jug of water and poured it into the radiator, "I believe you'll be alright now, Ma'am."

I gave him a big thank you and was on my way to Pineville. I found the little garage and asked for help.

"It will be a little while before I can get to you," the mechanic said.

I waited inside the office. He found the problem. "The thermostat is stuck."

"Go ahead and replace it," I instructed. "May I use your phone?"

"Help yourself," he said. "It's on the desk."

I dialed Ralph to make sure that Edwina wouldn't be alarmed if she called and was worried about the length of time I'd been gone from the hospital.

"Ralph, I have had a little problem with the car, but am heading home to pick up Hannah."

"The hospital called for you and asked that you return," he replied.

He had no further explanation. Of course, I assumed Edwina was being released. Feeling much relief, I headed back to the hospital. By that time rain had begun to fall.

Upon arrival I walked down the long corridor all prepared to take Edwina home. Suddenly a voice came over the intercom system, "Would the family of Edwina Burkhart please report to the nurses' station?"

A little startled, I flung open the double doors that led to the patient area, nurses' station, and I.C.U. Being a small facility, everything was in close proximity.

Dr. Vora stood at the nurses' station. He looked especially concerned as he said to me, "Edwina developed a severe headache after you left. A scan was ordered stat. She has a brain bleed and there is nothing I can do. It's in God's hands. Momma, you pray and pray hard! I have already prayed," he said.

I raced to Edwina's room before anyone told me she was in I.C.U. I found the room empty. I slowly sat down in a chair in front of the window that gave a view of the mountains beyond.

I lifted my eyes to the sky high above the mountains, trying hard to look through the misty rain and said, *"God, oh God, I don't believe I can loose another one."*

I hung my head in sorrow for a minute before I arose from my chair then began walking toward the nurses' station.

As I approached, I heard the nurse say to Dr. Vora, "The helicopter cannot maneuver through the fog and rain. An ambulance with paramedics is not available to transport Ms. Burkhart."

"Can I call for an ambulance to come from Harlan to get her?" I asked.

"No. Legally we are not allowed to do that. Harlan is out of our jurisdiction," the nurse explained.

"We are doing everything we can for your daughter," Dr. Vora assured me.

I walked into the ICU unit where Edwina lay. I looked down on my blonde haired, blue-eyed daughter lying flat on her back, but still conscious. There was a distant look in her eyes.

Her voice was weak as she whispered, "Mom… if I die… please, donate my organs."

I knew she, too, was thinking of the fate of her sister.

"Honey, let's pray," I said, taking her by the hand.

"Please, God, let me stay with my Hannah Grace," she prayed.

~~~~~

Shortly, Elizabeth and her sister-in-law, Carol, along with my brother, Harold, and his wife, Lela, arrived. We all gathered around Edwina and prayed. It wasn't a silent prayer. We all joined together praying aloud so that Edwina could hear. Dr. Vora stood silently praying with us. Edwina responded by looking toward us. We knew that hearing our prayers would strengthen and encourage her.

Shortly after our prayers, she was rushed outside into the rainy night to an ambulance that took her to Central Baptist Hospital in Lexington, Kentucky. As I stood watching, the sound of the siren was loud and seemed to be sounding a death warning. I covered my ears as I stood in the dark cool night trying to block out the sound that seemed to pierce the very core of my heart. It seemed that I was reliving the horrible day of Kimberly's death, exactly one year earlier to the day.

Harold and Lela drove me to Lexington. I sat in silence, feeling as empty inside as before. The drive was all too familiar. As we traveled up the interstate cutting through the farmland, the heart wrenching fear of the unknown overwhelmed me - not knowing what awaited me, wondering if by chance God would be merciful and spare my daughter. None of us spoke on our way. Even Lela was silent and she always had something to say.

When entering the emergency area at Central Baptist Hospital, my sister, Wilhelmina, had already arrived. She had driven from her home in Morehead, one hour west of Lexington and had arrived before us with her pastor, Rev. Potter and Deacons Jeff Buckler, John Tucker, and Forest Williams. Wilhelmina had a puzzled look about her.

"Pauline, the ambulance hasn't arrived." She knew the ambulance had left before we did. The news alarmed me somewhat, however I was still in shock.

When walking into the emergency room I asked, "Why hasn't my daughter, Edwina Burkhart, arrived by ambulance?"

"We have no information," they replied.

We were taken upstairs to wait. I thought maybe she had died on the way, but no one could confirm the news until the ambulance arrived. Many unpleasant thoughts pressed in. My mind was crowded with images and heartaches from the past.

Soon Edwina's brother-in-law, Toby, who lived in Lexington, came in to the waiting area. He had learned that the ambulance had broken down on the way near London, Kentucky. Another team had to come to the scene and transfer her to their ambulance.

Neurologists and neurosurgeons were called in. Angiograms and tests were done. The consulting physicians were pretty sure Edwina would live. By 2:00 in the morning my sister, Morine, and her husband, Bob, arrived. With family and friends pouring in, it was almost like a repeat of September 9, 2003 playing out before me.

Edwina remained in Central Baptist Hospital for almost a week while angiograms and tests were repeated. Our prayers were answered. The brain bleed had been contained. There were no signs of additional bleeding. No one ever figured out why the bleed had happened in the first place and did not expect it to happen again. The prognosis was good.

~~~~~

My heart breaks when I see the change in Edwina's life, but I am so thankful that she is able to raise her daughter. Edwina's medical conditions forced her to give up the job she had held as Coordinator of the Family Resource Center for Cawood Elementary School. She loved working with families and helping underprivileged children. She has had to adjust to living a quiet life since she retired with a total medical disability.

Even though they are divorced, it comforts Edwina that Hannah's dad is a good father and Hannah loves him with all her heart.

God truly has blessed Edwina by prolonging her life. He did work a miracle for her. A huge blood clot remains in her brain. She returns periodically for brain scans to make sure there is no further bleed from the original site.

Edwina moved into her new log home a year and a half after her illness. The two story home is built of hemlock with lots of windows and dormers to let in the sunlight. The three bedrooms and two baths allow plenty of room for Hannah and Edwina to invite relatives and friends to visit. It also has a living room with a fireplace, a kitchen, a dining room, a utility room, and a loft overlooking the living room. Two porches stretch across the entire width of the cabin in front and back. The metal roof allows her to enjoy the sound of falling rain.

The cabin sits beside the Martin's Fork River which makes a low rumbling sound over the small rocks. Between her front yard and the river is a still pond of cool calm bluish-green water. Hannah will be able to cast her reel into the pond from the front porch. Beyond the pond lies green pastureland where her horses graze. Behind the house a small mountain stream bordered by mountain laurels, dogwoods, and hemlocks makes a soothing sound as it passes to enter the river.

After the divorce from David, Edwina designed her own house plans for the log home. Her new home was one dream that became a reality.

Lindsey, David, Hannah, and Edwina

Hannah Grace

CHAPTER 42

Again I walk by the river as I did so many years ago, when the distress of my husband's breakdown and mother's illness brought me here in 1989.

The shining waters still ripple over the rocks and the spring rains have brought nature alive. I stop and lift my eyes from the clear gurgling water to the fresh green fields south of the river. There the horses graze in a row as if their places were marked for a perfect picture. The pastureland rises from one field to another until it reaches the foot of the mountains. In the mountains beyond the trees are springing forth tender leaves of many shades of green. The dogwoods and redbuds are in full bloom. Chimney Rock and Table Rock still stand as sentinels weathering the storms, standing in majesty among the new life that spring has brought.

I sit for a time listening to the flow of the river water, thinking of how Kimberly loved the freshness spring brought to the mountains. Coming back to reality, I look north of the river to see bubbling water sliding over the solid rock from high on the ridge and on either side of the cascade are dogwood and redbud trees. The tiny redbud petals fall like snow, drifting beneath the small yellow, white, and purple wildflowers scattered among the new foliage bursting through the rich soil.

I sit in silence for a while feeling the breeze blow down from the mountain summit and smelling the sweet fragrance of wildflowers released on the gentle wind. In the stillness of the moment my spirit speaks to me, "Like for you, this too was Kimberly's Camelot."

The water journeys from the Wild River, which flows out of the Brush Mountain many miles upstream. As it passes me by with its soothing sound, I think of the family I never met and wondered about so many times. I marvel at strangers who gave me their seventeen-year-old son's kidney, adding these past twenty-three years to my life. I remember that Kimberly was also seventeen when the young man was suddenly taken away. I think about how this unselfish family allowed me twenty extra years with my Kimberly and how I would love to tell them face to face what they have meant to me.

I look upward into the blue sky thinking of how time has made a change. I think of how many miles are behind me and how, regardless of what my destiny has been, I am still holding on, enjoying my grandchildren and children as well as my family, my friends, and my beautiful God given country. I treasure many precious memories of days gone by.

Only God could grant to me what I see and feel in this very moment. He truly is an awesome God! Only He can fill the void in my heart and soul that came September 10, 2003 when Kimberly Lynn Harber was suddenly taken away.

Robin Brock, JR Ginter, and Kim

Will

AFTERWORD

It is now 2007 and Codey, Lindsey, and Hannah get off the school bus at my home. Codey heads for a bowl of chocolate ice cream and a little relaxation before play time. As soon as Lindsey changes into her play clothes, she heads to the south barn to feed and curry the horses.

I look on as she enjoys her evening chore and fun time. I'm delighted to see an awesome resemblance to Kimberly's looks and mannerisms as Lindsey works.

Lindsey comes from the barn near the edge of the mountains and says, "Mammaw, you want me to tell you something?"

Her excitement overwhelms me.

"Please do," I reply.

"As I neared the breezeway of the barn, the horses were outside but they were neighing and running around. I looked to the side of the barn near a pile of tin and saw a big bear's butt facing me! I screamed, 'oh God' and ran as fast as I could. I was afraid to look back. I'm not sure I breathed until I was through the gate!"

I know I will smile as long as I live every time I think of Lindsey's bear adventure.

Hannah missed the excitement as she had an orthodontist's appointment. Usually when Hannah isn't helping me in the kitchen, she is in the pasture with Lindsey or playing in the barn loft. She, too, has a great love of horses.

I get such pleasure from watching Lindsey riding her horse, Smoky, her long hair billowing behind her. She's beside herself with pleasure since she will be taking Kimberly's horse, Flash, home with her as soon as some fencing is done. She and Hannah sometimes make me feel as though time repeats itself.

I look in all directions to locate Codey. He is usually around the yard and hay fields hitting golf balls. He and Will have developed a love for golf and have great potential. Codey looks forward to Will's summer vacation. They will certainly go to see Rodney Wilson at the Harlan Country Club every day they can; they think he's the best club manager around.

Will is a sophomore in Oklahoma. He has adjusted to his new life and has a good relationship with his dad. He has made friends with a few special boys who love to hunt, four wheel, golf, and do the things that young boys enjoy.

Of the other grandchildren, Corey is in nursing school in Harlan and loves the profession. Lee is in Seattle, excelling, as always, in the Air Force. Ashley is living in California and attending college.

Ralph is doing much better. The medical attention he resisted so long has made a world of difference. Jacqueline is pursuing her teaching career and really making a difference. Edwina is still in early retirement; she and Hannah are looking forward to their first spring in their log home.

While a beautiful part of my life is gone, a beautiful part remains. I realize that, if I live long enough, there will be other cups of bitterness to drink from in life. I also know that God is, and will always be, where I place my confidence and hope.

Edwina and Hannah

Lee today

Ashley today

Jackie, Brian, Codey, and Lindsey Hensley

www.ingramcontent.com/pod-product-compliance
Lightning Source LLC
LaVergne TN
LVHW021659060526
838200LV00050B/2425